The World According to Hollywood, 1918–1939

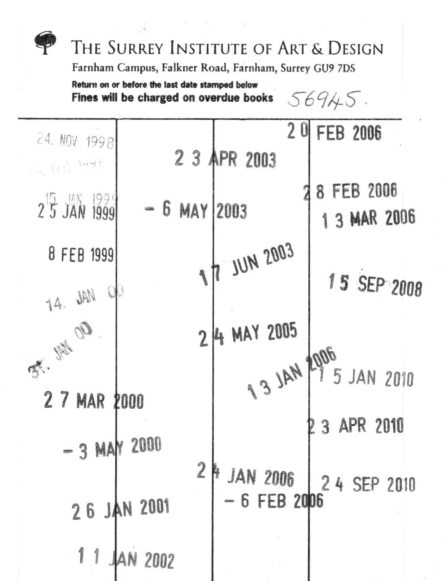

Exeter Studies in Film History
General Editors:
Richard Maltby and Duncan Petrie

Exeter Studies in Film History is devoted to publishing the best new scholarship on the cultural, technical and aesthetic history of cinema. The aims of the series are to reconsider established orthodoxies and to revise our understanding of cinema's past by shedding light on neglected areas of film history.

Published in association with the Bill Douglas Centre for the History of Cinema and Popular Culture, the series will include monographs and essay collections, translations of major works written in other languages, and reprinted editions of important texts in cinema history. The series editors are Richard Maltby, Professor of Film Studies, Sheffield Hallam University and Duncan Petrie, Director of the Bill Douglas Centre for the History of Cinema and Popular Culture, University of Exeter.

The World According to Hollywood, 1918–1939

Ruth Vasey

UNIVERSITY
of
EXETER
PRESS

First published in Great Britain in 1997 by
University of Exeter Press
Reed Hall, Streatham Drive
Exeter, Devon, EX4 4QR
UK

British Library Cataloguing in Publication Data
A catalogue record of this book is available
from the British Library

Paperback ISBN 0 85989 554 8
Hardback ISBN 0 85989 553 X

Printed in the United States of America

For my family

Contents

Illustrations

Figures

Tables

Acknowledgments

In 1985 I was working at my first film lecturing job in Sydney, wondering whether I was the only person in the world who was troubled by prevailing accounts of the historical relationship between Hollywood's production and distribution practices. Then Kristin Thompson, who was on an Australian lecture tour, gave an address at Sydney's Paddington Town Hall, and I discovered with relief that I was not entirely alone. In the decade that followed, Kristin became mentor, example, lavish host, patient editor, and valued friend. Without the encouragement that she originally gave to a very junior academic, this project would probably never have been attempted, and life would have been very different.

In its first manifestation, this manuscript was a doctoral thesis undertaken at the University of Exeter, England. I wish to acknowledge the financial assistance of the Association of Commonwealth Universities at that time. I am also indebted to the British Association for American Studies, and the University of New South Wales, both of which sponsored additional research. Portions of this book have appeared previously in the following articles and book chapters: "Foreign Parts: Hollywood's Global Distribution and the Representation of Ethnicity," *American Quarterly* 44, no. 4 (December 1992): 617–42, reprinted in *Movie Censorship and American Culture*, edited by Francis G. Couvares (Washington, D.C.: Smithsonian Institution Press, 1996); "The International Language Problem: European Reactions to Hollywood's Conversion to Sound" (with Richard Maltby), in *Hollywood in Europe: Experiences of a Cultural Hegemony*, edited by David W. Ellwood and Rob Kroes (Amsterdam: VU University Press, 1994), 68–93; and "Beyond Sex and Violence: 'Industry Policy' and the Regulation of Hollywood Movies, 1922–1939," *Quarterly Review of Film and Video* 15, no. 4 (1995): 65–85. I am grateful to the editors of these publications for their permission to reprint this material.

In attempting a project of this kind, one necessarily places oneself in the hands of archivists and librarians. Happily, those engaged in the area of historical film research often seem able to muster enthusiasm for even the most arcane quest. I am especially grateful for the cheerful collaboration of Sam Gill and Howard Prouty at the Margaret Herrick Library of the Academy of Motion Picture Arts and Sciences, Maxine Fleckner-Ducey and Harold Miller at the Wisconsin Center for Film and Theater Research, and Ned Comstock at the Doheny Library, University of Southern California.

During the past ten years I have been constantly surprised and delighted by acts of kindness and generosity from people in both the academic world and the professional film community who have given their time and energy to help me with the preparation of this book. I would particularly like to acknowledge the assistance of the late William K. Everson, who arranged for me to see *Woman Trap* when I had just about given up hope of tracking it down and who also commented on a section of the manuscript. Luigi Luraschi, of Paramount Pictures Corporation, gave up his time to be interviewed and provided a valuable firsthand perspective on many of the events that I was investigating. James Hay generously provided information about the Italian market. Both Thomas Elsaesser and Lea Jacobs read versions of the manuscript and offered constructive criticisms that influenced the final draft.

Other friends and colleagues played much-appreciated roles in this project throughout its evolution. Sabina Dunn and Geoffrey Webb have maintained a lively interest in the subject from first to last and have provided an indispensable home-away-from-home and communications base in New York City. Frank Couvares is one of the few other people I have met who is truly smitten with Production Code Administration correspondence; conversations with him have always managed to reinvigorate my own enthusiasm for trawling through archives and have reminded me that primary research is *fun*. Tino Balio has always put everything in perspective, both in conversation and in his own measured and thoroughly researched contributions to the field. Others who have helped to make the process of researching and writing this book an improbably enjoyable as well as a collaborative experience include Kate Bowles, Todd Gray, Elizabeth Christopher, Jo Seton, David Bordwell, and Mick Gidley. My colleagues at the School of Theatre and Film Studies at the University of New South Wales have also consistently provided a positive and convivial environment in which to work.

By far my greatest debt, however, in this as in so many other things, is to my partner Richard Maltby, who himself constitutes one of the more delightful discoveries made during this project. There is not a single page in this book which has not been influenced by conversations with him. Any virtue (except brevity) in the final version is testament to his inspiration, encouragement, and support. Finally, I must acknowledge the special contribution of Benjamin John Maltby, who imposed a nonnegotiable deadline of nine months on the completion of the final draft.

Abbreviations

AMPAS	Academy of Motion Picture Arts and Sciences
AMPP	Association of Motion Picture Producers
BBFC	British Board of Film Censors
MPPDA	Motion Picture Producers and Distributors of America, Inc.
MPTOA	Motion Picture Theatre Owners of America
NAMPI	National Association of the Motion Picture Industry
NBC	National Board of Censorship
NBR	National Board of Review
PCA	Production Code Administration
SRC	Studio Relations Committee

The World According to Hollywood, 1918–1939

Introduction

The world of the Hollywood cinema is both like and unlike the world which its audiences inhabit. A motion picture may be set in New York or ancient Rome, but if the movie is a product of Hollywood we know that the fiction will be governed by a set of narrative and representational conventions that will override the social, geographic, and historical characteristics of its nominal locale. The world according to Hollywood is an exotic, sensual cousin of the realm outside the cinema, simultaneously familiar and strange to its worldwide audiences, who are as certain about what is morally right and wrong in this utopia as they are about whether the star or his best friend will get the girl in the final scene. In Hollywood's fictional kingdom, the desires that viewers project onto characters are fulfilled and regulated by a narrative resolution that reasserts and reestablishes a deterministic moral order, by which the guilty are punished, the sympathetic are discovered to be innocent, and audiences "exhausted with the realities of life" are "improved" by what one of the authors of the regulatory Production Code of 1930 called "correct entertainment."[1] This book investigates some of the influences that helped to shape Hollywood's uniquely formulated view of the world in the interwar years, that part of the "Classical" period when the American cinema established its hold on the imaginations of the world. It describes a process of evolution, in which some themes and treatments survived, while others became displaced onto different forms, and some simply disappeared from Hollywood's horizons.

A consideration of major importance to this study is the extent to which the worldwide dimensions of Hollywood's audience influenced the nature of its products. At the most basic level, the size of the audience led to the economies of scale that underpinned the industry's output of more than four hundred movies a year in the 1930s. Production on this scale meant that the movies could not be understood as wholly distinct from one another, either at the level of manufacture or at the level of consumption. The "Hollywood movie" was itself a ge-

3

neric type, constituted by a broad set of conventions that embraced such content-specific genres as the backstage musical, the western, and the historical costume drama. Worldwide distribution supported the strong production values and reliable technical proficiency that are identified with even the most routine Hollywood product, and so helped to determine the physical environment—the "look"—of Hollywood's productions.[2] At the same time, the global reach of the movies helped to reinforce Hollywood's identity as an emissary of consumer culture, a fascinating sales catalog of twentieth-century goods, from motorcars to makeup. "Product placement" in more or less overt forms was well established by the 1930s.[3] The status of the movies as a medium of mass entertainment allowed Hollywood to define, as well as reflect, the latest fashions.

This book will, however, attend less to the implications of the sheer size of the audience than to the implications of its diversity. Allowing for the differences in marketing emphasis inherent in such production categories as romantic dramas and horror pictures, Classical Hollywood movies were broadly designed to be consumed by people of both sexes, all ages, and all levels of experience. As the first global medium of entertainment, the movies faced the problem of how to satisfy audiences of vastly different cultural, religious, and political persuasions with essentially the same diet of images and narratives. Even within the domestic American market there was no typical audience. American censorship classifications were not introduced until 1968, so children, their parents, and their grandparents regularly consumed the same entertainments.[4] Metropolitan theaters played to ethnically diverse immigrant populations as well as to majority "middlebrow" culture and the social elite; small-town and rural Americans were equally avid picture-goers.[5] Hollywood had to formulate a recipe for movies that could play in the North and the South, on the West Coast and in the East, and from Capetown to Capri. As if all this were not difficult enough on the level of audience response, distributors had to contend with different censorship standards at municipal, state, and national levels. Pressured by the demands of special interest groups and moral reformers, the movies needed to negotiate a very narrow path indeed if they were to arrive unscathed at their countless sites of exhibition.

Individual studios faced the challenge of fashioning their output for broad-based consumption, both local and international, with varying degrees of enthusiasm and competence. The extent to which the companies monitored their own products to ensure that they contained nothing that would jeopardize their chances in the marketplace depended largely on the degree of cooperation that existed between the financial heads of the companies in New York and the heads of production in Hollywood. To the New York executives, unimpeded distribution was a necessary condition for profit maximization, while West Coast producers were inclined to think that any attempt to "pasteurize" their products was inimical to the creative side of the industry. The physical separation of the centers of fiscal control in the East and the sites of production in the West reflected a deep-seated tension in the industry between pragmatic and "artistic" considerations, manifested in a struggle for institutional power between the New York company heads and the Hollywood "moguls." From the perspective of New York, the industry's interests needed to be protected as much from the self-indulgence and profligacy of its own production arm as from the puritanism of official censor boards.

A strategy for negotiating between the two centers of power emerged through the agencies of the industry's trade association, the Motion Picture Producers and Distributors of America, Inc. (MPPDA). From its founding in 1922, this association represented the mutual and noncompetitive interests of America's major producers and distributors, occupying a relatively neutral position in relation to conflicts within or between companies. The MPPDA was centrally involved in the industry's foreign trade and acted as its representative in negotiations with the U.S. Commerce and State Departments. It also promoted aspects of trade regulation and the standardization of business practices. During the 1920s the MPPDA gradually extended its regulatory functions to cover production as well as distribution and exhibition. By the beginning of the 1930s it had created a centralized authority empowered to scrutinize theme and treatment in all of Hollywood's output and to ensure that the movies could be distributed domestically and abroad with a minimum of disruption through censorship action or consumer resistance. This system of centralized regulation allowed Hollywood's world to acquire its consistent, if idiosyncratic, vision. Regardless of the "house styles" that characterized the output of the studios in the 1930s, all of Hollywood's products were under pressure to conform to an increasingly comprehensive set of narrational and representational guidelines.

The most conspicuous aspect of centralized self-regulation in the motion picture industry was the Production Code of 1930, with its strong emphasis on the "morals" of the movies and its implications for Hollywood's treatment of sex and crime. The industry's main public relations problem in the 1920s and 1930s was the widespread conviction that children would learn "sophisticated," violent, or antisocial behavior from watching motion pictures. The Production Code was largely designed to assuage these anxieties, which had been exacerbated by the introduction of sound. It was administered under the auspices of the MPPDA by the Studio Relations Committee (SRC) and its successor, the Production Code Administration (PCA). The existence of the Code was never an industry secret—on the contrary, the MPPDA wielded it as a public relations weapon in the 1930s—but the manner of its administration was a closed book until the archives of the PCA were opened to the public by the Academy of Motion Picture Arts and Sciences in 1983. Since then, several works have analyzed Hollywood's operations from the internal perspective provided by these records, which contain correspondence between the PCA and the studios. Among them are *The Dame in the Kimono* by Leonard J. Leff and Jerold L. Simmons, *The Wages of Sin* by Lea Jacobs, and *Hollywood Censored* by Gregory D. Black.[6]

The Production Code had a profound effect on the construction and realization of Hollywood's narratives, and in this book I will be concerned with its evolution and effects. However, the regulation of the world of the movies by the Studio Relations Committee and the Production Code Administration was far more broad-based than a reading of the Code would suggest. In practice, the regulatory policies of these agencies were determined by a wider set of parameters, relating to both domestic and international issues. The Code itself, with its particular emphasis on morality and obedience to the law, constituted only the most conspicuous subsection of industry regulation. Its purpose and operation can be more fully understood within the wider context of "industry policy." This was a set of constraints that gradually took shape throughout the 1920s and 1930s in response to factors originating in both the domestic and the international spheres. Industry policy influenced not only the depiction of sex and violence but also Hollywood's representation of religion, politics (domestic and foreign), corporate capitalism, ethnic minorities, the conduct of lawyers, doctors, and other professionals, and a host of other issues, large and small.

Because matters of industry policy were not central to contemporary public discourses about the potentially harmful effects of the screen, they were handled with less fanfare than those that concerned morals or the law. There was no particular public relations advantage to be gained by advertising the industry's accommodating attitude toward big business, the political process, isolated lobby groups, or governments of other nations. Indeed, it was important that the cooperative stance of the major producers should not be seen as impeding the "freedom of the screen," particularly when the industry was anxious to convince the Justice Department that it was not violating federal antimonopoly statutes. Consequently, the areas of industry regulation designed to respond to pressure from limited (if powerful) constituencies were subject to little publicity, even though they constituted a significant proportion of the work of the Studio Relations Committee and the Production Code Administration. Little has yet been published about this wider framework of industry regulation. This book will investigate its origins and development as well as its effects, with a view to illuminating the institutional processes by which pressures arising from sections of the audience, both national and international, were incorporated into Hollywood's mode of representation. In the process I hope to contextualize the Production Code itself and to demonstrate that, far from being a radical imposition on Hollywood's production practices, it operated within, and was consistent with, broader preexisting and contemporaneous regulatory procedures.

To date researchers have largely overlooked the influence of the foreign market on Hollywood production. Between the world wars, the principal film companies derived an average of 35 percent of their gross revenue from the foreign field,[7] a larger proportion of revenues than most other American export industries earned abroad.[8] Nevertheless, studies describing the effect of audience pressures on Hollywood have typically proceeded as if the audience in question were exclusively domestic.[9] Cultural analyses of Hollywood's international impact have also commonly made the assumption that the movie industry, as an imperialist monolith, promulgated ideologies uniquely expressive of, and responsive to, "American" attitudes.[10] In 1985 a detailed analysis of the early foreign market appeared, in Kristin Thompson's meticulous study of distribution patterns, *Exporting Entertainment*.[11] Thompson showed that revenues from abroad were an essential part of Hollywood's highly capitalized economic structure. She did not, however, attempt to identify the consequences of this situation for production practices. Other scholars have examined Hollywood's economic and diplomatic connections with specific customer nations, but none have analyzed the way in which, or the extent to which, Hollywood tailored its products to the requirements of its international audiences.[12] Ian Jarvie's *Hollywood's Overseas Campaign* is the most recent, as well as the most weighty, example of this approach. Although Jarvie documents Hollywood's relationships with Canada and Britain in scrupulous detail, he does not address the possibility that the content of the movies themselves may have been affected by these relationships.[13]

In fact, trade negotiations concerning motion pictures cannot be divorced from the issue of motion picture content after World War I. Foreign governments perceived movies not just as articles of trade but also as potential American commercial and political emissaries, which played a disproportionate role in the lives of their national communities. Just as the American industry had to persuade its domestic audiences that its products were harmless and morally sound, its domination of the markets of the world depended at least in part on its ability to convince its foreign customers that its output was inoffensive and ideologically neutral. The argument could not be made exclusively at the negotiating table. It had to be made in the movies themselves, and the MPPDA instituted procedures for scrutinizing Hollywood's products for potential causes of adverse foreign reaction, negotiating with producers over appropriate adjustments to motion picture content. As a result, the international field came to exercise a wide range of influences on Hollywood's physical, social, and geopolitical landscape. By the same token, motion pictures played a part in international diplomacy when they entered distribution, whether their producers liked it or not. Well before its more overt interventions in World War II, the State Department took an active interest in the kinds of representations that Hollywood sent abroad. Issues surrounding censorship and self-regulation can illuminate the significance of the foreign market in Hollywood's affairs in a way that purely economic approaches cannot.

Studies that concentrate on Hollywood's impact on particular "national" industries, or those that dwell on the American cinema's representation of particular ethnic groups, while valuable in themselves, tend to miss the point that Hollywood's approach to its foreign customers was systematic and generalized. Neither the industry's approach to trade negotiations nor its attitude toward the representation of ethnic types varied significantly from group to group. The history of the internal operations of the MPPDA opens a window onto the organizational and administrative procedures which underpinned this important area of industry policy.

In the early 1920s the handling of international public relations issues was not integrated with the handling of domestic issues, either within individual companies or at an industry-wide level. Within the MPPDA, foreign problems of all complexions were dealt with either by its Foreign Department or by Will H. Hays, the association's president, without reference to the organizational structures that had been set up to accommodate pressures arising from the domestic sphere. However, as the industry developed ever more sophisticated strategies for overseeing movie content, the administrative mechanisms employed to obviate domestic and international public relations problems substantially converged; after 1927 it is impossible to speak of international influences in isolation from domestic public relations initiatives. Although the MPPDA's Foreign Department, operating from its New York office, continued to be responsible for trade negotiations and diplomatic contacts, it was in regular communication with the association's Los Angeles public relations department, which was designed to transmit audience pressures of all kinds directly to producers at the point of production.

Some of the major anxieties characterizing the domestic and foreign sectors overlapped, especially those relating to sex and crime. Other matters were of more specific concern to foreign nations, typically those with racial, political, cultural, or religious overtones. The need to reconcile the long-term priorities of the MPPDA with the short-term priorities of its members—industrial stability on the one hand, and local and international box office profits on the other—contributed to the establishment of an institutionalized process of negotiation over the content and ideology of every movie produced by the "organized industry" in Hollywood.

This study takes a historical approach, tracing the evolution of mechanisms by which the MPPDA mediated between various market pressures and the processes of production, and then examining their effects. The changing relationship between the industry's organizational approaches to domestic and foreign public relations matters is therefore reflected in the structure of the book. Although at times it is necessary to treat the local and international issues separately—especially in the first part of the study, when their institutional administrations were quite distinct—at other times they merge sufficiently for their discussion to be closely integrated, as in chapter 4. It is, however, my contention throughout that the nature of domestic self-regulation cannot be fully understood in isolation from international considerations, and vice versa.

Chapter 1 outlines the state of the American movie business after 1918 and describes some of the factors that led to the formation of the MPPDA, including the industry's expansion abroad. Considering the extent of its eventual domination of motion picture exhibition around the world, the American movie industry was slow to occupy markets beyond its domestic sphere. Until World War I producers and distributors were preoccupied with consolidating their control over their home market, which had seen incursions from European producers. This concern forestalled effective exploitation of foreign territories.[14] After the war, however, the strength of the domestic market fueled the American industry's global distribution and sustained its occupation of foreign markets. By this time the industry had grown into a multinational enterprise of sufficient complexity and prominence to justify the establishment of the MPPDA to represent its collective interests with respect to international, political, and industrial matters.

When the MPPDA was first formed, its charter did not provide for any influence on production at all; its various initiatives regarding content regulation developed gradually, in response to changing circumstances. Chapter 2 describes the development of the association's public relations arm, from the formation of a committee drawn from influential public organizations to the establishment of an internal department able to communicate public pressures directly to producers. It also outlines the early history of the industry's public relations activities in the international sphere and discusses the first attempts to integrate foreign relations pressures into the industry's wider self-regulatory mechanisms.

Chapter 3 investigates the effects of the widespread adoption of sound technology on the internal operations of the MPPDA and on its domestic and foreign commerce. As long as movies were "silent," they could be modified in accordance with the predilections and sensitivities of their various intended audiences, both regional and international. Although major decisions about themes and characterizations needed to be made before the action was fixed on film, the flexibility of the silent medium allowed aspects of meaning and nuance to be adjusted for specific audiences during distribution, or even at the point of exhibition. Silent movies could be received by their patrons in any language, and with virtually any moral inflection. The difficulty that faced the industry when sound was introduced was that the flexibility of the medium was significantly reduced. It became far more important for movies to be "correct" at the point of production. As a result, the industry's mechanisms for overseeing content were progressively strengthened and streamlined.

One response to the problems posed by the sound film was the production of movies offering multiple levels of interpretation through the deliberate creation of textual ambiguity. Chapter 4 discusses the development of such textual strategies in the context of increasingly stringent mechanisms of industry self-regulation, including the Production Code. It examines the ways in which these approaches were used to cater to audience sensitivities in both the domestic and the international arenas, and it also considers the extent to which the Studio Relations Committee was able effectively to mediate between the exigencies of production and distribution.

In 1934 the Studio Relations Committee was reconstituted as the Production Code Administration. The second half of the 1930s was a period of unusual industrial stability, and during this time the industry's mechanisms of self-regulation developed to a point at which they incorporated a consistent set of representational and narrational strategies. Chapter 5 describes the evolution of the treatment of sex, crime, ethnicity, and other issues up to the point when World War II precipitated the reorganization of the industry's ideological agenda. This chapter also outlines strategies adopted by various overseas markets in the course of their attempts to influence Hollywood's representational practices.

While the discussion in the first five chapters is primarily concerned with tracing the evolution of self-regulation in the motion picture industry and with identifying the strategies that Hollywood adopted to placate public opinion, chapters 6 and 7 focus on the effects of these self-regulatory strategies. Chapter 6 concentrates on the effects that Hollywood's relationship with its foreign market had on what actually reached the screen. It examines the influence of international distribution on five movies in relation to their production status and their intended range of distribution. Logically, the influence of the international sphere was most perfectly absorbed when it ceased to be apparent. For example, words known to be vulnerable to foreign censorship, such as *lousy* and *bloody*, simply fell out of usage. Since the requirements of self-regulation were themselves evolving in response to changing historical circumstances, however, the permissible limits of representation were always subject to negotiation. These negotiations—major and minor—are apparent in the production histories and content of the movies. Moreover, the extent to which international influences were accommodated on the screen depended on both the cost of the movie and the attitude of its producers. Low-budget pictures were typically less constrained by foreign considerations than were prestige productions which needed the whole of the global field to generate profits.

Chapter 7 examines some particular characteristics of Hollywood's world that resulted from its unique system of "industrial structures and strategies."[15] Inasmuch as these strategies caused Hollywood's universe to differ from the depiction of the world inherent in other forms of cultural representation, their full implications were not necessarily anticipated by anyone within the industry. They resulted in a parallel universe structured according to rigid notions of virtue and sin, crime and punishment, with underlying political and social structures that were typically both conservative and benign. But for a world that eschewed any explicit representation of sex, it was strongly erotic; for a social world designed to be consumable everywhere on earth, it was strangely ethnocentric; and for an industry that was often denigrated for providing entertainment for the masses, its mode of representation was often extraordinarily sophisticated, ironic, and self-conscious.

The records of the MPPDA and the PCA form the main primary sources for this study. In addition, I have drawn upon studio archives, trade papers, and publications of the U.S. Department of Commerce. Often the movies themselves contain the most eloquent testimony of their institutional history, both in their confident assertions and in their hesitancies and contradictions. Since this book is based less on textual analysis than on historical interpretation, "case studies" are included to illustrate the demands, the limitations, and indeed the expressiveness of broader industrial and narrative frameworks, rather than for any intrinsic merit the films may have as "texts." Some of the most telling evidence for an approach such as this is in the form of scripts and treatments that were abandoned before or during the course of production. Hollywood's permissible field of representation is demonstrated as much by the topics that the industry avoided as by the images that eventually filled the screen.

1

Image Making

Managing the Expansion of the Motion Picture Industry

During and after World War I, the Hollywood film industry underwent a series of fundamental transformations. Companies representing different facets of the industry merged, leading to the creation of giant, vertically integrated corporations. Capital investment soared and output increased, with moviemaking reorganized along factory lines for greater efficiency. Average budgets increased from twenty thousand dollars in 1914 to sixty thousand dollars in 1920 and kept rising.[1] Before the war the American industry had been oriented toward its domestic market, but in the late teens it embarked on a major campaign of global expansion. In short, by the end of the war Hollywood had become big business.

The expanded industry required new bureaucratic structures to regulate its affairs, both aggressively and defensively. The major companies needed to act cooperatively in matters of mutual and noncompetitive interest, such as negotiations over access to foreign markets and the lobbying of the U.S. government for economic concessions. They also needed to arrive at a uniform response to censorship ordinances and to agree on terms for dealing with other producers, distributors, and exhibitors. Just as important, with the movies occupying an increasingly central position in the hearts and minds of audiences around the world, the major companies had to contend with considerable resistance to their cultural power, among both conservative factions within the United States and nationalists abroad. In order to ameliorate such resistance, it was necessary for Hollywood to find ways of regulating the business affairs of the industry and its products. Several earlier attempts to organize aspects of motion picture trade had proved unsuccessful, but 1922 saw the formation of a new high-profile trade association, the Motion Picture Producers and Distributors of America, Inc. The MPPDA promised to be a formidable agency for the coordination the industry's affairs.

Going Global

In the 1910s the buoyancy and scope of the domestic market was reflected in the American producers' relative neglect of effective methods of exploitation overseas. Although by 1906 the Vitagraph company had opened its own foreign offices in London and Paris, most American companies chose not to deal directly with the majority of their foreign customers. Instead, they allowed most of their overseas business to be conducted by foreign sales agents, who reexported American movies from London to destinations around the world.[2] Such an arrangement was ill designed to provide producers with direct information about conditions in specific foreign markets or to promote the American product abroad. The Americans' lackadaisical approach contrasted with the vigorous direct marketing procedures of their European competitors, especially the French and Italians.[3]

When World War I stalled European production, the American companies found themselves with a unique opportunity for foreign expansion. Nevertheless, it was not until the center of movie distribution shifted from London to New York between 1916 and 1918 that any significant change occurred in the attitude of the American producers to the foreign market.[4] The increase in American control over foreign sales and rentals, brought about by the reorganization of patterns of export, encouraged producers and distributors to take a more active stance in foreign trade. American distributor David P. Howells articulated this change in approach at the end of the war:

The time is passed when a distributor can buy the foreign rights for a production and then sell it to a European agent for circulation and let the matter drop. The distributor must make a judicious selection of all films bought for the foreign market. . . .

The picture that pleases the Chinese may not "go over" with picture fans in Argentine. The distributor must have an intimate first hand knowledge of the foreign market before he buys.[5]

Between 1916 and 1918 the extent of the American industry's representation overseas had increased markedly. The change from domestic to global scale would eventually affect every aspect of the industry, but distribution was the branch most immediately confronted with the need for new patterns of organization consonant with an international outlook.

Some companies preferred to sign agents overseas to act on their behalf, while others formed subsidiary branches for distribution abroad. Universal, which had established distribution facilities in Europe before the war, initiated new branches in the Far East, while Fox established a combination of agencies and branches in Europe, South America, and Australia. Famous Players–Lasky and Goldwyn both worked through agencies in South Africa, South America, Australia, Scandinavia, Central America, and Europe.[6] In 1920 American exports of exposed film stood at 175,233,000 feet, more than five times the prewar figure.[7] While such patterns of expansion involved a measure of competition between the companies concerned, particularly in Europe, these four companies together managed to encircle virtually the entire globe with regional networks.

The industry's approach to foreign expansion foreshadowed its hegemonic operations in the 1920s and 1930s, when a clique of powerful companies adopted a set of interdependent relationships that Douglas Gomery has characterized as those of a "chronically quarrelsome but closely knit family." Indeed, while Gomery has observed that only the oligopolists that emerged in the 1920s were able to construct effective world distribution networks, it was equally the case that a position of power within the industry depended on access to foreign distribution.[8] The reason lay in the structure of the production economy instituted during the period of global expansion. From about 1917, a movie's foreign sales—already representing 20–40 percent of its expected revenue—began to be calculated into the budgeting of its negative cost. This level of capitalization (representing more than fifty thousand dollars for a prestige feature in 1919) allowed production to be carried out on a sufficiently lavish scale to discourage potential competitors, both at home and abroad.[9] However, tying the industry's profit margin to global economies of scale also turned foreign revenues from a luxury into a necessity, particularly where high-budget, prestige productions were concerned.

The extent of the industry's dependence upon the overseas market was frequently a cause for discomfort among its executives. In his memoirs, Will Hays, president of the MPPDA from 1922 to 1945, recalled that the very success of capturing the foreign trade "created an endless string of problems and rivalries." Contemplating the crucial third of the industry's gross that was derived from overseas, he commented, "While this comfortingly proved the popularity of American films, it made it absolutely necessary to hold our foreign markets, in order to maintain both quality and quantity in production. This was the sword of Damocles always hanging over our heads."[10]

Growing Together

There were a number of pressing reasons for American film companies to work cooperatively after the war and to present a united front on issues of mutual concern. Conditions facing the industry were changing rapidly and growing ever more complex. At the same time as the industry's growth necessitated a change in organizational approach, a number of external threats faced producers and distributors on both the domestic and the foreign fronts.

The development of the leading companies, notably Famous Players–Lasky and Loew's, into giant corporations was characteristic of American big business in the 1910s and 1920s.[11] Like other corporate behemoths, these companies ran into trouble with antimonopoly legislation. Their vertically integrated operations, which had the advantage of guaranteeing both exhibition for their products and products for their exhibition outlets, arguably placed them in violation of the Sherman Anti-Trust Act of 1890. The larger companies were thus faced with an ongoing legislative battle simply to maintain the basic structure of their businesses. It was a battle they would ultimately lose, but until 1948, when the Supreme Court's ruling in the "Paramount Suit" forced the reorganization of the relationships between production, distribution, and exhibition, it was waged with feeling in a variety of legislative arenas and required the studios to be united in their own defense.[12]

The Sherman Act had been invoked to cause the dissolution of the monopolistic Motion Picture Patents Company in 1915. In that instance, the legal action had been initiated by production and distribution companies who argued that their trade was being unreasonably restrained.[13] Five years later, however, legal pressure was exerted on the major companies by independent exhibitors. Always a vocal and contentious lobby group, in 1920 they formed the Motion Picture Theater Owners of America (MPTOA) to represent their interests. It is not surprising that their relations with the vertically integrated companies were strained, since those companies had themselves originated in combinations of production and exhibition businesses, leaving the remaining exhibitors out in the cold, operating in the shadow of conglomerates motivated by new sets of industrial priorities. One of the MPTOA's first activities was "to place on record the producer-distributors who were invading the exhibition field." Adolph Zukor, whose Famous Players–Lasky company was most flagrantly in breach of the act, immediately promised that the company "would not extend its activities excepting where it was impossible for [its] pictures . . . to be given presentation," but this satisfied neither the exhibitors nor the government.[14] In August 1921 the Federal Trade Commission filed a complaint against Famous Players–Lasky, charging the company with unfair practices and the monopolization of first-run theaters.[15] Although this action did not result in a "cease and desist" order until 1927, it demonstrated the need for more effective countermeasures on the part of the major companies.

Another problem requiring a united response was official censorship, or "political censorship," as it was termed within the industry. In 1920 films were subject to censorship in Maryland, Kansas, Pennsylvania, and Ohio, and during the year bills proposing censorship were introduced in twenty-two other states.[16] With standards varying between states, and sometimes even between municipalities, nationwide motion picture commerce was becoming increasingly difficult and costly. Distributors not only had to pay for alterations to their products to make them conform to the requirements of official boards, but they were also obliged to pay a fee every time the movies were subjected to inspection. Thus local censorship became equivalent to a multiple taxation on motion pictures. The extent to which the major companies mobilized their resources in opposition to censorship can be gauged by the fact that industry representatives managed to block all of the twenty-two bills proposed in 1920. Nevertheless, when in 1921 censorship legislation succeeded in New York, the most important territory in the country to film distributors, industry leaders realized that they needed a more effective combined strategy for dealing with legislative action.[17]

The major companies also needed to find representation of their collective interests in the foreign field. Gathering adequate information about prevailing trade conditions was a formidable task in itself, considering the extent of the market. Universal, for example, had 175 representatives in foreign countries in 1920.[18] The U.S. Department of Commerce had long included motion picture items in its commerce reports, but officials in the industry felt that the level of governmental support did not adequately reflect the movie's status as a rising article of foreign commerce.[19] Protectionism, copyright problems, taxes, and the vagaries of foreign exchange all contributed to the mass of obstacles facing distributors in the foreign field. In 1921 William Sherrill, of the Froh-

man Amusement Corporation, urged the industry to apply pressure to
the government:

[I]t behooves the American producers to urge [the industry's] influence upon
Congress to engage in a trade or exchange agreement with foreign countries. . . . The motion picture industry has not wielded the influence it pos-
sesses and is altogether unmindful of its power, its privileges and its rights.
Congress has enacted laws to protect other interests that export its merchandise; so, too, should Congress be called upon to protect the fifth largest industry in the United States. That too little consideration is given by our Government to the export and import trade as far as it applies to motion pictures
is proven by the meager, slipshod and unsatisfactory information furnished
by American Consuls in foreign countries concerning conditions as far as
they apply to the motion picture industry existing in the countries of their
assignment.[20]

Action was required all the more urgently since postwar devaluation
of currency abroad had allowed foreign producers, especially the Germans, to undercut their American competitors, making Hollywood's
hold on the world's screens seem suddenly tenuous. The producers'
claims to deserving assistance were reinforced by the fact that they had
cooperated closely with the government during the war, disseminating
motion pictures abroad under the auspices of the Committee on Public
Information.[21] After this special relationship came to an end in 1919,
they found themselves without an effective platform from which to
impress the government with their importance and to insist on their
"privileges."

Meanwhile, censorship was a problem abroad as well as at home.
A range of specific cultural factors resulted in excisions: for example,
Japanese censors always deleted kissing, while their British counterparts were inclined to censor Christian ceremonies. Although American producers would have preferred their products to be shown intact, they were not particularly concerned if the films were trimmed
for exhibition in specific cultural contexts. The adaptability of the
silent medium enabled a movie to withstand considerable modification before it became totally incoherent. On the other hand, a movie's
being withheld altogether meant a definite loss of income. Australia,
Norway, and Canada—all relatively lucrative markets—were among
those nations which imposed particularly stringent censorship standards and were inclined to ban movies on the basis of their treatment
of sexual and criminal subjects. Distributors complained that producers completely failed to take the sensitivities of foreign censors into
account, with the result that many films lost revenue through being
withheld from foreign territories.[22] However, little action was taken

until a series of problems arose in the Mexican market, convincing producers of the need for industry-wide regulation of certain images intended for export.

The root of the Mexican problem was that the westerns that formed a staple of American film production regularly featured Mexican villains, following the precedent of popular "triumphalist" literature.[23] Peter Stanfield has shown that the Mexican villain was characterized as the antithesis of the Anglo cowboy hero as early as 1906, and by 1913 the "greaser" was stereotyped as treacherous, cowardly, and lascivious.[24] When in the course of international distribution these movies found their way to Mexico, the Mexican government was not unreasonably incensed at such a slur on the national character. Tired of complaining fruitlessly about individual instances of offense, the Mexican government banned the entire output of the offending companies in 1922.[25] The Mexican action helped in several ways to bring home to the American producers the implications of their participation in global distribution. First, movie content needed to be considered in relation to the intended range of distribution. Second, offense to a foreign nation by a single producer was a matter of concern to all the major companies, since it could damage the reputation and prestige of the entire industry in that market. Finally, the industry needed representation of its collective interests in foreign markets to negotiate and bargain with forces that opposed it.

As a result of the motion picture companies' various mutual concerns, the MPPDA was formed in March 1922. The association was not the producers' first attempt at cooperative action, but unlike its predecessors, it managed to endure and exercise a lasting influence on the industry. The MPPDA was much like other trade associations that appeared in response to the needs of consolidated industries in the 1920s, promoting stability within the industry, rationalization of business practices, and mutual cooperation.[26] Although the present study is primarily concerned with activities affecting production policies, these belonged to a wider context of industrial procedures. For example, in the 1920s the MPPDA was particularly concerned with regularizing relations between the production and distribution branches of the industry and was involved in protracted negotiations over a Standard Exhibition Contract. Its Legal Department promoted an innovative system of countrywide commercial arbitration to settle trade disputes within the United States. This system significantly reduced the time and money spent on litigation until 1929, when the Department of Justice found it to be a violation of antitrust legislation.[27] The MPPDA also formalized various agreements between authors and producers. Other areas of

concern included copyright and tax laws, the use of movies in education, nontheatrical distribution, and foreign trade.

Among the business transacted at the MPPDA's first board meeting
on 13 April 1922 was the formulation of a resolution to "do everything
possible to prevent the production of any new motion picture films
which present the Mexican character in a derogatory or objectionable
manner." The meeting also authorized the dispatch of an emissary to
Mexico, in the absence of official diplomatic contact between Mexico
and the United States. Will Hays recalled that "by that action the organized industry plunged into the sphere of foreign relations."[28] The
MPPDA agent, Bernon T. Woodle, spent three months negotiating
with the Mexican government and eventually managed to persuade it
to lift its ban. This is not to say, however, that offense to the Mexican
nation ceased as a result. On the contrary, despite early optimism that
the Mexican "Bad Man" could be "dislodged from the popular imagination," he continued to appear in a surprising variety of manifestations,
as we shall see in chapter 6.[29] Nevertheless, to the extent that the
MPPDA initiated negotiations at a diplomatic level, and in its designa-
tion of film content as a site of negotiation between the industry and its
foreign markets, this early Mexican episode anticipated practices that
would increasingly characterize the association's foreign policy in the
1920s and 1930s.

Image Problems

If the MPPDA was similar to other trade associations in its general industrial objectives, it was also different from them in its relationship
with the public. Although the motion picture industry was an object of
celebrity, the very nature of its merchandise as the material of popular
culture made it a focus of the anxieties and hostilities aroused by the
modern age. The MPPDA's unusual public relations problems caused
the association to represent itself, and especially its founding president, Will Hays, as moral "fixers" who would guide the industry in a
quest for social responsibility.

In the United States the members of the established middle class
perceived the movie as an object of suspicion as soon as it came to their
attention in the early 1900s. The bourgeoisie had ample reason to find
the movies objectionable, for in them converged many elements of the
new century that denoted change. The huge immigrant influx from
Europe, the creation of a large industrial proletariat, and the rise of
powerful corporations were recently established facts of American life
which contributed to a sense of anxiety among the country's forces of

conservatism. All three developments were implicated in the emergence of the motion picture, which seemed to be both symptomatic of and contributory to a revolution in social norms.[30]

The development of motion picture technology coincided with the rise of a mass urban and immigrant audience in the United States, which was particularly receptive to the movies.[31] For recent arrivals in the cities, cut off from their traditional communities and sources of amusement, the motion pictures proved an ideal entertainment not only because they were cheap but also because they required no specific cultural qualifications. Filmmakers were quick to exploit this market. According to Hays, "American films of the earliest silent picture era had to be designed to appeal to the less educated groups and to the large foreign-language sections of our own population. It was essential that the viewer should be able to follow the story whether understanding English or not. Hence our silent pictures early developed a style and form that commended them to all races and groups of people, without the aid of words."[32] The accessibility of movies to this polyglot community probably assisted the spread of American movies overseas, but at home it was an immediate source of worry for many members of the middle class. As the movies gained their independence from music halls and became the main attraction at primarily cinematic programs, many felt alarm at the prospect of a new venue for the large-scale dissemination of ideas and standards in which traditional moral guardians—parents, teachers, church leaders—had no stake and over which they had no control.

To make matters worse, the movies seemed to embody the threat posed by trusts and magnates to an established pattern of American life. In the late nineteenth and early twentieth centuries, anxiety about the pace and direction of social change was directed at the burgeoning businesses of the period, which seemed to be at the heart of an erosion of individuality and moral fiber.[33] The high profile of the motion picture business made its rapid expansion unusually conspicuous, and partly as a result of the monopolistic reputation of the Motion Picture Patents Company, the industry was widely deplored as an unholy and illegal combine.[34]

The producers might have been able to weather this criticism except for the fact that adverse public sentiment was liable to lead directly to restrictive legislation that plagued their practical and financial operations. Bad public relations had caused legislative trouble for the producers as early as 1908, when Mayor George McClellan of New York City expressed his dissatisfaction with the cinematograph as a medium of public amusement by revoking the license of every motion picture theater in the city. Although the order was not effectively enforced and devolved in any case on the unsatisfactory public safety standards at most cinemas, condemnation of the movies on religious and moral grounds was also a factor. At that time the exhibitors turned for help to the People's Institute, a philanthropic organization which had demonstrated a relatively benevolent attitude toward motion pictures.[35] The institute responded by establishing, in 1909, the National Board of Censorship (NBC), through which movie manufacturers could submit their products, on a voluntary basis, to the scrutiny of an independent committee.

The Board of Censorship considered the treatment of such sensitive subjects as sex, violence, crime, drunkenness, vulgarity, and moral outcome. Seals of approval were issued to movies judged to be inoffensive, setting a standard for the guidance of exhibitors throughout the country. Movies that fell short of the required standard could be revised in consultation with the board. The adoption of this system of self-regulation was to the advantage of the filmmakers because it promoted confidence in the industry and helped to institutionalize processes of distribution. At the same time, by insisting on domestically formulated standards, self-regulation helped to exclude the products of foreign industries and to concentrate control of the domestic market in the hands of American producers. In 1916 the distributor Walter Erwin outlined his interpretation of the board's origins in these terms at a Federal Motion Picture Commission hearing:

In 1909 there were some foreign films imported which had the continental standards of morals. The fathers of the industry at that time, Thomas A. Edison, Mr. Lubin, and Commodore Blackton . . . were proud of the industry and had every confidence and faith in its future. They were jealous of its reputation, so that they voluntarily went to Mayor McClellan and asked that he appoint a committee of citizens to review the pictures before they went out to the public. Mayor McClellan communicated with the People's Institute, and the People's Institute brought about the formation of this board.[36]

Although Erwin misrepresented these events—all the evidence points to the exhibitors, notably William Fox, having approached the People's Institute—the general point of his account is nevertheless telling. Thomas Edison, Sigmund Lubin, and J. Stuart Blackton were all key players in the Motion Picture Patents Company, which, as Kristin Thompson has shown, attempted to gain control of the American distribution field through the General Film Company and to exclude foreign competition.[37] Erwin's interpretation of events illustrates the principle

that the internal regulation of American motion picture content, undertaken in the name of moral improvement, was usually a matter of
sound business practice as well.

Whatever its other benefits, the National Board of Censorship did
not constitute a lasting solution to the industry's public relations problems. Its detractors were skeptical about the proposition of a "gentleman's agreement" with respect to motion picture practices. They complained that the voluntary aspects of the NBC rendered it impotent
and irrelevant, and they pointed out that members of the reviewing
committees mainly came from the New York area, where people were
alleged to have lower standards of morality than the majority of the
American public. Besides, they argued, since the expenses of the
board were largely met by the manufacturers themselves, the industry's claims of impartiality could hardly be taken seriously.

Although the voices raised against the industry constituted a minority, they were socially powerful. Lary May identifies the reformers as
"high" Progressives, "men and women aligned to rising business, professional, and political groups."[38] The men were active in the main-
stream of church and society, and the women were organized and
educated, often members of women's clubs, and committed to notions
of volunteerism and personal service in the community. Their influence was sufficient to have their complaints translated into calls for
governmental censorship at both the state and federal levels. The first
proposal for a permanent Federal Motion Picture Commission—
effectively a national censor—was introduced in Congress in 1914.
Although the commission was approved in principle at the committee
stage, the proposal was later set aside, only to be refloated in 1916.[39]
Indeed, public pressure ensured the reappearance of similar proposals
in 1926 and 1934. The Reverend William Sheafe Chase, one of the main
architects of the bills, voiced the reformers' principal concern in 1916:
"The wireless, the automobile, the various inventions make new conditions, and we have to meet those situations. Here is a new condition
with reference to the childhood of our country, a new danger that
confronts them. . . . Who do [the filmmakers] propose ought to have
control of this great invention? Who are going to be the people, if this
bill is not enacted, who will educate the children of our land? A few
motion-picture manufacturers, whose principal motive is making
money."[40]

In July 1922 Chase's character assessment of the manufacturers received support from Judge Harold J. Hinman of the Supreme Court
Appellate Division, in a ruling concerning the eligibility of newsreels

for censorship exemption. Agreeing with a decision of 1915 which had denied narrative films the protection of the First Amendment (*Mutual Film Corporation v Ohio Industrial Commission*), he reasoned:

The "show" business is clearly different from the newspaper business and those who engage in the show business are none too likely to confine their productions to the things which are just, pure and of good report; but in order to continue to attract patrons, many would cast discretion and self-control to the winds, without restraint, social or moral. There are those who would give unrestrained rein to passion. If the thing be true and real, they would reveal it in its utter nakedness. They appreciate the business advantage of depicting the evil and voluptuous thing with poisonous charm. Certainly there are some things which are happening in actual life today which should not have pictorial representation in such places of public amusement as are regulated by this legislation, places where the audience are not confined to men alone or women alone and where children are particularly attracted.[41]

Part of Hinman's case hinged on a political and aesthetic objection to the motion picture medium as an art based on photography. In the bourgeois press and stage, representations of events were necessarily mediated before reaching the public; before the development of the motion picture, the world that had been represented as social and political "reality" had effectively been a construct controlled by an educated class. Now newsreels threatened to propagate images of an unreconstructed world that might be inappropriate for the majority to see. It is clear, however, that Hinman's ruling was also crucially influenced by his distaste for the motion picture producers themselves, and for the industry as a whole.

Hinman, like Chase, expressed a particular anxiety about the effects of motion pictures on children: "The child soon becomes sophisticated, as he attends this school of experience . . . where character may be shaped most readily the one way or the other according to the sentiments conveyed."[42] This widely held anxiety was at the heart of public support for legislative controls. Modern society, as typified by the motion picture, raised the specter of the loss of traditional authority not only in the community at large but also within the home. Mothers testified before the Federal Motion Picture Commission hearings, saying that "we must have a uniform standard for the whole country, so that these plays will not creep in and injure the morals of our children."[43] Motion pictures were recognized as having a potent impact on the young because, despite the use of printed intertitles, they did not require literacy or mental sophistication to make them comprehensible. In this respect, their appeal to children was often conflated with their appeal to illiterate adults, who were themselves improperly distin-

guished from non-English speakers and immigrants in general. Together, these groups formed "the impressionable classes," for whose
protection censorship was an evident necessity. A women's club representative declared at a New York State censorship hearing that "we
think the most important thing is the safeguarding of the morals not
only of children but also of the vast throng of persons, who, while
perhaps they are not children in years, may be children in minds."[44]

At the same time, the expansion of the business overseas cast the
role of the producers as cultural arbiters into a new and alarming light.
If the industry was defining America's way of life to immigrants and
children, it was now doing the same for vast audiences in foreign countries. Those who perceived the movies to be controlled by ignorant and
unpatriotic producers were concerned about the international implications of their projection of Americanism abroad. In the early 1920s
these sentiments combined with anti-Semitic attitudes toward the Eastern European immigrants who were the most visible entrepreneurs in
the movie business, notably Marcus Loew and Adolph Zukor.[45] Their
Jewish affiliations rendered their influence alien in the minds of members of the Christian majority, who believed that these men lacked the
cultural credentials to occupy positions of social power. At best the
reformers felt that the prestige of their nation would be eroded and its
diplomatic missions undermined; at worst they worried that the
screen's irresponsible portrayals of international relations would lead
to further world conflict.[46]

Ellen O'Grady, a former New York deputy police commissioner, expressed the concerns of many at a state censorship hearing: "Why, in
the pagan countries to-day we read in our daily paper that they are
suppressing and rejecting the American film because it is demoralizing
their people. What is the natural conclusion to come to, but that those
men are dumping their filth on the poor pagan. Are they considering
the honor and glory of this country of ours? What consideration do
they deserve who have stigmatized our country to this extent . . .
those money-mad men?"[47] Testimonies of this kind reveal a devout
wish to wrest control of the movie industry away from the "motion
picture trust" and invest it in more dependable sections of the community. Chase mused that "the printing invention was seized upon at
once by the educational and higher influences of society. The remarkable thing is that the motion picture has been seized upon by the amusement agencies of civilization, and the great problem now is how to
change that situation."[48]

Yet the call for a "single standard" of acceptable content tended to
displace the more fundamental concerns of the reformers from the area

of industrial control to censorship. The women's clubs and the church-men tackled the problem on the level at which it confronted them in their everyday lives: on the billboards of their town, on their local movie screens, and in the mouths and swaggers of their children. The intricacies of the Sherman Act and the Federal Trade Commission were less tangible and confronted them less immediately. Thus the public war concerning cultural hegemony was destined to be played out as a series of bitter skirmishes over the border territories of permissible representation.

Defensive Measures

Even at the time when the National Board of Censorship was being formed to provide a measure of "voluntary" industry control, the larger producers might have welcomed an official system of national censorship if certain preconditions could have been met. Salacious or offensive products by fly-by-night operators only damaged the reputa-tion of the entire industry, and bringing these miscreants into line would have served the interests of the established companies. Another factor favoring federal control was the economic problem arising from the adoption of idiosyncratic censorship requirements by states and municipalities. A "single standard" could have saved the industry a lot of money and bother.

In 1916 the Zukor-Lasky group of companies even went so far as to cooperate in the framing of a bill for federal regulation of content.[49] However, there were several insurmountable obstacles to the indus-try's acceptance of a national censor. A federal commission would not have had the constitutional authority to override the prerogatives of the states; there was therefore the real danger that the industry would be saddled with both federal and local censorship requirements. There was also the obvious risk that the standards set by an appointed board would be so high-minded as to render movies completely uncommer-cial. In addition, the producers did not want to lay their business deal-ings open to governmental scrutiny. "Regulation" from the outside was a loaded concept; compulsory regulation on one front could soon open the door to regulation on others. At the same time there was the practical consideration that the wide-scale distribution of motion pic-tures depended to some extent on their capacity for adaptation to the requirements of different communities.

In 1915 an association called the Motion Picture Board of Trade of America was formed, comprising "the manufacturers, distributors, and some of the principal exhibitors throughout the country who are united for the purpose of common defense."[50] In the absence of a workable legislative compromise over a Federal Motion Picture Commission, one of the "defensive" tasks of the board was to guard against censorship initiatives wherever they arose. The association was short-lived however, and was quickly superseded by the National Association of the Motion Picture Industry (NAMPI) in 1916. This organization closely prefigured the MPPDA, as it dealt with trade relations, export conditions, and technical and logistical matters as well as censorship. In 1919, in an attempt to satisfy those who criticized the industry on moral grounds, its members submitted their products to the National Board of Review (previously the National Board of Censorship) for inspection. As the change of name reflects, however, the board had abandoned its "censoring" function in 1916 in favor of reviewing and classifying movies as a public information service.[51] The successful passage of censorship legislation in New York State in 1921 reflected the fact that the National Board was not perceived as an adequate check on motion picture standards. As far as public relations and the imminence of legislative controls were concerned, the industry was no better off than it had been in the mid-1910s.

Indeed, in some ways the industry's standing had deteriorated in the postwar climate. Where modernity flouted the ordered worlds of tradition, the movies often got the blame. For example, Cecil B. De Mille, who was working for Famous Players–Lasky, was notorious not for the spectacles with which he was later associated but for sexual comedies of manners conducted within the institution of modern marriage. As Lary May has commented, these movies marked a departure from the Victorian morality that had previously been enshrined in movie narratives.[52] *Old Wives for New* (1918), *Don't Change Your Husband* (1919), *Male and Female* (1919), *Why Change Your Wife?* (1920), *Forbidden Fruit* (1921), and *The Affairs of Anatol* (1921) employed contexts of American domesticity for comic explorations of such contemporary issues as divorce, female sexuality, and the pleasures of consumerism. Erich von Stroheim's *Blind Husbands* (1919) and *Foolish Wives* (1921), made for Universal, also challenged the institution of marriage, though with the lure of foreign eroticism rather than American modernism.

Meanwhile, one of the greatest threats to traditional norms appeared to be "Hollywood" itself, as it took root in the public imagination.[53] Inflated salaries provided successful stars with the means to adopt extraordinary lifestyles, apparently characterized by glamour and excess, and the popular press eagerly seized on any hint of scandal. The scale of the uproar surrounding the unsuccessful prosecution for manslaughter of screen comedian Roscoe ("Fatty") Arbuckle in 1921

and 1922 demonstrated the vulnerability of the industry to public condemnation, especially where a sexual implication was involved.[54]

In New York, the financial and management center of "Hollywood,"
the company heads realized that a dramatic public gesture of reform
was needed to halt the slide toward governmental control. The formation of the MPPDA in 1922 was represented as a turning point in the
industry's relations with the community. The association's membership comprised most of the major producers and distributors.[55] Their
selection of Indiana politician William Harrison Hays as their president
symbolized the statement they wished to make. In 1920, as chairman of
the Republican Party, Hays had been instrumental in Warren G. Harding's election to the presidency, and he had served as postmaster general in Harding's cabinet. Hays was a skillful political negotiator and
had the right kinds of connections to be able to do business with the
Federal Trade Commission, but from the point of view of public relations, his main qualifications were his reputation for high morals and
his prominent membership in the Presbyterian Church.

Hays was greeted in the press as a new broom who would sweep
the recalcitrant elements among the producers into line, in much the
same way as Judge Kenesaw Mountain Landis had been co-opted to
clean up the baseball industry after the scandal of a World Series fix in
1919.[56] The MPPDA's ideal account of Hays's intervention is encapsu-
lated in a chapter summary of a 1923 publication, *That Marvel—the
Movie:* "Grows up in the Slums—Used and Abused as a Money-
Getter—Goes from Bad to Worse—Will Hays Called to the Rescue—
Pulpit, Press and Playwrights Thunder Against It—The Responsibility of the Public—The Light in the Darkness."[57] The institution of the
MPPDA, with Hays at its head, laid the foundation for mechanisms to
"interpret the public to the industry and the industry to the public."[58]

2

The Open Door

The Industry's Public Relations

Hollywood has always had to tread a fine line between the short-term profits associated with sensational material and the long-term industrial stability promised by "responsible" entertainments. The MPPDA became instrumental in striking this balance in the 1920s. MPPDA president Will Hays was anxious to enhance the public's image of motion pictures: he tried to persuade the affluent middle classes to adopt the movies as a form of cultural expression, and he hoped that by increasing patronage from that quarter he would be able to transform the nature of audience demand. He reasoned that if "high-class" and educational products could be sure of returning a profit, producers could reasonably be expected to abandon the controversial subject matter that threatened the industry's status as widely consumable family entertainment. Hays experimented with strategies designed to give members of the educated middle class a positive investment in the industry, promising them a measure of influence over the nature and treatment of material adapted for the screen. Although some of Hays's initial ideas proved impractical, an "open door" was created for specific lobby groups to influence aspects of motion picture production.

Meanwhile, Hollywood's representatives abroad were equally preoccupied with the problem of how to reduce resistance to their products while maintaining consumer allegiance. Playing down the broader cultural impact of the American cinema as the vanguard of consumer culture, they tried to maintain the good will of foreign governments by encouraging the studios to tailor their products more specifically to the requirements of global consumption. If motion pictures were under pressure to become more middle class within the United States, abroad they were under pressure to submerge any elements that might be politically contentious and to concentrate on "universal" themes. Both subject matter and its treatment were offered as points of negotiation in the quest for the widest possible audience.

Toward a Department of Public Relations

The MPPDA was incorporated on 10 March 1922, with a membership comprising all the major companies involved in American production and/or distribution. Its stated objectives were "to foster the common interests of those engaged in the motion picture industry in the United States by establishing and maintaining the highest possible moral and artistic standards in motion picture production, by developing the educational as well as the entertainment value and the general usefulness of the motion picture, by diffusing accurate and reliable information with reference to the industry, by reforming abuses relative to the industry, by securing freedom from unjust or unlawful exactions and by other lawful and proper means."[1]

These aims encompassed industry-wide public and corporate relations but did not implicate the regulation of movie content in the association's industrial strategy. The omission was undoubtedly calculated. Barely a year before, the MPPDA's predecessor, the National Association of the Motion Picture Industry (NAMPI), had announced its intention to restrict content in line with community standards, only to find that its public relations were damaged rather than enhanced. NAMPI had passed a resolution known as the Thirteen Points, agreeing to avoid specific material deemed offensive, including "exaggerated sex plays, white slavery and commercialized vice, themes that make virtue odious and vice attractive, plays that would make drunkenness, gambling, drugs or other vices attractive, themes that tend to weaken the authority of the law, stories that might offend any person's religious beliefs, and stories and themes which may instruct the morally feeble in methods of committing crime or by cumulative processes emphasize crime and the commission of crime."[2] NAMPI's problems had stemmed from the fact that the Thirteen Points were openly published in the press. In the absence of any effective method of enforcing the observance of its self-regulatory code, the industry was highly vulnerable to criticism when producers were perceived to have violated its stated limits regarding themes and treatments. The public disapprobation that resulted was expressed in the passage of censorship legislation in New York State in April and May 1921, an event which signaled NAMPI's ineffectiveness in protecting the industry and ultimately led to the demise of that organization.

Will Hays decided to try a different tack in his bid to improve the industry's public image under the MPPDA. He initiated an innovative policy designed to recruit influential organizations in support of a publicly led program of motion picture reform. The cornerstone of the program was a Committee on Public Relations, made up of representatives of powerful community groups, which Hays hoped would serve to channel "destructive" censorship energies into a constructive drive toward higher movie standards. He called the committee "my special hobby—a creature of my own brain entirely," and he was still trying to convince company heads of its importance in September 1922, six months after the MPPDA was incorporated.[3] By this time the committee's operations were already under way. On 22 June 1922 Hays had organized a meeting at the Waldorf Astoria of 125 representatives of community groups, 74 of whom eventually served on the committee. Their reasons for interest in motion pictures were diverse: a representative of the YWCA, for instance, was concerned about the decline of U.S. prestige in the Orient, and a member of the National Safety Council was interested in promoting films on accident prevention.[4]

Partly because of the unwieldy size of the group and partly because of the range of individual members' concerns, smaller committees were organized, including a steering committee (the Committee of Twenty) and several subcommittees.[5] The Executive Committee comprised Lee Hanmer of the Russell Sage Foundation (chairman), Mrs. Oliver Harriman of the Camp Fire Girls, Charles McMahon of the National Catholic Welfare Conference, and James West of the Boy Scouts.

Hays's plan was that the Committee on Public Relations should be given facilities to preview coming releases. When the members reacted favorably, they would recommend the picture to the organizations they represented; adverse reactions would receive no publicity but would be forwarded in confidence to the producer concerned. This strategy would have cast the committee in a role similar to that of the National Board of Review: it would have been a source of information and advice without wielding any binding power. But even at the committee's inaugural meeting, several delegates voiced the expectation that they would play a much more active role in the affairs of the industry. They envisaged fulfilling a function more akin to that of the early National Board of Censorship, which had had the power to request changes in movies before distribution. National Catholic Welfare Conference representative Charles McMahon was among those who favored this expanded role, suggesting to the committee that "the exhibitors' problems would be greatly aided, the problem of cooperating with the exhibitor locally would be helped, if we could have some central organization, that would attempt to correct the key negative, so that the key negative and prints would be satisfactory before being sent out to the public."[6]

The Executive Committee insisted that the MPPDA should fund a permanent executive officer, resulting in the appointment of Colonel Jason S. Joy, a former executive assistant at the American Red Cross. Committee members claimed that the financial commitment involved in taking on a full-time employee would demonstrate that the MPPDA took the Committee on Public Relations seriously and would help to discount criticism that the producers were using the group as a public relations front.[7]

The committee's seriousness of purpose was brought home to Hays in December, when he spoke to the press about the blacklisting of Roscoe ("Fatty") Arbuckle, who had been locked out of the industry for nine months following his acquittal on charges of manslaughter. Hays sought to clarify his own position, namely, that it was not his job to judge individual conduct and that since Arbuckle had been found innocent, he ought to be allowed to return to work. The MPPDA was at once swamped with telegrams and telephone calls from members of the committee, expressing outrage that they had not been consulted on such an important matter of policy. Several delegates, including Julius Barnes of the Chamber of Commerce, tendered their resignations. On 4 January 1923 an emergency meeting was called, at which a chastened Hays explained, "I did not understand that the Committee would want to get into the attitude of responsible censors of pictures, that was not the idea and I thought the Committee did not want to get into the position of censors of morals or conduct of individuals."[8] With some difficulty he weathered the storm, which included censure in the press encouraged by the hostile Motion Picture Theater Owners of America.

Hays and the Committee on Public Relations were in accord, however, on the need to elevate public taste so that "clean and artistic" pictures would meet a greater response at the box office than those that were vulgar and sensational. Achieving this goal would involve recruiting the participation of the estimated 40 percent of the American public who did not generally attend motion pictures, especially those of "cultured outlook." Committee delegates agreed to Hays's whitelisting proposals to the extent that they were prepared to preview films and encourage their members to make box office hits of those that met their standards of art and morality. However, the delegates felt that the producers should be equally prepared to follow their guidance in modifying motion pictures in the name of higher standards. The Committee of Twenty recommended that their comments should be made available to producers on a regular basis: "After the pictures have been seen each organization represented will put in writing and forward to the Executive Secretary such comments as it believes will be of assistance to the producers in making changes in the picture previewed or as indicating things to be avoided or emphasized in future production."[9]

Since individual delegates had the task of mobilizing their respective organizations, it is not surprising that some took up the challenge more energetically than others. Among the most prominent were the Daughters of the American Revolution, the Boy Scouts, the General Federation of Women's Clubs, the International Federation of Catholic Alumnae, the Russell Sage Foundation, the National Congress of Parents and Teachers, the National Education Association, the National Catholic Welfare Conference, and the YMCA.[10] The Catholic organizations were particularly active, and since they had large and powerful constituencies whom the producers were anxious to mollify, they were able to exert an unusual degree of influence on the industry. Rita McGoldrick of the International Federation of Catholic Alumnae claimed in 1926 that her organization had been able to effect changes in objectionable sequences with little resistance from the producers.[11] When Catholic representative Charles McMahon took exception to *Between Friends* (Vitagraph, 1924), a drama featuring marital infidelity and suicide, he was able to have the film withdrawn from circulation for additional censoring.[12] However, many other committee members had neither the organizational infrastructure nor the interest to make their participation worthwhile, and their collective efforts lacked direction and cohesion. Jason Joy arranged meetings for film previews and discussions every two weeks, but enthusiasm for these soon waned.[13]

Among the more active of the subcommittees were the Committee on Historical and Patriotic Information, which cooperated with D. W. Griffith during the production of *America* (D. W. Griffith/United Artists, 1924), and the Committee on Pedagogic Pictures, which worked out the basis for a series of educational movies by Eastman.[14] The most conspicuous activity was that undertaken by the Committee on Children's Matinees, which was involved in the compilation of a series of special programs that were widely distributed for Saturday morning showings. Each program consisted of a package of seven or eight reels of recycled material supplied by different member companies of the MPPDA, usually comprising a feature, a short educational subject, and a short comedy. The service was a promotional activity rather than a profit-making exercise, and reduced-price arrangements with exhibitors ensured that a child's ticket price never exceeded ten cents. Most of the organizational work for the Committee on Children's Matinees was done by Joy's assistant, Ward P. Woolridge. Meanwhile, other subcommittees met infrequently, and several were inactive.

More seriously for Hays's long-term goals, many of the pictures recommended by the Committee on Public Relations failed at the box office. Although the committee claimed to represent thirty million citizens, its members had to admit that the policy of "boosting" pictures was not a success.[15] Only one film, *The Dramatic Life of Abraham Lincoln* (Rockett-Lincoln Film Co./Associated First National Pictures, 1924), benefited visibly from the committee's efforts. As Miss Leighton of the National Security League lamented, "I have worked so hard with clubs and have had clubs pass beautiful resolutions to get the local chairman to bring better films into the community and then they don't get out to bring the people into the theatres."[16]

At the same time, the producers did not seem to be making "wholesome" entertainment on a completely reliable basis, and public protests were brewing about the nature of material that was being selected for picturization. The thirty million who should have been supporting the efforts of the Committee on Public Relations were instead complaining about the production of movies from salacious books and plays. Against the recommendation of the Subcommittee on Adaptations from Books, *West of the Water Tower* was bought by Lasky and made into a motion picture in revised form (Famous Players–Lasky/Paramount, 1924). *Flaming Youth* (First National, 1923), *Black Oxen* (Frank Lloyd Productions/First National, 1924), and *Lilies of the Field* (Corinne Griffith Productions/First National, 1924) all caused indignation, less because they were salacious themselves than because they advertised notorious books. Suggestive titles and advertising were a particular problem, and Hays observed that fifteen out of forty titles in the Famous Players press book were suggestive.[17] Although the producers were aware of the trouble such titles caused, there was compelling evidence that movies with suggestive titles were disproportionately successful at the box office: Warner Bros.' flop *Lucretia Lombard* (1923), for example, drew "immense crowds" when retitled *Flaming Passion*.[18]

Hollywood's unabated inclination to cater to the wider public's preferences undercut Hays's efforts to improve the industry's public rela-

The Dramatic Life of Abraham Lincoln (Rockett-Lincoln Film Co./Associated First National Pictures, 1924), which depicted episodes in the life of Lincoln from his childhood to his assassination, typified the kind of motion picture that the Committee on Public Relations hoped to promote. The public was reluctant to attend such worthy entertainments, however, and *Lincoln* turned out to be the committee's only real success.

Flaming Youth (First National, 1923) was the kind of movie that threatened to bring Hollywood into disrepute among conservative members of American society. Although it was a melodrama with a "moral" conclusion, its depiction of Jazz Age libertarianism was considered to have a dangerous influence on the young, especially young women.

tions through the committee. Some delegates began to suspect that they had been cynically duped into participating, and several, including the representative of the influential National Congress of Parents and Teachers, publicly resigned.[19] In response, the industry tried to save itself from itself by instituting cooperative controls over source acquisition. In February 1924, the MPPDA Board of Directors passed a resolution requiring the reading departments of all member companies to submit synopses of any books or plays they were considering purchasing to the scrutiny of the association.[20] If anything offensive was discovered, the material was barred from production by any participating company, and no affiliated distributor or exhibitor was permitted to handle it should it be brought to the screen by an independent producer.

By the end of 1924 the strengths and weaknesses of the MPPDA's public relations program had become apparent. Useful cooperation had been established between the industry and several influential organizations, but the broader committee structure had proved unworkable. Energy and enthusiasm had been expended on meetings, letter writing, and positive initiatives, but the association lacked a department that could tackle problems as they arose. Significantly, a precedent had been established that allowed specific objections to be met with modifications to movie content, as happened in the case of *Between Friends*. Indeed, this approach was sometimes extended beyond the confines of the Committee on Public Relations: the National Billiard Association caused *Manhattan* (Famous Players–Lasky/Paramount, 1924) to be modified with cuts and retakes in response to protests on behalf of its "four million" members.[21] The industry required a smoother mechanism to transmit these kinds of pressures to the producers. It had to be able to accommodate professional and commercial groups and influential individuals, as well as religious and community organizations. Consequently, in March 1925, a Department of Public Relations was established within the MPPDA. It was essentially a reorganized and better focused version of the office of the Committee on Public Relations, and the department was headed by the former committee executive secretary, Jason Joy. Dubbed the Open Door, it was advertised as a direct channel of communication between motion picture producers and the public.[22]

The department continued to try to lead public opinion by disseminating pro–motion picture propaganda, but it also had a new, reactive function, which allowed Joy to emphasize the willingness of producers to eliminate from their products material which had proved to be offensive to specific constituencies in the past. At first the Open Door admitted mainly domestic complainants, but its function gradually widened to allow the possibility of access by foreign petitioners as well.

Projecting the American Image Abroad

The Committee on Public Relations had promoted the motion picture as "an instrument of international amity, by correctly portraying American life, ideals and opportunities in pictures sent abroad and the proper portrayal of foreign scenes and persons in all productions."[23] The foreign market only entered the committee members' considerations insofar as they were concerned about the image of the United States projected abroad; all the organizations represented on the committee had constituencies within the United States. By contrast, the Department of Public Relations invited participation somewhat indiscriminately from "every organization of every description in either this country or any other country which is interested in public betterment."[24] Some three years passed before the department's operations regularly incorporated foreign influences, but it is nevertheless significant that the international dimensions of the industry were recognized in the department's original charter, reflecting the fact that developments in the foreign field increasingly demanded the attention not just of the MPPDA's Foreign Department but also of the producers themselves.

The decision to send Bernon T. Woodle to Mexico in 1922 to resolve the impasse between Hollywood and the Mexican government had been taken by the MPPDA's Board of Directors; a separate Foreign Department did not become operational for at least another year. The head of this department from its inception until 1941 was Major Frederick ("Ted") Herron, who had been with Hays during his days at Wabash College in Indiana and had later joined the diplomatic corps and served as a military attaché.[25] Herron's job at the MPPDA was to keep track of conditions affecting foreign sales and to maintain communications between the industry and the U.S. State Department. He was also responsible for persuading the foreign managers of MPPDA member companies to act cooperatively in matters in which they had a noncompetitive interest. When taxes or other trading restrictions were introduced by customer nations, Herron would confer with financial advisers, lawyers, and foreign managers to draw up the industry's response, which ranged from compliance to boycott. When an Australian state sales tax threatened to spread from New South Wales to Victoria in October 1926, for example, he called a meeting of foreign managers and legal representatives to discuss the industry's response, warning them that "this problem is bound to spread if we don't meet it with a united front."[26] The MPPDA also maintained a three-man delegation in Washington, initially headed by Jack Connolly, with whom Herron maintained close contact in his dealings with government departments and agencies.

Hays himself took a considerable personal interest in the foreign situation. In September 1923 he accompanied Herron on a trip to England, where they conferred with the British Board of Film Censors and other industry representatives.[27] This trip probably helped to convince Hays that American exporters needed better recognition and support from their own government. European nations, especially those that had fostered film industries before the war, were coming to realize that Hollywood's domination of their home markets was not a temporary condition. Far from returning to prewar terms of trade, the American position looked more entrenched as each year passed. Not surprisingly, filmmakers in several European countries sought to change that situation. Agitation was building in countries such as Germany, England, and Hungary for governmental protection of national filmmaking enterprises—and, by direct implication, limitation of the free trading opportunities of the Americans.[28] There was pressure for quotas to restrict the numbers of American films allowed to be imported, and for special trade arrangements to promote the reciprocal circulation of European films in the United States. Filmmakers were also beginning to plan a European film cartel, which would pose a threat to the special advantage provided by the enormous domestic market of the United States.

In 1924 Hays began to press the U.S. Department of Commerce for a special Motion Picture Section within the Bureau of Foreign and Domestic Commerce, stressing the need for a comprehensive information service to back the industry in its fight against foreign legislative restrictions. Adverse legislation was rapidly gaining momentum overseas. The German market caused particular concern. Alone among the major population centers of Europe, Germany had been effectively closed to American films in the early 1920s, partly because of import restrictions designed to support its own domestic industry and partly because rampant inflation meant that German distributors did not have the hard currency to pay for American products. When the German currency was reformed and the quota restrictions were relaxed in November 1923, American producers hoped that Germany would become established as a lucrative sector of the foreign market.[29] They also hoped for improved access to Austria, Czechoslovakia, other countries of Eastern Europe, and South America, all of which were established customers of the German industry. On 1 January 1925, however, Germany implemented a new quota system designed to counter the American industry's penetration of its market. This "contingent" plan required, in substance, that only as many films could be imported as were produced in Germany.[30]

The major American companies took individual initiatives to bypass the effect of the contingent by organizing special relationships with German producers and distributors and/or founding subsidiary organizations within Germany.[31] At the same time, the MPPDA took steps on behalf of all of them. On 15 January a subcommittee of foreign managers decided to send an MPPDA representative to Europe. He was to be charged with keeping the association apprised of legislative developments and representing its interests in matters such as the contingent plan.[32]

Hays had initially sent Oscar Solbert, a former White House military aide, to make a preliminary report on the European situation.[33] However, the man eventually chosen as the MPPDA's representative was Colonel Edward G. Lowry, former managing editor of the Philadelphia *Public Ledger* and administrator of German property in London during the war. In February 1926 the MPPDA dispatched Lowry to England, where he was confronted with crises on several fronts. Hungary had passed a law which required compulsory production in that country by all importers of pictures; the German situation had not improved; in England a quota law was pending; Austria was considering its own contingent plan; and agitation for protective legislation was growing in France. Lowry found himself dashing from one trouble spot to the next, "the one fire horse on duty," as he described himself.[34] After two months, he reported:

Broadly speaking, this is the condition our industry faces in Europe: virtually everywhere there is being made an effort to overcome the predominance of the American picture. These efforts spring from a variety of causes. One of them is the intense spirit of nationalism that now pervades all Europe. For patriotic and political reasons, governments of the several countries now seeking to restrict the importation of American pictures desire the establishment of a national picture industry in their own country that will serve as propaganda and that will reflect the life, the customs, and the habits of its own people.[35]

He noted the economic rationale underlying the promotion of European national industries, including the employment opportunities for writers and actors and the spin-off benefits to the many suppliers of goods and services needed to support ongoing production. Theoretically, industry protection also offered European filmmakers a chance to negotiate entry to the lucrative American market. Above all, Lowry was impressed with the message he received everywhere on the Continent that a major element in the resistance to U.S. films was cultural and nationalist. While producers may have been behind the initial agitation, they found allies both in governmental circles and among certain sections of the public when they couched their protests in terms of the defense of national identity from the encroachments of an alien culture.[36]

Foreign claims about the "demoralizing" effects of the movies fed the anxieties of Americans about the capacity of the film industry to undermine their country's international prestige. In fact, foreign critics of the industry often responded to the medium in much the same way as their American counterparts, who saw the movies as subverting established morals and behavior. The expression of social license for which the movies were notorious was perceived as an assault on cultural mores in Prague and Pretoria just as it was in Pittsburgh. As in the United States, resistance to American movies abroad was sustained by a cultural elite. The great mass of people in most countries responded very well to the American product, with its action-oriented aesthetics and lavish production values; if the movies had not been popular they would not have constituted a problem. Those most opposed to the free circulation of U.S. films were those who felt they had the most to lose— not only the filmmakers and social conservatives but also governments themselves, who feared the erosion of their political and economic prestige through the cinematic equation of American values with glamour and prosperity.

Britain, always the most important foreign market for American motion pictures, was prominent among the countries on the defensive. At the Imperial Conference of November 1926, the British deplored the small proportion (approximately 5 percent) of Empire-produced films exhibited in British territories:

It is a matter of the most serious concern that the films shown in the various parts of the Empire should be to such an overwhelming extent the product of foreign countries, and that the arrangements for the distribution of such Empire films as are produced should be far from adequate. In foreign cinema pictures the conditions in the several parts of the Empire and the habits of its peoples, even when represented at all, are not always represented faithfully and at times are misrepresented. Moreover, it is an undoubted fact that the constant showing of foreign scenes or settings, and the absence of any corresponding showing of Empire scenes or settings, powerfully advertises (the more effectively because indirectly) foreign countries and their products.[37]

The protest was taken up by such popular newspapers as the *Daily Mail* and the *Daily Express*, and by the Federation of British Industries. In 1927 the British Parliament passed a Cinematograph Films Act, specifying an increasing proportion of British-made films to be shown on British cinema screens. Similar measures were contemplated in other parts of the British Empire.

As the British legislators realized, cultural and economic factors were virtually inseparable in issues surrounding the success of the American product. As long as the movies reflected American culture, they reflected consumerism. Whether their producers intended them to or not, Hollywood movies acted as extended advertisements for the product-oriented lifestyle that was the hallmark of twentieth-century America—and, more directly, for American products. The war had left the United States so far in advance of Europe industrially that modern technology represented on the screen was likely to be American by default. The force of association between the moving picture and the wider gospel of consumerism is suggested by an instance of a Chinese motion picture made in 1926. *Three Shanghai Girls*, which was wholly Chinese-produced, prompted the following report from a U.S. observer who saw it in Shanghai:

One of the chief points of value of this picture and its kindred pieces, from the American point of view, is the immense advertising value that it affords to modern American manufactured articles, which are always in view and being used by Chinese in a very familiar way. These articles are, of course, in rather common use in a relatively narrow circle of Chinese residents of Shanghai, who have had considerable contact with western ways and people; but they are for the most part utterly new to the people of the interior provinces of China, who will undoubtedly take a very live interest in discovering what strange new things these are that the Chinese of Shanghai employ.[38]

The items displayed prominently in the picture included Western furniture, a phonograph, typewriters and other modern office equipment, and "a snappy American roadster." The observer was convinced that this display of goods "must have its eventual influence on the increase in the volume of imports of the foreign articles going to make up the ensemble of the picture."[39]

As early as 1922 the U.S. Department of Commerce had coined the slogan "trade follows the motion pictures," and its spokesmen were fond of repeating the somewhat arbitrary claim that for every foot of film exported, a dollar was earned for the United States in spin-off sales of other goods.[40] In 1926 Congress finally responded to Hays's requests for a Motion Picture Section within the Specialties Division of the Department of Commerce, appropriating twenty-six thousand dollars for that purpose.[41] The Department of Commerce already reported on conditions affecting movies abroad in its *Daily Consular and Trade Reports*, which technically put the information-gathering capacity of forty-four foreign offices and four hundred consular offices of the Department of State at the service of the industry. Now this service was supplied with "commodity division backing." With C. J. North as chief and Nathan D. Golden as his assistant, the section was intended to "keep the Department [of Commerce], and through it the motion picture industry, in the closest touch with foreign market possibilities, and also the activities of our competitors in their endeavors to limit the showing of American films within their borders."[42] The Motion Picture Section provided information about foreign censorship regulations, tariffs, and duties, as well as trademark, copyright, and taxation legislation. It also published lists of producers, distributors, and exhibitors in foreign markets and kept track of theater capacity and construction. A special trade commissioner, George R. Canty, was appointed to investigate motion picture conditions in Europe. The new section reflected the growing importance of the motion picture industry to the U.S. economy, as measured in both capital investment and foreign exchange.

The MPPDA itself proclaimed the role of the movie as a sales agent for American goods. The association's secretary, Carl E. Milliken, told a gathering of salesmen that "the motion picture has dropped into your laps a selling agency, the like of which you advertising experts never even dreamed of. People are going to the motion picture as to an animated catalogue for ideas of dress, of living, of comfort."[43] The writer of an internal MPPDA memo of 1928 recognized that the impact of the movies was as much ideological as economic:

> Motion pictures are the most CONSPICUOUS of all the American exports. They do not lose their identity. They betray their nationality and country of origin. They are easily recognized. They are all-pervasive. They color the minds of those who see them. They are demonstrably the greatest single factors in the Americanization of the world and as such fairly may be called the most important and significant of America's exported products.
>
> They are such indirect and undesigned propaganda for the purveying of national ideals, modes of life, methods of thought and standards of living as no other country in the world has ever enjoyed.[44]

The memo conceded that, under the circumstances, foreign governments would have been justified in introducing restrictive legislation against American pictures sooner and more forcefully than they had already done:

[O]ur films were among the last of the exports from the United States against which trade barriers were erected. Motion pictures were not arbitrarily selected to be particularly discriminated against. They faced a general condition in Europe that affected the import to that Continent of a long and varied list of products and commodities. Indeed, it is a cause of speculation among persons most familiar with economic post-war conditions in Europe why American films were not among the first products to have trade barriers and restrictions placed in the way of their unhampered distribution.[45]

The main reason that legislative action was not immediately forthcoming was probably the fact that in foreign markets, as well as in the United States, the greatest financial investment in motion pictures was in exhibition outlets. Exhibitors around the globe depended on the American product to generate their profits, and despite the fact that exhibitors, as lobbyists, lacked the prestige of producers, they outweighed producers in terms of capital invested. American motion pictures were probably also protected by the fact that their status as amusements tended to obscure their function as purveyors of ideology. They were apparently apolitical, overtly concentrating on "problems of the human heart" rather than on economic or political relations. Will Hays liked to describe Hollywood movies as "entertainment pictures—fiction on the screen—and essentially free from propaganda."[46] When they were not making extravagant claims about Hollywood's success as the "silent salesman" of the American way of life, the MPPDA's spokesmen were insisting that movie consumption existed in a dimension of experience complementary to, but not essentially part of, the socioeconomic sphere: "The world must be amused. Men must have recreation and relaxation. They must be allowed to forget the grind of everyday existence. There must be a place for workers to rest, to laugh, to cry and to think when the day's job is done."[47]

The movie experience was ephemeral; even the materialism the movies portrayed was ultimately insubstantial, part of the phantasmagoria of the cinematic world.[48] The America of the movies presented itself less as a geographic territory than an imaginative one, and one also deliberately made available for assimilation in a variety of cultural contexts. Evidence of this territory's national origin was frequently expunged during distribution, to be replaced by local referents more directly relevant to its diverse audiences. The MPPDA encouraged the perception of the medium as universal, capable of transcending cultural boundaries:

Good motion pictures necessarily have an appeal to all men because good motion pictures, just as good literature and all good art, appeal to the basic human motives. Love of home, love of family, love of children, love of husband or wife, love of parents, worship of a Supreme Being, love of play, love of sport, love of country—these are basic elements in the makeup of all men. They mean as much to the German as they do to the American, as much to the English as they do to the Russian.

And, on the screen, these basic motives can be presented to all people. For the first time in history, a means of universal communication has been found.[49]

The elusiveness of "the movies" as cultural objects meant that the industry's publicists were in a position to determine how its products would be described and defined. Accordingly, the identification of the American Way of Life with consumerism provided the American film industry with a two-edged public relations weapon. At home its publicists could play up the consumerist emphasis in movie spectacles and their power to advertise American values, while abroad they could describe the same pictures as devoid of ideological substance. A necessary consequence of walking this rhetorical tightrope, however, was an insistent pressure on the industry to produce films that did not fly in the face of its apologists by being too politically or ideologically contentious.

The industry's representation of itself as culturally innocuous for the purpose of trade negotiations was clearly illustrated at a League of Nations conference held in Geneva in July 1928. This meeting supplemented an international convention for the abolition of import and export restrictions which had been signed in November 1927. The French delegation introduced a proposal that would have allowed the international community to restrict the exhibition of American films in defense of French "intellectual and moral traditions."[50] The motion failed, although the general restiveness of the French government probably prompted the establishment of an MPPDA office in Paris in March 1928 and the appointment of Harold L. Smith (a vice consul at the American consulate in Paris) as a Parisian representative of the association.[51] The point in this case is not so much the outcome as the way in which the case was argued.

The American representatives were Lowry; Hugh R. Wilson, U.S. minister to Switzerland, who was assisted by two commercial attachés; and Paul Koretz, an Austrian lawyer sometimes engaged by Fox but in this instance employed by the MPPDA. Koretz claimed that the French rhetoric about cultural integrity was an attempt to "camouflage" a "commercial purpose," namely the protection of the French industry.[52] The American delegation dismissed the argument that commercial transactions could have "intellectual and moral" outcomes. Wilson insisted that regulations governing motion pictures should be no different from regulations governing automobiles or typewriters, implicitly denying the significance or even the existence of the movies' ideological import. In the same speech he represented French fears about cultural imperialism as mere irritation resulting from "obnoxious" characterizations of French citizenry:

I, who am a very rare visitor to the films, have frequently seen my countrymen put in a position and represented in a way which is objectionable to me as an American citizen. France is not alone in suffering from this misrepresentation. . . . No one deplores more than I do the bad taste of an American producer who will caricature or falsify the characterization of a member of any foreign nation, and I the more deeply deplore this in that I am persuaded that one of the best forms of human understanding and one of the best lessons in comprehension between nations is conveyed by means of the motion picture films.[53]

The ideas expressed by Wilson were consistent with the American industry's tendency to dismiss expressions of cultural resistance as blatant protectionism and to displace broad-based cultural objections onto specific—and comparatively superficial—aspects of representation.[54] Frederick Herron, for example, commented in a memo to Hays: "Conceding [the] idea that films do have a cultural effect on the community, every one of these countries that are now passing laws against us has national censorship boards. Every motion picture that goes into that country from a foreign country must pass that board before it can be released. If there is anything harmful from a cultural standpoint in such films, there is the place that they can be stopped."[55]

Many countries, including France, did indeed censor or ban movies which they felt contained cultural slights. As a result, Hollywood was persuaded to make certain compromises concerning representation. However, the deflection of concerns about the movies' cultural impact onto content regulation did nothing to challenge Hollywood's cultural power in the long run. From the industrial point of view, amending details of representation was a trivial matter which cost nothing but the indignation of the occasional scriptwriter. By emphasizing specific elements of filmic texts, rather than the more fundamental character of the movies as the emissaries of consumer culture, content regulation shifted attention away from the more economically far-reaching consequences of patterns of distribution and exhibition and placed it squarely on production. Just as censorship debates within the United States clouded the antimovie lobby's protests about patterns of industry control, so the anxieties expressed by foreign governments about the influence of movies on national cultures were met, incongruously, with promises of stricter censorship and tighter industry control of narratives and characterizations. The need for the uniform implementation of such controls, especially following the introduction of the German contingent at the beginning of 1925, added to the impetus behind the development of effective mechanisms of self-regulation within the MPPDA.

Jason Joy Goes to Hollywood

At first the activities of the MPPDA's Department of Public Relations did not vary markedly from those of the Committee on Public Relations. Colonel Joy fielded domestic protests and generally did everything in his power to improve the status of the motion picture in the American community. His work continued to embrace the children's matinee program. He also produced various newsletters and other publications, as well as maintaining contact with the trade and religious press. Although the principle of community intervention in production had already been established, Joy's efforts to mediate between the public and the studios appear to have been haphazard until 1927, when his department transferred its operations from New York to Hollywood, where it was housed by the Association of Motion Picture Producers (AMPP). The AMPP was a West Coast association separated from the MPPDA mostly as a matter of legal convenience, in satisfaction of antimonopoly statutes.[56] The move put Joy in a far better position to negotiate with filmmakers over actual or potential causes of offense in their movies and was a logical outcome of the MPPDA's increasing vigilance over film content. The department officially moved on 1 January 1927, and throughout the year conditions on the domestic scene progressively favored tighter supervisory measures.

The most conspicuous development was a resolution adopted by the AMPP on 8 June 1927, listing eleven subjects that the producers would not, in future, represent in their motion pictures and twenty-five subjects that would only be represented with the exercise of "special care."[57] These "Don'ts and Be Carefuls" were formulated by a committee of industry executives headed by Irving Thalberg, closely guided by Hays, in anticipation of a Trade Practice Conference that would be held in October. The conference, to be conducted by the Federal Trade Commission, was primarily concerned with relations between distributors and exhibitors: the independent exhibitors hoped to be able to exert pressure on the major companies under the antitrust laws, especially in light of a recent court decision against Paramount's block booking activities. The Motion Picture Theater Owners of America, then the largest trade association for independent exhibitors, protested that block booking compelled its members to hire poor-quality and immoral movies along with the clean, high-class entertainment that they claimed their customers desired. However, the very formulation of the exhibitors' arguments left them open to the MPPDA's favorite strategy: rather than discuss the legal implications of their monopolistic business practices, of which block booking was a symptom, the producers and distributors assured the commission that their products were—or would be henceforth—entirely clean and wholesome. Through the self-regulation of movie content, they would make sure that the exhibitors would find nothing in any of the movies they were offered that could cause them or their audiences the least offense. The Don'ts and Be Carefuls were produced at the conference like a rabbit out of a hat in answer to the exhibitors' charges of salaciousness and irresponsibility, and they were incorporated into the conference's "industry fair practices" agreement.

In *The Hays Office*, a reverential account of the MPPDA published in 1945, Raymond Moley claimed that the Don'ts and Be Carefuls were "the first systematic statement of standards of decency and morality to be adopted by the industry."[58] Actually, the producers had committed themselves to a set of moral guidelines as early as 1909, when they agreed voluntarily to submit their products to the scrutiny of the National Board of Censorship. The standards of the board were, in turn, closely followed when NAMPI announced its Thirteen Points excluding "vicious" themes. Notwithstanding the minor idiosyncracies of local ordinances, these same strictures had recurred time and again in the statutes of municipal and state censorship boards. The self-appointed moral spokesmen of the middle class claimed that "there can be no dispute as to what constitutes wholesome entertainment."[59] The Don'ts and Be Carefuls were themselves, according to Moley, derived from "a formal study not only of all the eliminations made by official censor boards over a period of several years, but of the criticisms, objections and suggestions of the public-relations groups."[60]

Perhaps the consensual nature of the guidelines had not done much to promote their observance in the past, but it gave Joy the leverage he needed to begin the process of systematically overseeing movie content in Hollywood. Following directions from Hays, he organized a Studio Relations Committee (SRC) consisting of himself, John V. Wilson, James B. Fisher, Douglas Mackinnon, and Miss J. Plummer, to review questionable material with studio representatives when movies were still in the preparation stage. Producers submitted synopses and scripts on a voluntary basis, although Joy could seek to intervene if a project seemed to be particularly dangerous. He based his methods of persuasion on economic rationality: he argued that any departure from the Don'ts and Be Carefuls was virtually guaranteed to cause financial loss through censorship action and/or damaging publicity. The SRC met formally with studio representatives once a fortnight, although it had more frequent contact with studios about specific projects. In January 1928 Joy reported that 349 stories and treatments had been submitted for comment. Of the 163 that had already been released, all but 2 had passed the censor boards without major eliminations and had "caused no difficulty among groups in this or other countries." He acknowledged that producers had not consistently followed his advice on the 186 still in production, and that the 349 represented a minority of the industry's total output. On the whole, however, his report was encouraging:

> The whole-hearted and sincere attitude evidenced by the members when they adopted the Resolution (June 8, 1927), signifying their intentions to watch their own efforts regarding the theme and treatment of pictures, has not diminished. On the contrary, to their sense of responsibility as the principal custodians of the reputation of their industry has been added a realization that in this machinery lies a means of stopping a considerable wastage in production costs and reducing to a minimum the losses due to mutilation and often costly rejection of finished pictures; and finally of removing the causes which may inspire further disastrous legislation in this country and abroad—which in the long view is perhaps the most costly and limiting obstacle this Industry will ever be required to face.[61]

With the mechanisms to combat adverse legislation at the level of "theme and treatment" in place, conditions were established for the activities of Herron and Joy to converge in the systematic accommodation of pressures arising from the domestic and foreign spheres.

Channeling Foreign Influences to Production

After facilitating the Mexican agreement of 1922, Bernon T. Woodle seems to have served as a kind of roving ambassador for the MPPDA. He was sent to Australia in 1924 on a mission "to find out how American films could be made more acceptable to Australian audiences."[62] A more common form of diplomatic contact took place when projects were filmed abroad. The cultivation of official favor was important in these instances both because it expedited practical matters surrounding production and because it enhanced the American industry's prestige and trading status. The MPPDA offered its assistance not through its public relations wing nor even through its Foreign Department, but through the Office of the President, with Hays himself being involved in making top-level contacts. In 1923 he personally enlisted the help of the Italian ambassador for the Rome-based production of *The Eternal City* (Madison Productions/First National, 1923), produced by Samuel Goldwyn:

I called up Prince Caetani, the Ambassador to the United States from Italy, and I told him we wanted to make this picture correctly. I asked him if he was interested. He came to New York the next day and we spent the afternoon together. Three times he visited me. He appointed a representative, and for three weeks, this representative sat with the producer, the scenario writer and the director developing the scenario for *The Eternal City*. A member company went to Italy to make the picture. We employed a foreign princess that they picked out at a high salary and we made a picture that pleased Italy, pleased Mussolini himself; and we told the story of Italy as Italy would have it told, that all other nations might understand it.[63]

In Goldwyn's version of the Hall Caine story, the hero became a lieutenant of Mussolini, and the violent revolutionary ending of the book was replaced with a peaceful one. Shots of Mussolini and King Victor Emmanuel III on the balcony of the royal palace, reviewing troops entering the city, were introduced as if the two leaders had been "cajoled by Goldwyn himself into making guest appearances." The publicity for the picture emphasized the fact that it was filmed "at Rome, Italy, and New York, with the Co-operation of the Italian Government."[64]

Similarly, in 1925 Hays worked through the U.S. State Department and the French embassy to secure the cooperation of the French government in the production of the Gloria Swanson comedy *Madame Sans-Gene* (Famous Players–Lasky/Paramount, 1925). The movie, which was based on a Sardou play about a washerwoman elevated to the nobility by Napoleon, was shot in and around Paris and in the palaces of Fontainebleau and Compiègne. The French authorities reportedly even loaned Napoleonic costumes and relics from museums in Paris to the studio.[65] The cast was mostly French, and Frenchman Léonce Perret, who had worked in Hollywood from 1917 until 1921, directed.

Despite such conspicuous instances of international cooperation as these, Hollywood still had a long way to go in cultivating amicable relations with its customer nations. Apart from the underlying sensitivities attached to the American domination of the world's screens, the main stumbling block was the negative stereotyping of nations and ethnic groups in pictures routinely made in Hollywood. Cases that involved high-level protests from diplomatic missions were usually handled by Hays. The kind of negotiation conducted over such material is

Madame Sans-Gene (Famous Players–Lasky/Paramount, 1925) was one of several prestigious Hollywood productions shot in European locations in the 1920s—in this case at the
Palace of Compiègne, with the cooperation of the French government. Most "foreign"
locations, however, were shot on Hollywood back lots, a practice which frequently led to
international complaints about inaccurate, stereotypical representations.

illustrated in the production history of *The Woman Disputed* (United Artists, 1928). In the original play by Denison Clift, set before and during
World War I, the French heroine submits to the lustful advances of a
German officer in order to secure the freedom of her five companions,
one of whom is a French agent disguised as a priest. When her fiancé,
an American soldier, learns of the reasons behind her sacrifice, the play
ends happily. The MPPDA kept a close watch on current plays, seeking
to be forewarned about any particularly controversial material, and *The
Woman Disputed* was reviewed as a matter of course by Jerome Beatty, a
member of the New York staff, in October 1926. He reported that the
material was unsuitable for motion pictures for three reasons: the heroine was a former prostitute, one character was a spy disguised as a
priest, and the villain was a German of the "typical Hun" variety.[66]

In 1918 the industry had turned out such virulently anti-German
productions as *The Kaiser, the Beast of Berlin* (Renowned Pictures/
Renowned Pictures; Jewel), *My Four Years in Germany* (My Four Years in
Germany, Inc./First National) and *Hearts of the World* (D. W. Griffith/

States Rights; Road Show), but in 1926 Germany was a relatively important source of foreign revenue, providing just over 5 percent of foreign income despite its import restrictions. Moreover, as the country responsible for the original contingent, it required particularly sensitive handling. Adding these considerations to the other problematic elements in the play, Beatty's judgment of *The Woman Disputed* was not very encouraging: "It would offend the Germans, the Catholic Church and all the women's clubs. I don't think there is any way to patch it up so that it could be made into a picture that would get by."[67]

Nevertheless, Joseph Schenck announced plans for a movie adaptation. The German consulate responded swiftly. In a letter to Hays of 20 December 1926, the acting consul general stated candidly that such a production would jeopardize the industry's commercial prospects in Germany: "Alone the fact that the proposed action would become known in Germany might easily spoil all your and our efforts to bring about peace and cooperation on the field of film production and film presentation." Hays sent the letter to Schenck on 21 December, explaining, "The negotiations to which he refers have been extending over a period of some months and touch the whole matter of developing better relations with the German Government, their nationals and the press. It is one of the most important activities which we now have on. It has to do, of course, with the ultimate handling of the Kontingent and the whole matter of the treatment of the industry in Germany." Hays urged Schenck to treat the production with the utmost care to avoid any hint of offense to Germany. Schenck assured him that there would be no problem: "The girl will be an Austrian girl, the hero an Austrian and the villain a Russian. It will be laid at the time when the Russian army marched into Austria and there will be nothing in the picture that either Austria or Germany could have any objection to."[68] In 1928 the film was finally released in this version.

While the modifications to the plot of *The Woman Disputed* doubtless offered comfort to Germany, they evinced scant regard for the feelings of the Russians. This was of little concern to either Schenck or Hays, however; in the mid-1920s Russia, unlike the capitalist nations of Europe, welcomed American films and erected no barriers to their importation. Because the Commissariat of Foreign Trade held a monopoly for the Soviet Union, it could bid unopposed for American products, acquiring them cheaply and exhibiting them at relatively high prices. Hence between 1922 and 1928 the Soviet administration freely imported foreign movies to generate revenue from exhibition, which was then applied to Soviet production. Ironically, then, while the Soviets were rebuilding their own industry, the "silent salesmen" of capitalist

Norma Talmadge's character in *The Woman Disputed* (United Artists, 1928) was originally a French girl, and Gilbert Roland was to play an American soldier, but both became Austrian to avoid fomenting trouble in the German market. The German villain became a Russian. So little profit was derived from Russia that the switch involved no financial risk; this ploy became standard for filmmakers anxious not to offend other European nations.

consumerism were used to keep cinemas and cinema-going alive, with the blessing of the state.[69] Even so, the market was never a lucrative one for the American industry. According to *The Film Daily Year Book*, the total value of the U.S. films sold to Russia in 1925 was only $10,500, although the fact that most American films were sold to the USSR via German agents renders such figures unreliable.[70] The Soviets did not recognize international copyright conventions, and although Hollywood distributors took the precaution of sending them positive prints rather than negatives, unauthorized duplication was always a problem.[71] Throughout the 1920s the number of Soviet productions increased—from an estimated 4 in 1921 to 109 in 1928—and toward the end of the decade there was a corresponding drop in the number of imports.[72] In the 1930s importation virtually ceased, not only because foreign films had "served their purpose" in keeping Soviet exhibition afloat but probably also because of increasing ideological objections and because of the inability of exhibition to keep pace with the technical requirements of sound.[73]

Thus the Russians were never in a position to influence Hollywood's field of representation because they did not attempt to introduce contingents or quotas. Other countries had to accommodate the conflicting demands of their own producer and exhibitor lobbies, which meant accepting the American product on a conditional basis. As a result, these countries gained a certain amount of bargaining power over the nature of the product they received. The position of the Russians, by contrast, was unilateral and nonnegotiable: either they admitted foreign products, as was the case in the early 1920s, or they did not, as was mostly the case in the 1930s. Because there was no basis for discussion, film content was not introduced as a bargaining chip by either side, and Hollywood producers could characterize their villains as Russians without worrying about reprisals and boycotts. Indeed, as villains the Russians offered the rare combination of minority market status and recognizable national characteristics. In most cases they also offered more feasible alternatives to European villains than did the long-suffering and increasingly troublesome Mexicans and Chinese. In dollars and cents, Russian indignation was cheap.[74]

Germany, on the other hand, was handled with kid gloves even when it came to reissues. For example, when MGM decided to rerelease the hit *The Four Horsemen of the Apocalypse* (Metro Pictures, 1921), the company was keen to ameliorate the movie's fundamentally anti-German tone. In 1926 Hays held a number of discussions with the German ambassador about possible revisions, as well as "at least a dozen" conferences with the acting consul general. The studio not only agreed to numerous eliminations in the domestic negative but also constructed a separate version for use in the German market, a precaution that was not unusual in the silent period. In the new version the content of the original was "rearranged" so that "it is still a good picture but so altered in regard to the German elements in it that it is so pleasing to Germany that the German representatives want it shown in Germany."[75] Chaplin's *Shoulder Arms* (Charles Chaplin/First National, 1918) was another reissue that had to be brought into line with the MPPDA's standards of diplomacy: a sequence showing Chaplin single-handedly capturing the Kaiser, the Crown Prince, and General Hindenberg was entirely eliminated. By the late 1920s Hollywood was not simply avoiding German villains but also actively promoting German heroes: in the World War I drama *The Awakening* (Samuel Goldwyn/United Artists, 1928), the romantic lead is Count Karl von Hagen (played by Walter Byron), a lieutenant in the German army who falls in love with a French peasant.

By 1928 the SRC was fully operational in Hollywood, allowing Colonel Joy to accommodate the sensitivities of the foreign market in the course of his general supervision of production, not just in response to specific expressions of concern. Offenses to national groups were technically guarded against by the Don'ts and Be Carefuls, which directed that special care should be exercised in the treatment of international relations and that filmmakers should avoid "picturizing in an unfavorable light another country's religion, history, institutions, prominent people, and citizenry." This clause was something of an anomaly in the document, as it was the only stricture which did not refer to sex or crime.[76]

In practice, national groups had more in common with other special interest groups than with moral lobbyists. Although many organizations which sought to influence the movies by way of the Open Door had a moral agenda, many others did not: the majority of contacts came from "professional organizations, unions, and individuals, who felt that their trades and professions were being shown, however unintentionally, in an unfavorable light."[77] Joy encouraged the producers to accommodate the interests of these groups during production as a matter of "industry policy," to avoid creating bad feeling in influential sections of the community. Some organizations received more consideration than others: the American Association for the Advancement of Atheism got short shrift when it complained about the prejudicial treatment of atheism in *The Godless Girl* (C. B. De Mille Productions/Pathé, 1929).[78] On the other hand, the interests of foreign nations, especially those that were important or sensitive customers, received regular consideration, the objective being less to respond to criticism than to obviate it.

Frederick Herron became an increasingly important figure in articulating the interests of the foreign market. He was in daily contact with foreign trade and diplomatic representatives in the course of his work in the Foreign Department, and he gradually assumed responsibility for much of the diplomatic negotiation that had been conducted by Hays. Hays, however, still occasionally took an active role when particularly sensitive matters were involved. Herron kept an eye on material acquired for production and alerted Joy to potential foreign hazards; he often contacted producers himself when he detected dangerous material, and he occasionally worked directly with scenarists. All productions handled by the SRC were reviewed upon completion

The World War I German soldier as perceived by Hollywood underwent a regeneration between 1918 and 1928. In *Hearts of the World* (D. W. Griffith/States Rights; Road Show, 1918) he was a raping, baby-killing "Hun." By the time *The Awakening* (Samuel Goldwyn/ United Artists, 1928) was produced, however, Germany offered a reasonably lucrative foreign market, and the German protagonist had become both heroic and romantic.

by a member of the staff, usually James B. Fisher or Miss J. Plummer. The staff member noted any potentially contentious elements, including foreign problems, and a copy of the report was sent to both MPPDA secretary Carl Milliken and to Herron. The convergence of Herron's work at the Foreign Department with the activities of the SRC is exemplified by his contact with producers over French sensitivities in 1928.

In addition to their proposals at the Geneva conference, the French also formulated aggressive quota legislation, with the intention of limiting American access to their market. Hays himself visited Paris in March 1928 and managed to have much of the sting removed from the measures by threatening to boycott the market. In reaching agreement on compromise measures, he specifically offered as a bargaining chip the assurance that the American industry would make no films presenting the French in a derogatory light.[79] It was thus essential that the treatment of French themes demonstrate appropriate tact.

An especially sensitive point was Hollywood's representation of the French Foreign Legion. *Beau Geste* (Famous Players–Lasky/Paramount, 1926) had been a great box office success, and producers saw considerable further promise in the Legion's romance and exoticism. From their point of view, the Sahara was a mythical landscape of the heart, like the American West. Unfortunately, the French were wont to interpret the movies more literally, and they saw them as insulting slights on their methods of colonial administration. Herron had difficulty communicating the French sensitivity to producers. As he explained in exasperation on the release of *Plastered in Paris* (Fox, 1928), a Foreign Legion spoof starring the comedian Sammy Cohen, "The French Foreign Legion is one thing that you cannot burlesque under any circumstances, any more than you can burlesque the English Royal Guard. We have nothing in this country that corresponds to those outfits which are old and have traditions that they consider sacred."[80]

Beau Geste had been the subject of diplomatic protests, and French officials attempted to stop its exhibition in many centers around the world. Then in March 1928 Universal brought out *The Foreign Legion*, which contained many of the elements that had caused such an uproar over *Beau Geste*. The imitation of a proven money-spinner followed the usual logic of production cycles, but from the point of view of foreign relations it was a show of exceptionally poor timing. Upon viewing it, Herron wrote urgently to N. L. Mannheim, Universal's export manager:

I don't think it is necessary to tell you that if this film is issued with this material in it that you will not only hurt your own company in France, but will hurt the whole American industry throughout the world as a result of the agitation which will follow this. At the present time, the French are in the midst of passing a decree which gives them the privilege to do just about anything they want with the films. They can prohibit a company from doing business in their country if they feel so inclined. I feel so strongly on this film that I hate to even show it to the French Ambassador in its present condition. However, before releasing it in any condition, I would suggest that it should be sent to Washington and shown to the French Embassy, because just as soon as this is released in any form at all we are going to have a bad reaction in the French newspapers.[81]

The picture was shown to Lowry and Canty in Paris, and they advised against its release in case it jeopardized their negotiations with the French government. Robert Cochrane of Universal cabled Hays that he would reedit the film in any manner requested, even shooting new scenes if necessary, but he would not consider permanently shelving a negative worth a quarter of a million dollars.[82] Finally the changes were made, apparently to everyone's satisfaction, although the French commercial attaché could not be persuaded to put his approval in writing. Herron was particularly pleased, as he wrote to Joy in May: "Someone is certainly to be congratulated in Universal on having done a beautiful piece of work in cleaning up a very bad picture. When I say bad, I

The French Foreign Legion offered opportunities for narratives incorporating mystery, violence, heroism, and betrayal. Its locations were colorful yet equal to the American West in their broad, mythical qualities. If it had not been for French objections to the "inaccuracies" in such movies as *Beau Geste* (Famous Players–Lasky/Paramount, 1926), the Foreign Legion might have featured more regularly in Hollywood's output.

mean, of course, from the French standpoint. The work in this picture is cleverly done, and I believe they have eliminated all the points that were so strenuously objected to by the French attachés, and smoothed the edges off so that they still have a story and a film just as good as the original one which will not cause a frightful kick back."[83]

One of the changes the studio officials had promised to make in the new version was the renaming of the evil Arnaud as Markhoff, but in the end they reformed the character instead. Nevertheless, their tactic suggests again the representational price routinely paid by the Russians for failing to impose conditions on their American purchases.[84] The Russification of the villain was becoming a more or less routine practice, in the interests of avoiding offense to other Europeans. Sometimes plots had to be considerably contorted to achieve this. For example, Russians were a less than perfect choice for Universal's proposed production of *Grease Paint* in 1928, as Herron indicated:

This may or may not cause objection from the Austrians. They are very sensitive people and one never knows what they are going to object to. One must take into consideration the fact that today Europe is frightfully anti-

American as far as films are concerned and they are looking for every loop hole to attack us that they possibly can.

In Austria we are under a contingent system already. If possible, I would suggest that this locale be switched to Russia where there is not a chance of a protest. I realize, of course, that the Viennese waltz and the atmosphere may make this impossible, but it is better to lean backwards in a proposition of this sort than to go ahead and take a chance on stirring up bad publicity.[85]

It seems that in this case the difficulties presented by introducing a Viennese waltz to a Russian locale were insurmountable, as the movie was never made.

A scenario typical of those that met an early death at the hands of the SRC was Universal's property *I Take This Woman*. The company submitted the synopsis for review in June 1928, declaring with a hint of hollow confidence: "It is a war story, involving Austria and Italy, and while we do not see any possible objections that might arise in any part of it, still we would appreciate it if you would give us your opinion." The story involved a beautiful Austrian girl who came under threat from various brutal Austrians and Italians. Joy wrote to Hays that he was "naturally a little worried because of the international angle" and suggested that Herron might take up the subject with the Italian consul. Upon reading the script, however, Herron advised that it would be "inadvisable to even present the script to the Italian Ambassador in present form."[86] Joy proposed that he hold a conference with Universal about the matter, but the idea was carried no further.

In some cases strong representation of national groups within the United States blurred the line between domestic and foreign public relations issues. The Italian ambassador, for example, was apt to protest to the industry about national slights at the behest of both Italian Americans and the Italian government. The Irish, in particular, represented a powerful combination of interests, the least influential of which was the Irish state. *The Callahans and the Murphys* (MGM, 1927) was forced out of circulation by a combination of Irish societies in America and the National Catholic Welfare Conference, on the grounds that it was "a gross insult, deliberate or otherwise, to the ancient faith and culture of the Irish people."[87]

Even when the studios chose to submit synopses for review, they were not strictly obliged to adopt Joy's or Herron's suggestions. *The Gallant Gringo* (MGM, 1928), also known as *The Adventurer*, treated the kind of subject that was virtually assured to run into problems in the foreign field. The movie was an action melodrama that revolved around the exploits of a U.S. hero in the context of a Latin American revolution. Latin American countries always resented the implication

The producers of *The Gallant Gringo* (MGM, 1928) failed to follow the advice of the Studio Relations Committee and came up with a film that proved highly offensive to Latin America. Many excisions and modifications had to be effected before the film could be released internationally.

that they were subject to the predations of colorful and brutal dictators, especially when the restoration of order depended on the arrival of a contingent of U.S. Marines or, as in this case, the intervention of a lone Yankee visitor. Nevertheless, despite the problems inherent in the project, Herron agreed to work with the studio on a treatment that would, he hoped, be comparatively inoffensive to Latin America. To the chagrin of the SRC, however, when the picture was released it contained all the sensitive sequences that the studio had agreed to eliminate or change. The result so compromised its chances of general distribution that the film had to be withheld from circulation and modified, at considerable expense to the studio.[88] Such cases of noncooperation demonstrated the advantages of more careful selection and treatment of subject matter, not just in terms of good will but also in terms of dollars and cents.

An inevitable result of the work of the SRC was the narrowing of the field of representation normally attempted by filmmakers. After losing money on the script of *I Take This Woman*, Universal was unlikely to buy another story with equally contentious European elements. Joy or Herron would only have to request the substitution of a Russian for an Austrian so many times before scenario writers beat them to it. As Joy gathered expertise on the likely reception of different themes and treatments, filmmakers learned to limit some of the most obvious causes of agitation.

Meanwhile, sound technology had already become a reality. During the next few years it would revolutionize the motion picture business both at home and abroad. It made the development of effective mechanisms for accommodating global influences in motion picture content both more complex and more imperative.

3

Sound Effects

Technology and Adaptation

The introduction of sound had an immediate effect on the centralized regulation of Hollywood's products. Because sound movies were difficult and expensive to modify once they entered distribution, it became economically imperative to ensure that anything likely to lead to censorship action or public protest was removed at the point of production. The machinery of self-regulation was refined and systematized, with domestic and foreign pressures being increasingly integrated in the work of the MPPDA. The foreign market was an unusually conspicuous factor in Hollywood's day-to-day operations at this time. Experiments with multiple-language versions of movies, dubbing, and subtitling reveal the determination of the major companies to retain the global scope of their distribution.

The displacement of silent movies by talkies affected patterns of exhibition as well as production. The expense of wiring theaters for sound eventually forced thousands of small cinemas out of business, especially in the foreign market. Larger, more upscale movie houses replaced them, changing the status of the medium and indirectly affecting market demand. The industrial reorganization that took place during this period demonstrates the complex interplay that existed between the production, distribution, and exhibition branches of Hollywood's operations.

Silent Movies in the American Market

As "texts," silent movies were inherently unstable; it was the nature of the medium that metaphor and allusion should predominate.[1] To some extent intertitles could determine the specific import of a scene, but the titles themselves could also remain vague and euphemistic. In Universal's 1916 picture *Where Are My Children?* for example, an unwanted pregnancy was indicated by the title "It was the old, old tragedy, and one of the 'unwanted ones' was called to earth."[2] Members of the audience were left to construct their own interpretation of the title from visual cues.

Even as objects, silent movies were themselves never so precisely fixed as their talkie descendants. Film historians Kevin Brownlow and David Gill have suggested that the movies seen by audiences in the United States sometimes differed quite markedly from the products circulated under the same title abroad: "Silent films were normally shot on two cameras—one for domestic use, one for foreign. (Duping was of unacceptably poor quality in those days.) But where a film was shot with one camera . . . the European negative had to be pieced together from alternate takes. These alternate takes were often less effective than the take selected by the director for the American version. Where there was no alternate take, an alternate setup was used instead—a long shot instead of a closeup."[3] Silent movies could also be modified with comparative ease once they had entered distribution. Because Hollywood needed to sell its products throughout the United States and at destinations abroad, movies needed to adapt to a wide range of cultural requirements.[4] Different communities required adjustments in detail and emphasis, and individual movies commonly underwent a range of adaptive treatments during the process of distribution and exhibition.

The most overt manipulation of a movie's content after its release took place during regional distribution, at the hands of censors. In 1927 the MPPDA estimated that approximately 80 percent of its total business was subject to censorship, including the 30 percent conducted overseas, virtually all of which encountered censors at least once. At home, more than a third of the business conducted by domestic distributors was reviewed by state censorship boards, and an additional 15 percent faced scrutiny at the municipal level.[5]

The mechanical process of censoring a silent film was relatively simple. Changes could be effected by excising and/or rearranging shots, without necessarily disrupting the continuity. A deleted title could be rewritten by the distributing agent at a cost of about five dollars.[6] Yet for the producers and distributors, censorship provided a continual source of irritation and expense. This was partly because wherever censorship existed, *all* films were subject to a reviewing charge of two to three dollars per thousand feet of film, whether they required modification or not, with an extra charge for all additional prints distributed. At the same time, the studios incurred losses in the cost of expensive footage that was thrown out before it reached the screen. In the United States alone, the combination of these factors cost the industry an estimated $3.5 million a year in the late 1920s. The MPPDA lobbied to end "confiscatory" reviewing charges, while Jason Joy and the Studio Relations Committee gained their bargaining power with the studios by holding out the hope that their advice would help to keep waste to a minimum. The SRC offered advance information about the proclivities of troublesome censor boards that enabled both producers and distributors to make protective modifications, with more finesse than the "butchering" that they complained of from the censors. Even with the best advice, however, there was no guarantee that movies could be made consistently censor-proof, and the major companies were resigned to a certain level of modification to their products across the United States as well as internationally.

The practice of modifying movies to meet the requirements of regional audiences was consistent with the status of movies as commodities, rather than texts with a specific privileged arrangement of content. Function was the priority, not form, reflecting the movies' origins as program fillers, not "works of art" to be considered independently of their conditions of exhibition. By the mid-1910s their status had risen, but there was no question of their being distributed in a single immutable form. In 1914 Orrin Cocks of the National Board of Censorship articulated a common assumption with regard to local censorship: "Moral questions will never be solved for the whole people. . . . When one appreciates the foreign population, the extent of the country, and the various social classes in the United States, he must concede to the various communities modifications of a minimum national standard."[7]

At the same time, the comparative ease with which modifications could be introduced to silent movies also encouraged the practice of censorship of an unofficial kind, at the point of exhibition. Aaron Brylawski, an exhibitor from Washington, D.C., testified before a 1914 House of Representatives committee that individual exhibitors regularly exercised the right of censure over material shown in their theaters: "The first time the picture is seen the owner or manager looks at it to see if it comes up to the standard and will not offend his patrons, and as from one-third to one-half of his day patrons are ladies, and he knows they come almost daily, he is careful to see that there are no objectionable features. If he thinks a scene or part of a scene can be misconstrued he cuts it out. After it is out, it stays out."[8] By 1922 exhibitors were prepared to take an active part in determining not only the morals of the movie but its aesthetics as well. Donald Ramsey Young, a contemporary commentator on the industry, noted that

many theatres, especially the larger ones, run over the films before the public showing and eliminate what is believed to be objectionable to the audience for which it is intended. This practice is so common even in states and communities which have little or no legal censorship that it excites no trade comment. It is taken for granted that each manager will use his own judgment. Such cuts are frequently made to shorten the program or to improve the "action" of the picture from a technical point of view, but they are also made in order that the patrons may not be offended.[9]

The "shortening" of the program refers to the practice, then common, of trimming multiple-reel pictures to make them fit into a two-hour program format. In the case of large-scale productions that received their initial release as "road-shows," playing for high prices in selected prestige venues ("legitimate" theaters and picture palaces), the movies were trimmed for their regular release by their distributors, commonly losing two to three thousand feet.[10]

Modification by exhibitors continued to the end of the silent era. Exhibitors who attended the Motion Picture Trade Practice Conference in 1927 argued that they needed to be able to edit movies "to satisfy public sentiment," especially in cities not regulated by official censorship. Although the presiding commissioner, Abram Myers, would later take up a paid position with the independent exhibitors' trade association Allied States, he was in this case sympathetic with the producer-distributors, who objected to exhibitors meddling with their products: "As I understand the course of conduct of business the film is leased or rented and the title to it remains in the distributor. It is his property. I assume he has some interest in its mutilation. Also I think the public has an interest in the proper presentation of the picture and ought not to see fragmentary parts of a story after they have paid their admission to see a film." The producers eventually succeeded in passing a resolution that "the changing by exhibitors of motion pictures or the cutting by exhibitors of motion pictures with no other purpose than to shorten their length, is an unfair trade practice."[11] They cannot have been satisfied with this compromise, however, for it allowed the exhibitors to do as they wished with the movies on any pretext *except* shortening the length.

While the film itself was vulnerable to the improving hand of the exhibitor, a further level of textual instability was inherent in the musical accompaniment that formed an essential element of the "silent" cinema. Specially prepared orchestral scores could be distributed to first-run houses, to be performed with greater or lesser degrees of sensitivity and expertise, but in most neighborhood theaters the local accompanist would improvise on organ or piano, reinforcing, undercutting, or commenting on the action. This wildcard musical element helped to ensure that, outside metropolitan centers, movies were rarely presented to audiences in exactly the same form twice—even in the same cinema. The importance of the musical accompaniment's contribution to the audience's interpretation can be gauged from European reactions to early sound films, some of which were distributed abroad with sound tracks but no dialogue. Both German and Italian audiences, accustomed to local accompaniments to Hollywood films, objected that the recorded music was "too American" for their taste.[12]

The assumption of regional variation was so widespread that the industry was nonplussed when France attempted to impose a new import condition as part of its program of restrictions in 1928, requiring that all films be submitted for censorship in "the identical form in which they have been exhibited in the country of origin." The point of the legislation was to prevent films containing material detrimental to the prestige of France being released in the country of production, with the offensive sections only being excised for the French market. But which version should be construed as the American standard? As Carl Milliken, secretary of the MPPDA, remarked: "It would be virtually a physical impossibility to meet this requirement. Pictures released in this country necessarily undergo certain changes in the adapting process which follow diverse censor rulings in various states which may change the complexion of a picture, or else the picture may be shortened for its theatrical presentation, yet the ruling requires submission of the pictures in their original form."[13] With the MPPDA, distributors, censors, and exhibitors all taking a hand in the silent movie's progress to the screen, the "original" form of the film was chimerical. The filmic "text" itself was ultimately determined by the specific context in which it was exhibited.

Adapting Silent Movies to the Foreign Market

The chameleonlike nature of the silent cinema helped to free it from cultural specificity and facilitated its ability to adapt to the requirements of audiences all over the world. As in the domestic sphere, adjustments could be made to silent movie content to assist international distribution. For example, a screen version of Tolstoy's *Resurrection* (Inspiration/United Artists, 1927) was found to be acceptable in most markets, but it ran into trouble with the Irish censor, who stated, "This gloomy story of seduction, prostitution and murder is a sincere work which undoubtedly conveys a moral, but I consider it unfit for general exhibition." This opinion, however, by no means ruled out the film's circulation in Ireland, for the censor went on to suggest that "if the renter will deal with the film, treating the story with greater reticence, I may be able to grant a certificate."[14] The film was eventually passed for general viewing in Ireland after eliminations had been effected in eleven scenes—nine with sexual connotations, one with excessive violence, and one deemed "irreligious."

As in the United States, modifications for the foreign market could take place at any stage throughout production, distribution, and exhibition and could affect virtually any aspect of a movie's presentation. In Switzerland, for example, some exhibitors ruthlessly cut all the movies they received so that *two* features could be packed into a two-hour program, causing the U.S. Department of Commerce to complain that "whole slices are taken out which are of the utmost importance to a clear understanding of the picture."[15] In Brazil, the speed at which films were projected reportedly depended on the exhibitor's estimation of the literacy of his patrons, so that even slow readers could follow the intertitles.[16] The most decisive interventions were those made in Japan, where a *benshi*, or narrator, accompanied the action, elaborating the narrative with all the resourcefulness of the traditional storyteller. According to Joseph Anderson and Donald Richie, "The more famous had different techniques and sometimes differed widely in interpreting the same film."[17]

In general, however, the intertitles themselves constituted the principal site of international adaptability in the silent format. While the visuals could be cut or rearranged, intertitles could be changed entirely to cater to diverse national and cultural groups. Hollywood characters could speak any language or dialect. Indeed, in the Baltic States they spoke three languages at once, since historical and political circumstances required the intertitles to be rendered in German and Russian as well as the local language. Theoretically, at least, the process of translation allowed anything inappropriate or potentially offensive to be changed. Even minor cultural differences could be accommodated, as Sidney Kent, general manager of Paramount Famous-Lasky, explained in a lecture to Harvard students in 1927: "The titles are translated from English into some thirty-six languages. As a matter of fact, our English at times has to be translated into other forms of English in order that it may be understood. The titles that are used here cannot be used, for instance, in England. Many expressions that we have here are not understood by the rank and file of the people there, and so the titles are translated into the average language of the country, in other words, the language that is intelligible to the great mass of people."[18]

Intelligibility was not the only matter at issue. By "naturalizing" movies, the producers were encouraging a tendency already present among foreign audiences, to adopt the imaginative content of the movies as part of their own cultural territory. The Hollywood universe was not a foreign country to its aficionados, whatever their nationality. As active interpreters, audiences made sense of Hollywood in their own cultural terms. The movie-going habit was a familiar, domestic ritual around the world, and American movies and their stars were a significant part of millions of non-American people's daily experience: American movies made up most of the world's motion picture diet (see table 1). Foreign audiences constituted a market not only for the movies themselves but also for fan magazines which encouraged personal identification with American stars.[19] Douglas Fairbanks and Mary Pickford visited Norway in 1924 and Moscow in 1926, and on both occasions they were given rapturous receptions by spectacular crowds.[20] Harold Lloyd was familiarly known in the USSR as "Harry," as Charlie Chaplin was known as "Charlot" in France.[21] Even in Japan, where a thriving national industry produced more than half the films exhibited, American stars had become household names, and they were thoroughly assimilated into the popular imagination. According to David Bordwell, in Japanese film production "Hollywood pictures were cited, copied, remade, and even inserted into Japanese ones."[22]

American producers had an interest in encouraging the idea that Hollywood belonged to the world, rather than to the United States alone. By obscuring the American origins of the movies, the producers enabled them to take on some of the cultural coloring of their customer nations, subtly combating consumer resistance arising from patriotic sentiments. Thus *Peter Pan* (Famous Players–Lasky/Paramount, 1924) was filmed in "a score" of versions, with Peter running up a different national flag over Captain Hook's pirate ship each time. The *Christian Science Monitor* reported that "the children of one country after another are now taking Peter to their hearts assured by the glimpse of their familiar national banner that the triumphant fairy boy is, as they suspected all the time, their very own."[23] In the same spirit, the American flag was routinely excised by distributors in several foreign markets. As

Table 1
American Films as a Proportion of Total Films
Shown in Foreign Areas, 1925

Region	Percentage
United Kingdom	95%
Australia and New Zealand	95
Canada	95
Brazil	95
Mexico	90
Spain and Portugal	90
Argentina	90
Scandinavia	85
France	70
Austria, Hungary, and Czechoslovakia	70
Italy	65
Germany	60
Japan	30

Source: William Victor Strauss, "Foreign Distribution of American Motion Pictures," *Harvard Business Review* 8 (1930): 309.

the Central American agent for Paramount Famous-Lasky reported in 1929, when explaining the disappearance of the flag from *The Rough Riders* (1927), "Strange as it may seem, too much showing of the American flag never fails to bring catcalls and whistles from the gallery."[24] Ironically, foreign censors sometimes collaborated in clouding the origins of American films. For example, when United Artists submitted *She Goes to War* (Inspiration Pictures/United Artists, 1929) to the Australian censors, the studio eliminated all titles reading "Back to America" or "Back to the U.S.A." and substituted "Back home," or "Back to my home town."[25] The Australians also altered any American spellings that the distributors had allowed to slip through.[26] Canada eliminated the American flag as a matter of course.

Some censor boards required elaborate revisions to bring the moral tone of the movies into line with local standards. When the crime melodrama *The Big City* (MGM, 1928) was prepared for its Australian release, the censors' requirement that the forces of the law should be seen to be triumphant prompted MGM to replace the noncommittal title " 'Twas midnight in the city and the lights were burning low" with something more explanatory: "In every big city today, picked members of the police force are playing a part in the underworld. Cleverly they hide their real identity until the time to strike is ripe—then the net closes! And yet another nefarious gang goes behind iron bars." The Australian board also required strict observance of moral propriety in romantic subjects. *Love Me and the World Is Mine* (Universal, 1928) was not unusual in being rejected by the antipodean censors. After Universal lodged an appeal, the film was allowed to be reconstructed, with the following modifications, typical of the requirements of the board:

1. Alter the character of the woman Mitzl from that of a woman of loose morals to that of a member of the Opera House ballet;
2. Completely remove all suggestion that Franzl was a libertine and make his love for Hannerl something of a sacred nature;
3. Remove all suggestion of any intimate relationship between Franzl and Mitzl.[27]

The necessary cuts, including the excision of twenty titles, reduced the length of the picture by 998 feet, but these cuts were partially offset by the preparation of 205 feet of new, morally acceptable titles. Universal's representative was pleasantly surprised by the result: "In most cases when a film is reconstructed here it loses a certain amount of its punch, but . . . this picture has rather benefitted by the alterations."[28]

The Australian censors themselves were given to some exceptionally cavalier rewriting. For instance, in *Breakfast at Sunrise* (Constance Talmadge Productions/First National, 1927), one title originally read, "An evening with Reginald was an evening indeed. Taxicabs often quivered for twenty minutes after he left them." This the censors mysteriously rejected in favor of their own creation: "Madeleine found her evening with Reginald somehow vaguely disappointing."[29] In a more predictable vein, in the same film they changed "We—we would have to live together" to "We can be married immediately and settle down and make them both mad with jealousy."[30] If in the United States extramarital relationships in movie fictions could not be consummated, in Australia they could not even be contemplated. Such different moral stances could be easily accommodated by the same movie because the intertitles formed an integral part of the narration.

While the Australian board constituted an extreme case, Hollywood's products had to be capable of responding to the restrictions that extreme cases imposed. Censors throughout the world engineered adjustments to silent movie content to varying degrees. In Cuba, the censorship commission worked in close cooperation with local distributors. According to a report by the U.S. Department of Commerce, "The [Cuban] commission depends upon the distributors to delete such parts or texts in their films as may be inappropriate with the regulations governing the exhibition of features, such as those that may tend to offend the national dignity of friendly nations or their political institutions, those that are pornographic or likely to propagate vice, and doctrines, such as communism, prejudicial to the public welfare, especially in regard to the graphic exhibition of means for transgressing the law, that might unduly influence children and minors."[31] Similarly, the MPPDA reported that in Czechoslovakia, where censors were especially sensitive to violence, crime, indecency, and the supernatural, a much larger number of American pictures would have been disapproved if local distributors had not anticipated the action of the censorship board by changing captions and making excisions in advance.[32] In China it was up to the cinema managers to "edit all their films along the lines of the censorship provisions."[33] Where the more economically significant German market was concerned, positive action on the part of American distributors was sometimes recommended. A commercial attaché stationed in Berlin told a meeting of the SRC in November 1927 that Germans "desire their pictures long and drawn out" and proposed that the German negative should be cut "one or two thousand feet longer than that used in the United States."[34]

The Studio Relations Committee at the End of the Silent Era

The SRC was central to the MPPDA's strategy for anticipating specific market requirements and communicating them to the producers. The committee was specifically charged with forestalling censorship action, with a view to saving money while improving the public relations image of the industry, both at home and abroad. The SRC encouraged the studios to beat the censors at their own game by making appropriate adjustments at both the production and the distribution stages. The issues likely to offend domestic sensibilities were not difficult to ascertain, since the MPPDA was centrally involved in a national discourse on cultural representation. The vagaries of foreign censorship, however, were more difficult to predict. Rowland V. Lee, who worked as a director at Fox, outlined the problem this created for filmmakers at a conference of the Academy of Motion Picture Arts and Sciences in July 1927:

During the last four years I have spent about a year and a half in Europe and I have been to theatres in about 18 different countries, and I have been astounded to see what has happened to those pictures in all those different countries. There have been sequences cut; there have been close-ups cut. We know what censorship is in this country. You ought to see what happens to some of our eight and nine reel pictures abroad. Some of them are cut down to five reels. Now to my knowledge, what happens to a picture after it leaves the director's hands never comes back to the director. There is no way in which he can find out what happens to his picture. There is no way in which he can find out why his picture did not go well in Italy, because maybe they had an Italian that was a heavy and that did not go over, and we have learned that we can not have a Mexican heavy in a picture. It seems to me that every picture should have a history, a production history, and that production history should be a part and parcel of the knowledge that goes to the director and a part of the director's duties should be to find out why his picture didn't do well in the South, why his picture didn't do well in England, why his picture could not be shown in Germany. We have not the slightest idea what happens to our pictures.[35]

The SRC initiated just such a system of dossiers, providing producers with information that would help to keep their movies out of trouble around the globe. It kept production files on individual films, based on member companies' reports and information supplied by the MPPDA's Foreign Department. Reports from the Motion Picture Section of the U.S. Commerce Department, in the form of *Commerce Reports, Trade Information Bulletins,* and a newsletter called *Motion Pictures Abroad,* were collated at the offices of the SRC and forwarded to member companies. In 1928 the SRC announced its intention to keep files on "each foreign country with which we usually have trouble, on each group representing a section of public opinion, and on each subject of picture material usually objected to."[36]

Because the studios did not always choose to cooperate fully with the SRC, its records remained partial. Studios often released films without the SRC's review and did not consistently submit their foreign censorship reports for the record. This was a source of considerable frustration to Joy, even though his team barely had time to process the mass of information that it did receive, on top of its reviewing and consultative work.[37] Nevertheless, evidence suggests that the SRC counted the foreign market among its major priorities, perhaps because of the ever-present threat of tighter legislative restrictions abroad.

The minutes of the SRC's monthly "dinner-meetings" recount an order of business that usually began with a briefing on cultural sensitivities in specific foreign markets, typically by an eminent foreign visitor. Studio delegates were given digests of censorship action encountered by the industry since the previous meeting. At first eliminations were listed by company, but they were later organized into categories according to type, including sex-suggestiveness, crime, vulgarity, liquor, kissing, profanity, sacrilege, nudity and indecent exposure, offensive and smart-cracking titles, and nose-thumbing.[38] Derived from current censorship actions, these categories overlapped with the Don'ts and Be

Carefuls of 1927 but were generally concerned with more detailed and less consequential issues. Nose-thumbing was at issue rather than drug trafficking, "smart-cracking titles" rather than white slavery. Such eliminations as are listed in the minutes of these meetings show that while the movies were generally innocuous, they continued to violate the conventions governing sex-suggestiveness, crime, and vulgarity to an extent guaranteed to keep the censors in work. The organization of the minutes is also significant: foreign and domestic eliminations were listed together, reflecting the MPPDA's conception of its global dimension as equal to, and not methodologically different from, its involvement in the United States.

Foreign issues were also integrated with domestic concerns in the SRC's script conferences, as shown by Joy's periodic reports to Hays. Meetings with studio representatives in May and June 1928 involved negotiations over subjects possibly offensive to France, Germany, England, and Nicaragua. In the case of *The Red Sword* (FBO Pictures/RKO, 1929), Joy was worried about any foreign reaction that might be adverse to a theme with a "revolutionary flavor."[39] Foreign concerns were at issue in five out of the twenty-four pictures discussed during this period. The rest of the negotiations concerned the treatment of crime, sex, and religion—matters of concern to both domestic and foreign markets, and the subjects always demanding the greater part of the SRC's attention.

In May 1928 George Kates of Paramount's New York Foreign Department was sent to Hollywood to help the studio avoid difficulties with foreign governments. Paramount also had someone in-house to advise them on the domestic censorship situation, probably John Hammell. In June, Joy wrote to Hays,

I am in the process of conducting a series of personal conferences with the various studios on the whole matter of censorship. During the interim since the last report I have met with the people who are important in this activity at Paramount, F.B.O., De Mille, Fox, Metro-Goldwyn-Mayer and Educational. If you have had a chance to observe the eliminations from these companies you realize that there is a vast difference in the manner in which these companies are handling this question. I am very hopeful that we will be able to demonstrate to the less careful studios the wisdom and economy of following such a procedure as Paramount has inaugurated. While Paramount continues to have eliminations made, they are of a more trivial nature and are not apt to cause trouble for themselves or for the industry.[40]

This comment encapsulates Joy's policy for overseeing silent movie content: he was satisfied if major causes of offense could be eliminated at the point of production, since details of a less controversial nature could be modified at the time of the picture's release. However, Paramount's "careful" cooperation was probably less a consummation of the old system than an anticipation of the new, for at this time Hollywood's elastic capacity to adapt to the demands of its many markets was being challenged by the widespread adoption of sound.

Sound Technology and Industry Regulation

Sound pictures were originally conceived as incorporating music and sound effects rather than dialogue. The earliest sound programs, which reached the screen in 1926, emphasized vaudeville acts, trading on their ability to bring Broadway talents before a wider public. By mid-1928 most major studios were experimenting with "synchronized" features, with music and special effects, including revamped versions of silent successes, but filmmakers were relatively slow to explore the dramatic potential of speech. Early talking pictures contained only brief snatches of dialogue, with most movies depending on silent movie techniques, including intertitles, to put the story across. In August 1928 Warner Bros., the sound pacesetter, released *The Lights of New York*, its first all-talkie. Yet as late as November 1928 an MPPDA spokesman commented that while sound effects such as wind, rain, and "elevated trains" had an assured place in future productions, there were "decided differences of opinion about the future of the talking film itself."[41]

Will Hays quickly apprehended the dangerous public relations implications of sound pictures, with or without dialogue. Addressing the SRC on the subject at its monthly meeting on 24 July 1928, he reminded studio representatives of the industry's widely publicized public commitment to regulate the content of their pictures. He also pointed out that censors were still finding reasons to cut member companies' films, to the tune of 2,132 excisions in the first six months of the year. This situation was bad enough for public relations, but with the growing trend toward the production of sound pictures, such infractions could prove economically disastrous:

It is pretty difficult to save your situations if there is an oath, for example, by lip movement. It is more difficult if the oath is in a subtitle, but the last word in trouble will be found in the spoken word. If you do not eliminate objectionable things from pictures that are to be synchronized to sound effects, the financial loss will be so great and the damage to your pictures so extensive that it will just happen once. An immediate illustration is of a loss now imminent on account of the cut in one state of a picture made with sound accompaniment. What the state requires will cost the producer nearly $35,000, if the picture is to be shown there. This sort of thing does not have to happen very often to attract the attention of the financial heads of the companies. If a talking picture is made and any part of the dialogue is cut and the movement depends on it, the picture is lost. There is no immunity.[42]

The situation was made more critical by the fact that the sound system used by Warner Bros. and its associated company Vitaphone utilized a sound track recorded on wax disks, played on an attachment to the projector. Within a few years this technology was to be supplanted by the system developed by their principal competitor, Fox, which involved an optical sound track printed on the edge of the film. However, in 1927 the Fox system was used almost exclusively for newsreels, and in 1928 it was not yet clear which system would become the standard.[43] Fox's optical track offered some limited flexibility: although the predominance of fully scored musical accompaniments made excisions highly disruptive, not to mention the problems posed by rearrangements of shots, at least sequences could be snipped without ruining the entire reel. Wax disks, however, were absolutely inflexible. If a single word, or indeed a single visual detail, was to be eliminated, the reel's sound track would need to be recorded again to regain proper synchronization. The nature of this technology threatened to restrict the medium in a more profound sense than the limitation of camera mobility that is often cited as a major effect of the sound revolution.

Hays told the SRC: "Because the responsibility is not elsewhere than with us, I suggest for your consideration that you make every possible effort to eliminate everything from these pictures out here before they are completed for release, and we at the other end (New York) will undertake to organize all of the Censor Boards into some cohesive or similar purpose by visiting them and making them understand the seriousness of the new situation and how careful we are out here. We might get them to act more or less together."[44] Hays recognized that, with the advent of sound, the preparation of many versions for as many markets was no longer possible. He wanted to see the production of censor-proof material that could be played in any state in the Union and in virtually any nation on earth. But no one knew for sure whether such an idea was feasible, and the studios urgently sought strategies that would restore some of their previous margin of latitude in organizing film content. At Paramount, the manager of the New York exchange suggested that several different versions could be made available by submitting movies to the major censorship boards *before* they were synchronized with music, since it seemed inevitable that "we would have no end of trouble if the picture were synchronized first." At the same time, he felt that extreme care should be exercised in choosing sequences to be furnished with dialogue. Bedroom scenes and "low-life" scenes, for example, were so vulnerable to the censors that spoken lines should be permanently foregone in favor of intertitles.[45] Bell Laboratories—a research branch of AT&T, which manufactured Vitaphone's equipment through its subsidiary Western Electric—sought a more mechanical method of maintaining the medium's flexibility by investigating a means of fading the dialogue in and out of the soundtrack in the event of interruptions by censorship.[46]

Actually, sound movies were not yet technically subject to censorship restrictions in the United States. The decision of the Supreme Court in the case of *Mutual Film Corporation v Ohio Industrial Commission*, which had denied the movies the right to free speech in 1915, referred only to the silents. The MPPDA, which had often argued that the movies should be granted the same freedom of expression as the press and the stage, recognized that the talkies provided a new opportunity for questioning the constitutionality of censoring the screen. Since all pictures, including newsreels, were subject to equal controls, the MPPDA decided to make test cases of speeches made by Herbert Hoover and Al Smith as they accepted nomination as presidential candidates at their party conventions in 1928. Following an agreement struck between members of the MPPDA and orchestrated by its general counsel, Gabriel Hess, Fox refused to submit the sound tracks of its Movietone newsreels of the speeches for the approval of the state censors in Ohio and Pennsylvania. The censor boards refused to take the bait, however, and granted licenses for the exhibition of the newsreels without vetting them, "because of the subject matter."[47] Hays wrote to the members of the MPPDA, urging them routinely to withhold their sound tracks from the censors in order to bring the matter to a head. Success depended on the industry's presenting a solid front, but Warner Bros. refused to cooperate. That company had the most to lose, since its sound output was far more substantial than that of any other studio. By August 1928 Vitaphone was producing an average of four short synchronized segments and one full-length talking picture every week.[48]

The nature and extent of Vitaphone's output made the company the focus of Hays's concern about the industry's response to sound. Writing to Jack Warner about Vitaphone's violations of the Don'ts and Be Carefuls, he attached a list of transgressions that had been noted by MPPDA officials and warned, "Whether or not the present censorship laws where they exist shall apply to sound is a question to be settled. . . . If such laws do not apply now, they will be passed and they will be passed in many states where they do not now exist, if many mistakes are made in talking pictures as indicated in the attached. Thus, what is done now in this connection becomes a very vital industry matter."[49] "The attached" refers to violations observed in *The Beast,* a "playlet" starring Irene Rich, John Miljan, and Barry Townly. The list gives an idea of the kind of material that Hays considered dangerous:

"Their memories are damned short."
"Damn those drums."
"Those Damn niggers are at the gates again."
"Good God, the niggers have got her."
"—Stinking blacks—"
"—kisses hot on my lips—"
"—my teeth on your white shoulder—"
"—after two years of wanting you—"
"Oh pity, for God's sake, pity."
"Carlysle, thank God."
"I'm damned glad I killed him."

Perhaps surprisingly, "sex-suggestiveness" is quantitatively outweighed by profanity as a problem in these "spoken titles," as the MPPDA termed them. Profanity was a sore point with Hays and his team, because it offered no margin for dispute or interpretation. The Don'ts and Be Carefuls expressly forbade swearing, and the use of profanity was therefore completely indefensible from a public relations perspective. In sound movies the danger was greater, not just because profanity was difficult to remove, but also because the comprehension of the spoken word did not depend on the literacy of the audience. The movies' influence on the young and impressionable, previously restricted to visual representation, was now at issue in language as well. As a result, sound movies were simultaneously more vulnerable to censorship action than the silents and less able to accommodate it. Ironically, the loophole which made them technically exempt from censorship had the immediate effect of restricting content still further, since the MPPDA wanted to demonstrate that the irreproachable content of the movies rendered official supervision unnecessary. Even visual content became inherently more vulnerable, because, as William C. de Mille commented, "We cannot put in a title to tell the audience they haven't seen what they thought they saw."[50]

The main consequence of these developments was an increasing watchfulness on the part of the industry itself over film content. Jason Joy's hand was greatly strengthened by the added economic hazards that attended "rejectionable" material in the talkies. Cooperation with the SRC not only acquired heightened economic importance for individual companies but also proved more crucial in the efforts of the industry as a whole to avoid legislative intervention. Rita McGoldrick of the International Federation of Catholic Alumnae remarked with satisfaction on the producers' attitude in her regular radio broadcast "Endorsed Motion Pictures" on 9 May 1929:

It is a pleasure for us at this time to pay very sincere tribute to Universal Pictures for their willingness to cooperate with the public groups toward the ideal of better pictures, and for the good faith which actuates their efforts. SHOW BOAT, that highly elaborate, lovely story of the Mississippi, was carefully pruned of any possible features that might have been objectionable to certain localities in this country. The story of Julie of the Show Boat, the clever and exquisite young actress of the boat's stock company who is happily married to a white man although she has the inheritance of negro ancestry, has been left out entirely in the motion picture version of Edna Ferber's novel. In the book, as well as in Mr. Ziegfeld's interpretation of it, this episode becomes the pivot of fine and dramatic action. But the motion picture producers, realizing the difficulty that the miscegenation theme would present in many sections of the country, *did not hesitate* to sacrifice what would ordinarily have been splendid motion picture material, alive with suspense, dramatic emphasis and moments of emotion. *We cordially compliment Mr. Laemmle on his courage.* Producers who show in this manner that they are making a sincere effort to raise the standards of the screen entertainment deserve the endorsement and cordial support of organizations such as ours.[51]

It is difficult to read this passage now without a sense of irony. But McGoldrick was accurate in her estimation of Carl Laemmle's motives: he wanted to be able to sell his picture, one of the earliest musical features, in "all localities," and if miscegenation was going to cause problems in the South, it would not reach the screen anywhere, "splendid motion picture material" notwithstanding.

To accommodate early sound production, which was centered in New York rather than Hollywood, an East Coast version of the SRC, the Eastern Studio Relations Committee, was set up.[52] By the time the committee became operational in May 1929, under the direction of Hays's executive assistant, Maurice McKenzie, the tide of production had already turned back to Hollywood. However, the fact that the Eastern SRC continued to operate until the mid-1930s, when its jurisdiction was formally restricted to short subjects, demonstrates the determination of the MPPDA to oversee 100 percent of its member companies' output.[53] In 1930 the new regimen was officially formulated in a Production Code, discussed in chapter 4. The Code superseded the Don'ts and Be Carefuls of 1927, mainly by providing fresh terminology for the debate over permissible limits of representation in the cinema. While it was specifically occasioned by the introduction of sound, it should be viewed in the context of the trend toward industry regulation of movie content that had been gradually increasing since 1922.

Foreign Agents

Although sound was causing upheavals in American exhibition by 1928, it had not yet found its way overseas. Ironically, given the problems that language diversity was soon to cause, many industry figures initially felt that the use of language would cause fewer problems abroad than in the United States because the non-English-speaking market would necessarily be confined to synchronized music and sound effects. At any rate, the problem could be avoided temporarily, since most overseas exhibitors had not yet taken up the challenge of wiring for sound.

Meanwhile, the SRC's policy of increased vigilance led it to seek links with consultants who could negotiate matters relating to foreign countries in a more or less official capacity. Following the procedural precedent established by Hays, it was not unusual for the SRC to submit international material to the relevant embassy for comment, both during and after production. However, this was often a slow and bureaucratic process. Moreover, the studios and the agencies of the MPPDA could expend time and energy in negotiating with consular representatives over details of narrative structure and characterization, only for the government in question to go ahead and ban the movie anyway.[54] Jason Joy was interested in identifying individuals with whom he could have regular contact and who would be able to approve properties on behalf of their governments, thereby forestalling official objections.

Several such connections were initiated during 1928. Raúl Spindola, honorary commissioner of the Department of Education in Mexico, was temporarily assigned to the committee as "a friendly advisor in the matter of pictures with a Mexican background."[55] The Chinese had had an active representative since at least 1926.[56] The Canadian Mounted Police offered to send a consultant, although there is no evidence that he ever arrived. Sometimes a consular official was nominated as a regular contact, as in the case of C. F. Borcosque, the Chilean vice consul, who was responsible for informing the industry on matters concerning South America, and Chile in particular. The presence of these advisers in Hollywood was well publicized, to the extent that some lobbyists, misunderstanding the economic rationale behind their appointments, complained that native Americans did not receive representation equal to that accorded foreigners.[57] The amount of influence wielded by these individuals on behalf of their various national interests varied according to the economic importance of the market they represented and the current state of trade negotiations. They were mainly concerned with details of historical or cultural accuracy, but in cases where they genuinely had the authority to speak for their governments, it was possible for them to affect more significant aspects of a movie's complexion. The most extreme example of intervention in production involved Baron Valentin Mandelstamm, who represented France.

Mandelstamm gained his influence through a chain of association with the French minister of foreign affairs: he was a friend of the assistant to the assistant to the minister. Tenuous as his standing may appear, he seems to have commanded the confidence of the French government.[58] Herron recognized this in a letter to Joy of August 1928: "We simply must cultivate the French embassy and their hirelings if we ever expect to quiet that country down. Much as I hate to take on people such as Mandelstamm, it seems to be the only solution of our problem."[59]

The tiresome thing about Mandelstamm was that he saw himself more as a professional script consultant than as a "friendly" adviser on details of cultural representation. Consequently, he not only wanted to be paid for his services (his commissions from the studios constituted his only apparent source of income), but he also expected to have a major influence on script development. The problem of his status is typified by his collaboration on *Condemned to Devil's Island*, also released as *Condemned* (Samuel Goldwyn/United Artists, 1929). The story was in obvious danger of running afoul of the French sensitivity about the representation of its penal institutions. Acting in cooperation with the studio in August 1928, Mandelstamm secured permission from the French Foreign Office for Goldwyn to proceed with the production, on the condition that the studio supply him with details of the scenario. In May 1929 he wrote to the company, reminding executive Arthur Hornblow that "the story should be submitted to me for a final O.K. before starting to shoot."[60] As Goldwyn explained in subsequent correspondence with Hays, "In pursuance of the above arrangement we submitted an early draft of the story to him. It quickly became evident, however, that Mandelstamm intended to use his quasi-official capacity to inject himself into the situation as a story collaborator. He maintained that his comments upon the story, which had been submitted to him pursuant to our understanding with the French government, were in the nature of literary suggestions for which he should be paid. Thus, a delicate and embarrassing situation arose."[61] Goldwyn broke off his discussions with Mandelstamm on this occasion, but the Frenchman was still busy as a consultant the following year and was still requesting payment.[62]

The nature of Mandelstamm's attempted editorial interventions can be discerned from his comments on the script of *Du Barry, Woman of Passion* (Art Cinema Corp./United Artists, 1930), a "romantic costume-melodrama" set in the court of Louis XV. Mandelstamm objected to the portrayal of the king of France as an "old roué" and took issue with the "incorrect" characterizations of the king and Du Barry on historical grounds, pointing out that Du Barry was shown as "a mixture of Kiki and a vixen, when it is well known that she was very ambitious." Indeed, in his opinion, most of the action was implausible, and he identified "fundamental errors" in the script's depiction of locales, customs, the army, and Paris and its topography, and in its use of dialogue: "Summing it up it is an impossible story, and should it be produced as it is, it will surely provoke formal protests from the French authorities and it will also be severely criticized by the civilized world. I am at your disposal to make constructive suggestions, should they be required." Much of Mandelstamm's advice was dismissed by the studio, especially in matters that were outside his area of authority, such as psychological plausibility. Joe Schenck of United Artists told Jason Joy that he did not believe the French government was especially interested in what their kings had done. Nevertheless, he promised to treat the subject with great caution. Frederick Herron confided to Joy, "I wouldn't touch this picture without the help of Mandelstamm because it would take the very finest type of finesse to handle such a picture without causing trouble, not only for this picture, but for the producers of the picture, as well as the whole American industry."[63]

Concrete instances of Mandelstamm's influence can be found in *Morocco* (Paramount, 1930), in which he was the author of several changes. For example, he objected to action in the original script in which a Foreign Legion officer, Adjutant Caesar, was shown shooting an American private, "Sam" ("Tom Brown" in the finished film) in the back. Mandelstamm persistently argued that the sequence constituted a slur on the honor of the officers of the Legion. Eventually, at his insistence, an element of ambiguity was introduced into the sequence through the insertion of a shot of an enemy machine-gun nest, at which Caesar could have conceivably been aiming.[64] The late introduction of the shot helps to explain the confused screen direction in the middle of the sequence.

Valentin Mandelstamm failed to appreciate that *Du Barry, Woman of Passion* (Art Cinema Corp./United Artists, 1930) was designed to be more sheer entertainment than historical document. As a representative of the French government, he condemned the producers for the "inaccuracies" in the movie. Producers had to keep Mandelstamm's opinions in mind to some extent if their movies were to be allowed access to the French market.

Darryl Zanuck at Warner Bros. decided to risk ignoring Mandelstamm's advice concerning the comedy *Fifty Million Frenchmen* (1931). He brushed off the complaint that the picture showed French women as "loose and leading immoral lives." When Joy warned him that this could lead to trouble, he replied flippantly: "In reference to Baron Mandelstamm: In the French point of view he asked me not to use any French girls in *Fifty Million Frenchmen*, so I therefore used American girls. They play all the parts." Mandelstamm was not prepared to let the matter drop. According to both Herron and Harold Smith in Paris, he lodged the worst possible report of the film with the French Foreign Office. Herron thought he was probably bitter because "Warner Bros. did not buy him off." As a direct result of Mandelstamm's recommendations, France not only rejected the film but also put a temporary ban on Warners' products.[65]

Mandelstamm certainly had the last laugh. In a letter to Warner Bros. executive William Koenig on 22 July, he wrote:

On Saturday last, July 18th, you invited me by phone to come over to First National Studios to see you, which I was glad to do. You informed me that the French government, following the release of *Fifty Million Frenchmen*, had put a ban on all the Warner Bros. First National productions in France and French colonies, and you requested me to do all that would be in my power to be instrumental in helping to lift said ban. With the utmost frankness you admitted that there was no excuse for your organization, after all the reiterated warnings I had given you, either verbally or in writing, which may be proved from many records on file. You expressed to me your regrets on behalf of your organization and told me that this would never occur again and that you were eager to reinstate me in my former capacity of French counsellor for your company; that I would be given every facility to perform my duties, and that all my advices and suggestions would be from now on strictly followed.[66]

Mandelstamm demanded that he be given assurances of this situation in writing. Otherwise the ambassador, who was already "very much displeased" with Warners, might not be prepared to view the studio's situation sympathetically, "in spite of all my good will."[67]

The presence of Mandelstamm in Hollywood represents one of the most idiosyncratic sites of foreign influence on the movies. His function was similar to that of the consular representatives in that he was responsible for eliminating potential causes of national offense, but he differed from them to the extent that he tended to recommend what should be in the movies as well as what should stay out. The studios, while choosing a path between heeding him and humoring him, had to reckon with him as an added pressure on their production practices.

The Foreign Market and the Introduction of Sound

From the time the American domination of the foreign market stabilized after World War I until the end of the silent era, films were adapted for release in overseas markets wherever their potential revenue outweighed the cost of modifying, distributing, and advertising them. The value of individual markets to American producers depended on many factors, including the disposable income of the population, the number of cinemas, the availability of alternative entertainments, governmental regulations, seasonal conditions, and exchange rates. The quantity of film traded therefore cannot be taken as a reliable indicator of a market's revenue-producing status. The region that imported the most American film footage in 1927 was Latin America, and the single nation that imported the most footage in that year was Australia; but foreign earnings, excluding revenue from Canada, were distributed otherwise, with Great Britain clearly constituting the most

Table 2
Sources of Hollywood's Foreign Income (Excluding Canada),
1927

Region	Percentage of Income
Great Britain	30.5%
Australasia	15.2
France	8.5
Argentina and Uruguay	7.5
Brazil	6.8
Germany	5.25
Central Europe	4.0
Italy	3.5
Scandinavia	3.5
Japan	3.1
Spain and Portugal	2.25
Mexico	1.5
Cuba	1.25
Chile and Peru	1.25
Canal Zone, Trinidad, and Colombia	1.0
South Africa	1.0
China	.8
Holland	.8
India	.6
Philippines	.4
Guatemala	.5
Puerto Rico	.25
Bermuda	.00
Other small places in the world	.52

Source: J. H. Seidelman (Paramount Foreign Department),
memo to Frederick Herron, 28 November 1928, Electrical Research file, reel 4, MPPDA Archive.

valuable international customer (see table 2). Canada was an exception
because for all practical purposes the industry treated distribution and
exhibition there as an extension of the domestic field. Canadian territories had more stringent censorship standards than most of the United
States and were to some extent categorized with states that had strict
censorship boards, such as Pennsylvania and Ohio.[68]

Because of the nature of distribution patterns, the American movie
industry could not cater to the individual needs of every customer nation. For example, Haiti, Martinique, Guadeloupe, and French Guiana
all happened to obtain their American films through Latin America, so
they had to put up with Spanish intertitles instead of French. Naturally,
lucrative or potentially lucrative markets received the most consider-

ation from American companies, and economically or politically powerful factions within a society attracted much more attention than the
impoverished or colonized. Generally, however, during the silent era
each market was accommodated according to the same strategy: that is,
by avoiding censorable or objectionable material during production,
and by modifying content during distribution and exhibition. The advent of sound altered Hollywood's relationship with its market abroad
by changing the nature of both audiences and films.

Although sound pictures were relatively slow to find their way overseas, they proved popular when they arrived. *The Jazz Singer* (Warner
Bros., 1927), which conventionally marks the beginning of the sound
era, opened in London on 27 September 1928, nearly a year after its
premiere in New York. Although there was reason to fear that spoken
dialogue would disrupt the American producers' hold on non-English-
speaking markets, the enthusiasm with which the new technology was
greeted abroad made the industry initially sanguine, if not complacent,
about the future.

Nineteen twenty-nine was a boom year for American motion picture
exports. Sound was suddenly in demand in all the major revenue-
producing markets. Theaters were wired wherever sufficient capital
could be found, and American producers were in advance of their
competitors—mainly German, British, and French—in the techniques
of sound production. Ironically, foreign earnings were also boosted by
a large increase in silent exports. This came about partly because of the
desire of producers to divest themselves of their silent products before
they became unsalable, and partly because many rival foreign producers were effectively paralyzed by the speed of technological change.
The fact that the earliest experiments in sound involved synchronized
music and effects rather than dialogue helped to delay the inevitable
confrontation with the problem of language, although complaints from
the German and Italian markets that the music on Hollywood sound
tracks sounded too American gave the first hint of the cultural problems that would beset the talkies. Silent versions of most sound pictures were still being produced for the unwired section of the American
market, so silent programs could be substituted where the use of the
English language was an obstacle. In Sweden, for example, alternative
silent versions were distributed with all American sound pictures except revues, operettas, and pictures that exclusively involved singing.[69]

In several ways, sound pictures arrived at precisely the right time for
America's foreign trade. For several years before 1929 a glut of pictures
had created a buyer's market, especially in Europe. The U.S. Department of Commerce had repeatedly warned the industry to select fewer

films for export, apparently with little effect.[70] The new technology now acted to the industry's advantage by reducing the number of films available, thereby increasing the value of each movie to the distributor. Indeed, the arrival of sound raised the stakes involved in the motion picture business at every level. In the silent days, movies could be shown virtually anywhere there was a flat space, including in small rural halls that masqueraded as cinemas one or two nights a week. These tiny operations in foreign territories were of little or no value to the American producers and distributors, who earned most of their profits from key cinemas situated in the large cities. In the United States, approximately 85 percent of total revenue was obtained from a third of the theaters, and overseas the differential between first-run and subsequent-run was just as dramatic.[71] For example, in Belgium in 1928 a prestigious American film could be rented for fifty thousand francs to a large first-run venue but could only hope to bring four hundred francs in a small subsequent-run theater several months later. In Romania the disparity was even greater, ranging from six hundred thousand to two thousand lei.[72] In Latin America, 80–90 percent of all revenue was derived from the key cities.[73]

Europe was Hollywood's best regional customer, providing more than two-thirds of all foreign income. In Britain, even suburban cinemas were often lavishly appointed, but this was not the norm for Europe. Americans perceived the large numbers of small and medium-sized cinemas in Europe as a blight on the territory. For example, George Canty observed that "there is to be found in Germany the usual preponderance of small, inadequate motion-picture houses that do so much to hinder necessary growth."[74] Throughout Europe, the lower end of the exhibition field was already upgrading to more substantial operations; this trend was most marked in Poland, where the number of cinemas decreased from 800 in 1924 to 450 in 1927 without any notable decrease in the total number of seats.[75] Nevertheless, Europe's cinemas were far less advanced than those in the United States, which had seen a concentrated program of building and improvements in the late 1910s and early 1920s. The arrival of sound provided an incentive for cinema owners abroad to speed up this process.

The Commerce Department's report on the European market in 1929 remarked on the progressive disappearance of smaller cinemas and their replacement by larger, more centralized establishments, "constructed purposely with a view to the exhibition of sound films."[76] In the United States, public relations pressures had persuaded the MPPDA to take special measures to help keep struggling exhibitors afloat during the change to sound, but overseas the association was frankly pleased to see such exhibitors go.[77] Sound cinemas in Turkey made large profits, while 50 percent of small provincial theaters closed; in Hungary, the new seating provided by two new and three reconstructed theaters in 1930 was sufficient to compensate for the seats lost in the closure of forty-nine minor houses.[78] During 1931, Europe saw the closure of approximately two thousand small, unwired cinemas, and the world economic depression added an extra burden to small exhibitors whose only choice was to gamble on expensive new technology or to be starved for product as the supply of silent films dwindled.[79] Remarkably, building and reconstruction in Europe kept pace with closures, even in the depths of the Depression, and the switch to sound was ultimately accomplished without a significant drop in the total number of cinemas. Yet the character of the business had been transformed. Canty commented at the end of 1931 that "with the advent of talkies, the cinema has become more than ever dependent on mechanical and electrical machinery, and is therefore definitely headed away from the 'shooting gallery' classification and very possibly toward better direction and greater public respect, [which] augers very well for the future."[80] Fewer, more carefully selected movies played in larger, more expensive cinemas, with longer runs. Many individual theaters had been absorbed by cinema combines. In general, the changes wrought by sound seemed to point to bigger and better business for American companies abroad. However, the industry's enthusiasm about the prospects of the foreign market was tempered by two factors: the perennially vexing issue of legislation hostile to the American product, and the inflexibility of the sound medium, especially as it affected sales in non-English-speaking markets.

The Impact of Sound on Foreign Legislation

Although most quota and contingent legislation was intended to limit the volume of American imports, to some extent it acted in Hollywood's favor by encouraging the more careful selection of products for export and hastening the elimination of the bottom of the range. The British Cinematograph Films Act of 1927, for example, specified a gradual increase in the proportion of domestically produced films to be distributed in the British market, beginning with 7.5 percent in 1928. The idea was to stimulate investment in British films, but the U.S. Department of Commerce saw the legislation as useful for the American industry as well: "Conservative estimates place the American share of the annual [British] feature import market henceforth at practically 70 per cent. This figure is healthier than previous larger percentages, since increased British and Continental competition, forcing the American contribution down to this figure, has only eliminated the poorer output of the American companies, pictures which in the past have been used principally in so-called block-booking transactions."[81]

A similar pattern prevailed in many parts of the British Empire and in many of the quota-regulated countries in Europe. Fewer movies not only meant a better return per picture but also assisted the American industry by boosting the prestige of the Hollywood product. From this perspective, the assumption by some commentators that a reduced market share constituted a loss of "power" for Hollywood in Europe seems ill-founded.[82] Germany, where contingent legislation seems to have genuinely eroded American profits, was the exception rather than the rule.[83] The real problem with most quotas from the American point of view was not that they were restrictive but that they were subject to change without notice, which made long-range planning for the foreign field a nightmare. As one government official complained in 1929, "It is impossible to foresee market conditions when these indefinite restrictions remain, just as it is extremely hazardous to make financial investments in an attempt to strengthen demand for motion pictures."[84]

For a while in 1929 the American companies hoped that the development of sound might cause quota legislation to be universally abandoned.[85] They reasoned that if public demand for sound pictures continued, most foreign industries would lack the necessary capital and expertise to be able to fulfill their side of quota agreements.[86] If exhibitors could not obtain the films that their patrons wanted to see, the major financial sector of the country's movie trade was put at risk. Hence the hope arose in American circles that the limited number of sound films available would enable Hollywood producers to distribute their products without encountering official interference, as a result of lobbying by local exhibitors.

The relative strength of the American position is illustrated by the misadventures of the French quota in 1929. The Americans had shown themselves more than ready to resolve diplomatically the demands of their European customers, especially the Germans and French. But in 1929 the organized French film trade, the Chambre Syndicale de la Cinématographie Française, recommended quota changes to the governmental Film Control Commission that would have reduced the ratio of imported films to those produced domestically. Previously seven to one, the ratio was now proposed to be three to one. This time the American industry responded by withdrawing completely from the French market; it did no business there for six months. American wiring and recording companies joined in the boycott. When business resumed in September 1929, after exhibitors (and arguably their patrons) had endured considerable privations, the old ratio of seven to one was restored, and the Chambre Syndicale announced its intention to devise "some new system of protection to the native industry which does not savor of the present contingent system."[87] The Hungarians followed suit by scrapping their contingent the following year, replacing it with a system of import certificates that could be secured for a fixed fee.[88]

Although these early developments supported the contention of the Department of Commerce that sound films had "dislocated" the basis of quota and contingent legislation, the official analysis proved to be overly optimistic. Restrictive legislation continued to survive in various forms, as the department conceded in 1931: "[The] restrictions are either generally becoming sharper or assuming different trends, or are springing up in entirely new quarters, thus requiring increased study as they continue to be based on different plans."[89] The Depression also seriously eroded profits from the foreign market in the early 1930s, mainly because of currency depreciations and restrictions on international monetary exchange that kept Hollywood revenues tied up in foreign territories.[90]

Yet in Europe the development of sound did partially thwart plans to restrict the American product—not at the national level, but across the continent as a whole. The so-called Film Europe movement consisted of various European initiatives, between 1924 and 1928, aimed at joint production and reciprocal distribution.[91] The general idea was to counter the advantage of Hollywood's huge domestic market by breaking down sales barriers to European movies within Europe. The project was ambitious even in the silent era. To compete with the Americans on their own economic terms, the Europeans needed to gain a proportion of the wider global market while also achieving dominance in their own territories. Nevertheless, by 1928 coalitions had been established, treaties forged, and a display of European solidarity achieved.[92] A struggle between U.S. companies and a German-led European consortium, Tobis-Klangfilm, over the control of patents related to sound technology represented a site of tenacious resistance to the domination of American companies in the European industry: the "patents war" managed to forestall America's entry into the German sound market for twelve months, from mid-1929 to mid-1930, and to interrupt its progress in several other nations.[93] Ultimately, however, the effect of sound, when *sound* came to mean "talking," was to splinter this incipient unity into its component language groups. Any sense of cohesion that had arisen from the shared determination to resist the American industry was undermined by the local cultural imperative of hearing the accents of one's own language.

In Italy, for example, a law was passed in 1929 prohibiting the projection of a movie in any language other than Italian, and similar strictures were temporarily instituted in Portugal and Spain. Producers in France and Germany found themselves alienated from the highly lucrative British market, leaving that field wide open for the Americans. British manufacturers themselves adopted sound film production with enthusiasm, but they were more interested in the ready-made English-speaking market of the British Empire than in the problematic European arena. They were also quick to recognize the new opportunities available to them for trading in the American market and were accordingly inclined to enter into deals across the Atlantic rather than across the English Channel.[94] Several Hollywood companies, including Warner Bros., United Artists, Universal, and RKO, organized alliances with producers in England or entered into production there themselves, encouraged by the need to secure product to satisfy the British quota.

But if language was an important factor in the failure of the European trading bloc, it was also one of the major conundrums facing the exporters of American movies. Film, the international art, suddenly found itself language-specific. The problem now was how to reinstitute the flexibility of form and meaning that had enabled movies to be sold around the world.

The Language Question

By late 1929 the non-English-speaking world was getting tired of patched-up synchronized versions and unintelligible dialogue. C. J. North, chief of the Commerce Department's Motion Picture Division (which had been elevated from the status of a section on 1 July 1929), reported in 1930 on the disaffection of foreign audiences: "While talking pictures a year ago had passed beyond the novelty stage, English dialogue pictures were still being shown with a fair degree of success. . . . But this situation has undergone a revolutionary change. Films in the English language stand little or no chance in most non-English-speaking areas."[95] Yet the Department of Commerce remained confident that the industry would meet these developments by a process of "bookkeeping and experiment."[96] Hollywood would have to adapt to the new conditions through economically rational adjustment of its business and production practices. Dubbing was not yet fully viable because of technical limitations, although most major studios experimented with it. The only available alternative was a vastly more expensive and complex operation: namely, the production of several different talking versions of selected films, each in a different language. Stars could retain their own parts if they were multilingual; otherwise, foreign replacements could be used. According to Kristin Thompson, each foreign version produced involved an average outlay of thirty thousand to forty thousand dollars beyond the cost of the original language production, compared with the twenty-five hundred dollars that it had previously cost to subtitle the average silent feature.[97] Yet despite the financial risks involved, the industry pursued this solution energetically, led by MGM, which launched a two-million-dollar program of French, German, and Spanish versions in November 1929.[98]

The production of multiple-language versions demonstrates the extent of the American industry's commitment to its markets abroad. As long as overseas trade was accommodated by the financial and distribution sectors of the industry, it remained relatively inconspicuous, but once the onus shifted to the production sector, the importance of the foreign market was dramatically revealed. By 1930 all the major companies were producing foreign-language versions, and language professors were busy on the lots, coaching the actors in the subtleties of French, German, Italian, and Spanish pronunciation.[99] In addition, the major companies embarked on multiple-language production in Europe. Paramount took the most conspicuous initiative: in 1930 the company established a large studio at Joinville, outside Paris. In its first year of production the studio completed sixty-six features, including some movies made in twelve different languages.

The language problem affected the whole basis of Hollywood's approach to its foreign trade by forcing it to make status differentiations among its customers. Companies had to consider which territories were economically significant enough to be supplied with products in their first language. Canty suggested the following hierarchy for Europe:

Group I, which can be supplied with films in one of the leading languages (English, Spanish, German, and French) are Great Britain, Germany, France, Belgium (French), Switzerland (French and German), Spain, and Austria (German).

Group II, whose territory is too small for economic production of films in the domestic language and where the exhibition of films in the second language is risky, are Sweden, Norway, Denmark, Italy, Czechoslovakia, Hungary, and Poland.

Group III, small countries where films should be released in the second language (indicated in parentheses) that are merely sound synchronized or have native titles superimposed on the screen, are the Netherlands (German), Portugal (Spanish), Turkey (French), Greece (French), Bulgaria (French or German), Rumania (French), Yugoslavia (German), the Baltic States (German), and Finland (German).[100]

In theory, the production of films in the languages of the major customer nations meant that, for those markets at least, the inflexibility of sound film could be offset by meeting national requirements during production, obviating the need to introduce expensive modifications during distribution and exhibition. In practice, foreign-language films presented a whole new range of problems that caught both the studios and the MPPDA off guard. As an industry executive observed in 1929, "International questions are ever as stubborn as [they are] delicate and have a way of developing subtleties in inverse ratio to their initial simplicity."[101]

Although the English-language version of *The Bad Man* (First National, 1930) posed a number of public relations problems for the studio, particularly with respect to the Mexican government, the history of the Spanish version, *El hombre malo*, is more relevant in the present context. The movie was the first Spanish-language production attempted by First National. Its production manager, Henry Blanke, found himself with an immediate problem when trying to decide what kind of Spanish should be used in the production. As he explained in a letter to the SRC,

You know that in the play of *The Bad Man* you are dealing with two different nationalities—an American family on one side and Lopez and his gang, being Mexicans, on the other side. The contrast between these two nationalities is shown in the English stage play in the following way: the American family speaks English while Lopez and the Mexicans speak a broken English. In order to get the same contrast in the Spanish picture, we decided to have the American family speak the Spanish of the stage—the Castilian, and to have Lopez and his gang speak Mexican.[102]

Some disaffected Mexican members of the cast gave details of the production to the Mexican press. The implied status differentiation between Castilian and Mexican Spanish was strongly resented, and the movie was denounced in Mexico even before its release. The newspapers also found fault with the movie's casting. Although Mexico frequently protested at Hollywood's reinforcement of the Bad Man stereotype, in this case Mexican national pride was offended when a Spaniard, Antonio Moreno, was cast in the Bad Man role of Pancho Lopez. Blanke insisted that the company had tried to enlist the services of Leo Carrillo, a Mexican who had been recommended by the

Mexican vice consul, but that the actor had been in Australia and unavailable for the part. In any case, the complexities of the language
and cultural problems involved in *El hombre malo* pointed to a new
range of problems for future production.

A different array of diplomatic problems arose in relation to the Spanish version of *Mr. Wu* (MGM, 1930). Colonel Joy wrote to Irving
Thalberg expressing concern about the possibly offensive representation of the Chinese in the film, "in view of the very strong Chinese
influence in most Central and South American countries."[103] The potential for cultural indiscretion did not stop there, however:

> The second, and most important consideration is the likelihood of offending
> the English, whose influence is also great in Latin American countries as well as
> Spain, by making English the characters in the story who are in unsympathetic
> conflict with the Chinese. In view of the fact that the actors who will play these
> parts will probably be Latin types and will speak in Spanish, and that the charac-
> ters represented by the Gregory family might just as well be Spanish, it may
> possibly seem illogical and be offensive to the English that they should be sin-
> gled out for no necessary reason.[104]

In the end diplomatic and economic considerations were indivisible, as
Joy reminded Thalberg: "In view of the limitations involved in marketing this picture, we feel sure that you will want to give careful consideration to everything that will make the picture acceptable to the fullest
extent in that market."[105]

The MPPDA specifically charged John V. Wilson of the SRC with the
responsibility of keeping in touch with studios during their prepara-
tions of foreign-language versions. Theoretically, he was supposed to
make sure that all such productions conformed to standards laid down
for American distribution—a requirement necessary to allay the fears
of the industry's critics, who remained worried about the pernicious
effects of American motion pictures abroad.[106] But foreign-language
productions were often made with crews, casts, and scriptwriters different from those who had worked on the original versions—émigrés
were typically employed on American lots—and were intended to satisfy very different sets of cultural requirements.

The problems inherent in trying to enforce a single standard are illustrated by correspondence relating to the French version of *Bachelor Father* (MGM, 1931). In the English-language version of the film, the
MPPDA had required the insertion of a scene indicating that the father
in question had been legally married to the mothers of his various children but had subsequently been divorced from them. The studio, with
Wilson's compliance, omitted the scene from the French version, caus-

ing Hays to complain to Joy: "It is a serious matter, indeed, if critics are able to point to a case and prove that we have a different version abroad of any picture or in any phase of any picture from that used as the standard version in this country under the Production Code. If it can be shown that we observe the Code here and violate it in versions that are sent abroad, we will loose a very large amount of criticism and justify a very large number of powerful critics."[107]

Wilson's response reflects the extent to which motion pictures had been subject to local interpretation throughout the silent period. He recognized the incompatibility of differing cultural demands and could not conceive of a single format sufficiently adaptable for international distribution: "It would be illogical to say that a production of this character would fully satisfy requirements if it were made to satisfy the moral standards of American audiences who will never see it, even if no regard is given to the satisfaction of the moral standards of the French people for whom the picture is especially made. This would be dangerous, because many things innocent enough in our language would be quite offensive to the French and because some of our moral standards are less moral to the French than standards which we consider immoral." Wilson claimed that from the French point of view it would be far more objectionable for a man to be shown continually marrying and divorcing than indulging in a series of youthful affairs. He stressed that the production staff of foreign versions were attuned to the "religious and moral standards, the racial and national beliefs, institutions and traditions" of the countries for which the movies were intended. These people were qualified for their jobs by "experience and nationality." Wilson insisted, "I think we will confuse the issue very much if we require studios to make foreign language pictures in conformance with American standards because it will so much detract from our very serious efforts to concentrate upon the satisfaction of the requirements of the various countries for which those pictures are expressly made."[108]

Whether it was a result of cultural differences or not, Hays was right in concluding that directors of foreign versions took extra latitude with content, making movies that were more risqué than was allowable in the United States, possibly because of less stringent censorship standards in some markets. Herron backed up Wilson's decision to allow a little more "sophistication" in foreign versions: "You are exactly right in your opinion on this matter, although I would hate to be quoted outside in this. You can be more sophisticated in your foreign versions than you can in the domestic ones, but the productions must be kept on a high level, even with this sophistication, and not allowed to drop into the mud at any time."[109] *Variety* reported that MGM's German version of *They Knew What They Wanted* (MGM, 1930) took extra license with the language, since "without a worry as to domestic censorship, the studio had more leeway for Continental consumption."[110] In response to the omission of the scene in *Bachelor Father,* Colonel Herron commented, "In fact it makes it more spicy, of course, not to have this in, and on the Continent I think it will get by."[111]

By 1931, however, it was already becoming clear that the production of special-language versions was economically impractical. The Department of Commerce reported gloomily that such movies were less popular in Europe than silent features, although this preference may have developed partly because the larger exhibitors, who had already wired their theaters, would only play silent films if they were of the highest quality. American films specifically designed to be synchronized with music and effects also had more drawing power than special-language versions. Unfortunately for Hollywood, markets that were large and lucrative enough to warrant special productions, especially the French and German territories, were able to support their own film industries, the products of which were apt to compete successfully with those of the American companies. Despite the efforts of the studios to produce culturally authentic special-language versions, the films always seemed compromised. They were neither genuinely expressive of a local sentiment nor adequate to the prestige of the Hollywood silent cinema, with its "super productions" and international stars.

Where its foreign-language versions were concerned, Hollywood was, ironically, caught in the same set of circumstances that had frustrated its foreign competitors since World War I: high capitalization was impossible, since the movies' intended markets were too small to recoup large investments, but less expensive productions did not have sufficient drawing power to justify their relatively modest costs. The difficulties confronting the Paramount enterprise at Joinville were compounded by the inability of the company to secure adequate numbers of established French and German stars. The studio halved its foreign-language productions in 1931, to a total of thirty-one: nineteen French, five Spanish, four German, one Swedish, and two "international" versions containing sound effects but no dialogue.[112] By 1932 it was barely managing to produce two French films a month, while other companies, including MGM, had largely closed down their foreign-language units, eventually converting foreign-based studios into dubbing units. Spanish-language production continued on a small scale in Hollywood until the end of the decade, but versions in other languages virtually disappeared after 1932.

Sound Solutions

Foreign versions adapted from English-language originals, which retained the original songs and sound effects but deleted the dialogue in favor of titles, had early appeared on the international scene and were still in circulation in 1930, but they had lost their attraction with the appearance of native-language movies. RKO had tried to streamline its foreign production and cut down on costs by using a technical process which allowed foreign casts to act against back-projected scenery filmed for the American original, but the results were disappointing.[113] Foreign exhibitors had improvised a range of translation methods, typically involving the projection of titles on a separate screen, but these practices had never provided more than temporary solutions. By 1931 the most promising long-term answers appeared to be either subtitling or improved dubbing methods.

Subtitled movies were finding a satisfactory response in several markets, particularly in South America. The titling process was straightforward and inexpensive: the dialogue was analyzed in the New York offices of the major producers and condensed into a key list of English titles, which could be translated into any number of languages during distribution. In Europe, however, the performance of titled prints was patchy, especially in the larger markets, where local productions offered more competition. It was with a view to the European market that the American companies continued to experiment with dubbing.

The original problem with dubbing had been that the existing technology had not been capable of mixing or accurately synchronizing sound tracks. By late 1930 the invention of the multiple-track Moviola had overcome these limitations, enabling music and effects to be mixed with separately recorded vocal tracks.[114] Dubbing an individual print was not particularly expensive—United Artists estimated the cost of dubbing a picture into Spanish at thirty-five hundred dollars in 1933—but it depended on the maintenance or rental of a dubbing plant and the employment of associated personnel.[115] This was only economically feasible for the major language groups—Spanish, German, and French—and for Italian, which constituted a special case because of Italy's governmental restriction on foreign languages. Germany and France introduced regulations requiring that dubbing into their native languages be carried out on their home soil, in an effort to secure at least part of Hollywood's business and presumably to keep some control over the application of their languages.[116] Even for these markets, by no means all of Hollywood's products were dubbed, since the process was only considered appropriate for action pictures with little dialogue. In 1937 United Artists subtitled at least some of its movies in every market except Italy, which amounted to twenty-three subtitled versions. In several countries, including Belgium, Albania, and Greece, some versions were simultaneously dubbed and subtitled in different languages.[117]

In Latin America, audiences often preferred subtitled movies to those dubbed, or indeed produced, in standard Castilian Spanish. As one United Artists branch manager explained, "It must be hard for New York to understand the jealousy with which each of those Spanish-speaking countries regards its own Spanish as correct and all other dialogues [as] something to be treated with derision. . . . In past Spanish talking pictures, Argentine audiences were vastly amused at artists speaking pure Castilian. The manner of pronunciation would cause laughter among the audiences and ruin otherwise really dramatic sequences."[118] The same problem occurred in reverse for the Portuguese, who found the Brazilian Portuguese of the casts employed by American companies to be unendurable and pleaded for subtitled versions instead.[119]

As these examples suggest, subtitles not only solved difficulties of translation, but they also managed to ameliorate some of the problems produced by the cultural specificity that characterized sound production. Although audiences could hear the action being played out in a foreign tongue, the meaning of the dialogue was less specifically located through being indicated, in condensed form, in the local language. Thus the spectator was granted a certain amount of freedom with which to elaborate the import of the dialogue. Indeed, subtitled versions involved an interpretive latitude somewhat similar to that which had characterized the silent cinema, with its compressed and imprecise rendering of dialogue in titles. Specific cultural sensibilities could be accommodated by adjustments and naturalizations in the titles themselves, although radical modifications of content were generally implausible at the local level, and responsibility for meeting the wider requirements of the international audience passed back to the point of production.

Dubbed versions were culturally and semantically more inflexible, but they allowed some latitude for adaptation during the movie's progress from studio to audience. Small-scale causes of offense could be eliminated in the process of translation, and in Europe the use of a population's first language might have helped to localize the action and mitigate the foreign origins of the product. At the same time, the perceptible disjunction between the actors and their voices helped to ameliorate a problem inherent in the multiple-language versions, identified by Nataša Ďurovičová. She points out the absurdity of having Swedish actors, for example, speaking perfect Swedish but nevertheless comporting themselves exactly like Americans. Speaking of the Swedish version of *The Lady Lies* (Paramount, 1929), she comments, "What ultimately makes the film so difficult to watch . . . [is] that the sense of comfort with which the Swedish actors speak their lines is essentially incompatible with the manifestly non-Swedish social mannerisms, surroundings and psychological types of the characters."[120] An effect of dubbing is to cancel out this effect of dissonance with an additional kind of dislocation; since dubbing is necessarily an imperfect process, it is always clear at some level that American actors on the screen are not actually speaking Swedish. The imposed dialogue consistently announces its status as a product of technical intervention designed to facilitate local consumption, and the action remains firmly located in Hollywood, where it belongs.

Once these solutions to the language problem were in place, Hollywood's major international preoccupation became, ironically, its English-speaking territories, and especially Great Britain itself. This concern was partly occasioned by the sheer size of the markets: Britain accounted for more than 30 percent of foreign income, and the British Empire for more than 50 percent. In addition, because negatives sent to London were substantially similar to those circulating in the United States, British cultural imperatives had to be accommodated in the preparation of versions intended for the domestic American market.[121] This initially posed so many difficulties that the MPPDA mooted the possibility of making special British versions of "all pictures that would normally be construed as being contrary to their policies . . . in order to take advantage of the profits to be made there."[122] Indeed, the same mixing technology that had facilitated dubbing made possible the "reconstruction" of sound movies for difficult English-language markets. However, this expensive option was tenable only as a last resort. Instead, it became normal practice to anticipate British cultural requirements at the scripting stage and to build into the production process latitude for special "protection shots" to be taken for incorporation into the British version. An even cheaper strategy was to find ways of shooting culturally sensitive material that would prove acceptable to both Britain and the United States. Ironically, after the introduction of sound it was the English-speaking market, more than any other, that had to be taken into consideration at every stage during the preparation of Hollywood's products.

4

Sophisticated Responses and Displaced Persons

Content Regulation and the Studio Relations Committee

The public relations problems posed by talking movies took considerably longer to solve than the technological challenges that sound presented. "Sophisticated" material, often based on controversial Broadway plays, threatened to undermine the status of the industry's efforts to establish the cinema as "pure" entertainment. City conservatives, sections of rural American consumers, and significant areas of the foreign market, already concerned about the cultural impact of Hollywood, balked at the thought of contemporary social themes being discussed in front of their children.

Sound also exacerbated other public relations problems. The treatment of criminal subjects threatened to become more sordidly realistic; the characterization of foreigners became more immediately susceptible to offensive interpretation; and the nature of precise locations was more difficult to evade. This last point was especially problematic where social decadence or political corruption was part of the local color. Thus sound called into question Hollywood's suitability for general consumption, both vertically across age groups within individual theaters and horizontally across ethnic and geographic boundaries.

In response to these issues, the producers, encouraged and coordinated by the Studio Relations Committee of the MPPDA, developed an overall strategy by which to maintain the suitability of their products for broad-based consumption. Levels of ambiguity were deliberately introduced into motion pictures to allow multiple interpretations by multiple audiences. Treatments of "adult" themes were characterized by innuendo and ellipsis, so that the movies could not be accused of educating innocent viewers in methods of sexual or criminal behavior.

Part of the MPPDA's public relations strategy was the declaration of a Production Code, a set of representational guidelines primarily concerned with sexual and criminal matters. While the movies were still marketed as "sensational," they had to reassure their critics that they would not use their position of cultural centrality to undermine existing social structures. If their appeal was often in their very modernity, this was all the more reason for their narratives to be contained within apparently innocuous frameworks.

During the early years of the Production Code, foreign issues intruded much less obviously into the daily operations of production companies than they had done during the difficult transition to sound. In the early 1930s most of the major studios recruited personnel from their New York international sales offices to act as contacts with the foreign press in Hollywood and as in-house advisers on foreign issues. These appointees soon found themselves heading "international" departments, responsible for advising the studios about material that could inhibit their products' distribution abroad, in cooperation with the MPPDA.[1] Once acceptable methods of dubbing and subtitling had been developed, pressures from the international market could be integrated relatively smoothly into regulatory procedures designed for the domestic sphere. The major public relations crises confronting the industry during this period were domestic in origin, springing largely from the moral insecurity that enveloped the United States at the time of the Depression. However, the integration of domestic and international regulatory procedures nevertheless ensured that the foreign market was in a position to influence aspects of motion picture content regularly, indeed routinely, in a way that had not been possible before the introduction of sound. "Foreignness" became less clearly associated with particular ethnic and national groups and became abstracted into an amorphous category of the alien, so that specific interest groups could find fewer grounds for complaint. Even geography became less distinct, with "mythical kingdoms" often standing in for exotic locations in Latin America, Africa, Europe, and the Far East, so that film commerce abroad would not be affected by the casual insult of national stereotyping.

The Problem of Source Material

The advent of sound affected motion pictures thematically by influencing the nature of material acquired for screen adaptation. The studios had a policy of acquiring successful material from other sources, especially hit stage productions, best-selling novels, and short stories from current popular magazines. Although the acquisition of such properties was expensive, they had the advantage of having been pretested in the public arena, and their existing reputations constituted advance publicity. As the screenwriter Clara Beranger explained in 1929, story editors favored such material, because of the "stamp of approval" that the public had given to a successful play or book.[2] Also, because the copyright status of a well-known property was relatively easy to clarify, companies could avoid the legal hazards that sometimes accompanied unsolicited "original" material. Robert Gustafson, in his study of source acquisition at Warner Bros., claims that popular pretested material performed consistently well at the box office, to the extent that its success offset the comparative expense of the original properties. From 1930 to 1933 only 14 percent of source material used at Warners was written directly for the movies by staff writers.[3] When trying to defend their choice of material against criticism from the MPPDA, producers could argue that they were not responsible for the kinds of themes that reached the screen. Jesse Lasky maintained that "we are really in the hands of the men and women writing the current fiction, the literature of the day. THEY ARE OUR REPORTERS and they are the ones that set the standards for the present type of entertainment."[4] The introduction of talkies encouraged the studios to derive their subjects from the stage, despite the fact that plays were the most expensive story sources of all. According to Gustafson, of the six hundred thousand dollars that the Warner Bros. Story Department spent on source material each year from 1930 to 1933, 63 percent went toward the acquisition of plays, which constituted only 33 percent of material acquired.[5]

The derivative nature of screen material had long been a point at issue between the producers and the administration of the MPPDA. Hays claimed that the material available to the public in print or on the stage was not necessarily appropriate or admissible on the screen. "There is a greater degree of responsibility on motion picture producers for the effect that their product will have upon the minds of those who view it than there is on either the novelist or the dramatist," he told a women's club in Philadelphia in 1925. "The man who publishes a book or the man who produces a stage play appeals to a more or less limited group. Not everyone can or will pay $2 for a novel. Not everyone can pay that much or more to attend a dramatic performance. But everyone can—and nearly everyone does—pay the small price that grants admittance to the motion picture theater. . . . The book stalls and the dramatic theaters appeal, it might fairly be said, to the 'sophisticates.' But this is not the case by any means with motion pictures."[6]

Hays was concerned about the effect of the movies on the "impressionable classes" of children and immigrants. At the same time he worried about the public relations implications of exhibiting "sophisticated" material to the conservative population of rural and small-town America, "the vast majority of Americans, who do not fling defiance at customs and conventions, but who cling with fine faith and devotion to the things that are wholesome and healthy and who live lives similar to those of their forefathers."[7] The industry could not afford to alienate these communities by presenting them with the more controversial or risqué products of the popular press and stage. An exhibitor from Baraboo, Wisconsin, insisted in 1927 that he needed pictures that would cater to a general family trade "with a thorough guarantee against showing a single item that could possibly offer the remotest offense."[8]

Adaptations from the stage posed particular problems for domestic distribution since they tended to accentuate the gulf—both actual and imagined—between Broadway and Main Street, where Broadway signified New York City and every other large metropolis, and Main Street signified the small towns and rural districts of the American heartland. With the increase in dependence on the stage occasioned by sound, the industry found itself having to deal with properties that had a comparatively specific appeal—albeit to first-run metropolitan theaters—at the same time as the motion picture medium itself was at its least adaptable and accommodating. Carl Milliken, secretary of the MPPDA, indicated the extent of the problem in an interview with the *Cleveland Plain Dealer*: "We must tone down the vaudeville wise-cracker, make him understand that he is not only going on Broadway but into Podunk where the folks aren't accustomed to the sight of girls not fully clothed and where the wise-crack, which is amusing to you and thousands of others, may create offense. Don't let anyone tell you our tasks are easy just now."[9]

The problem of preparing a product for consumption throughout the demographically diverse regions of the United States is reflected in MPPDA correspondence relating to the early talkie *The Trial of Mary Dugan* (MGM, 1929). Frank Wilstach, one of the MPPDA's public relations consultants, wrote to Jason Joy expressing concern about scenes in the play, a courtroom drama in which Mary gave testimony about her life with her four lovers. Wilstach was worried about the implica tions for the future of screen entertainment if such material was allowed to pass. "If . . . censor boards will let dangerous material like this get by," he warned, "then it seems to me that the motion picture will very soon reach that stage of freedom of speech that has brought the speaking stage into disrepute, in late time." He continued, "Here, then, the whole matter will come to a test. If it be that they are making pictures that cannot be shown except on Broadway, as the saying goes, one mad howl will be set up; and that is exactly what I expect." Maurice McKenzie, Hays's executive assistant, agreed. He wired Joy: "Here some talk among industry that perhaps inland districts are not yet ready to receive with open arms themes like *Dugan* and *The Letter* [Paramount Famous-Lasky, 1929]."[10]

The difficulties created for the industry by the comparatively conservative standards of "inland districts" within the United States were exacerbated by the stringent censorship codes of customer nations such as Australia and Canada. It was becoming imperative for producers to refine their strategies for coping with the problems posed by their sociologically diverse audience.

The Ambiguous Text

The vexed relationship between the screen and its source material had led to the industry's 1924 adoption of the "Formula," which had the avowed purpose of preventing "the prevalent type of book and play from becoming the prevalent type of motion picture."[11] Initially the producers had resolved to exercise care in the selection of material and to avoid those properties which could not be adapted without radical revisions.[12] In effect, material considered too risky—for either domestic or foreign distribution—was relegated to a blacklist.

The Authors' League of America, however, recognized an infringement of authors' rights when it saw one and managed to get the procedure changed in 1927 to allow certain avenues of appeal. From then on an author could argue in favor of his or her property and if necessary could "prepare a new story, with the unsuitable material removed and with a new title . . . using such dramatic incidents and interest as may be used and making certain the elimination of the unsuitable material."[13] The author was then free to submit the new story to producing companies for "picturization," on the condition that it would not be advertised or publicized in a way that would suggest a connection with the original property. This compromise, which Richard Maltby has characterized as "the apparently preposterous process by which a story was rewritten, retitled, and then sold on the basis of the value of what was no longer in it," is an extreme case of the more general practice of revising properties for presentation on the screen.[14] The "property" for which the producers were prepared to pay such high prices was less the literary source itself than its reputation and the attendant advance publicity, which could be secured for the price of the movie rights. As in so many of Hollywood's business dealings, the most negotiable factor in the transaction was film content.

The assumption implicit in the 1927 agreement, that a controversial property's notoriety would survive any public attempt to divorce it from its source, suggests something of the complexity of the relationship between the movies and their audiences. For example, when Michael Arlen's best-seller *The Green Hat* reached the screen as *A Woman of Affairs* (MGM, 1928), it seems likely that a sizable section of the audience would have been aware of the source of the film from the ballyhoo in the press, even if some ads for the movie had not proclaimed the connection in contravention of the industry agreement.[15] Although the novel's controversial reference to venereal disease was expunged in the movie adaptation—the pivotal figure was portrayed as guilty of embezzlement, and thus morally rather than physically diseased—it is unlikely that this somewhat arbitrary substitution was read at face value by those members of the audience who were alert to the reputation of the book.

On the contrary, the charge that the movies encouraged the sale of salacious literature, often repeated by critics of the industry, must have been in part a response to the fact that the movies themselves were sufficiently coy to drive some spectators to buy the book, to find out what had "really happened" in the movie they had just seen.[16] From one point of view the filmmakers were taking the responsible course and protecting the innocent from corrupting or disturbing information; from another they were encouraging a sophisticated mode of audience response that involved reading through the action on the screen to identify deliberately displaced meanings. Either response—the "innocent" or the "sophisticated"—was open to individual members of the audience, as Jason Joy recognized in the advice he issued to Walter Wanger concerning *Applause* (Paramount Famous-Lasky, 1929): "[T]he dialogue between Helen Morgan and Fuller Mellish, Jr., in which she urges him to marry her because of the return of her daughter, might well be eliminated, allowing anyone who will to assume that they either have been or have not been married, depending upon the desire of the person who looks at the picture. The assumption that they are married is clinched further on in the picture, when she speaks of him as her husband."[17]

This man, David Furness, has a dark secret that causes him to commit suicide on his wedding night without consummating his marriage. Does he have a venereal disease? He does in the original novel (*The Green Hat*, by Michael Arlen), but in *A Woman of Affairs* (MGM, 1928) two mysterious government agents interrupt his honeymoon at a crucial stage and attempt to arrest him for embezzlement. The performance of the actor, John Mack Brown, belongs as much to the plot of the novel as to the plot of the film. His bride, Diana (Greta Garbo), also continues to insist that "David died for decency."

In other words, Joy suggested that at first the nature of the relationship between the two characters should remain moot, to be determined in the minds of individual spectators. Later, when the movie offered evidence that the couple had been married all along, the assumption of those who imagined them to be legally bonded would be upheld, while those who assumed them to be unwed would have two options. They could change their minds, in which case they would nevertheless have been given the license to consume much of the movie as if it *was* about an illicit relationship, or they could bring to bear sophisticated external information—such as knowledge of the source material or, indeed, knowledge of the moral imperatives governing Hollywood's narratives—to discount the denial presented by the film itself. Hence the movie would have presented at least two stories to at least two audiences at once, maximizing revenue while minimizing offense. In fact, in this instance Wanger did not follow

Joy's advice, as the two characters involved do get married during the course of the film. However, the correspondence provides an early instance of the kind of thinking that increasingly typified the regulatory operations of the SRC and that came to be widely accepted by producers in the 1930s.[18]

In correspondence relating to *Du Barry, Woman of Passion* (Art Cinema Corp./United Artists, 1930), Joy overtly articulated his concept of sophisticated and unsophisticated audience members for whom the movies needed to provide simultaneous attractions: "[T]he fact that there is an attempt to accurately portray historical facts is a justification for a story dealing as broadly as this one does with the theme of a woman's sale of her virtue for riches and power. Even then, however, the theme should be so delicately presented that it will not offend the unsophisticated although made perfectly plain and understandable to people of broader experience and knowledge. Therefore, any direct statement of this relationship or any action portraying its licentiousness should be avoided."[19] Ambiguity and suggestion, nominally kept within moral bounds by a transparent principle of "deniability," offered Hollywood a way out of its untenable liaison with its source material.

Such strategies underscore the fact that, from the point of view of the SRC, the underlying subject matter of a movie was of less concern than its treatment. As Maurice McKenzie remarked in 1928, "These days we are not thinking so much about restriction of themes as we are about the care with which themes are handled."[20] The development of a consistent mode of treatment that could be applied to virtually any property, regardless of its original formal or ideological complexion, was central to the way in which the American industry, through the agencies of the MPPDA, responded to the demands of wide-scale distribution and exhibition. A glance at a list of Hollywood titles between the world wars, with its dependence on popular plays and literature, might suggest that both Lasky and Hays were right, in their separate ways, in asserting that the profile of the industry's source acquisition determined its social, moral, and political outlook. On closer investigation, however, source acquisition proves to be a relatively poor indicator of Hollywood's priorities; the subsequent treatment of those properties reveals much more about the movies' worldview. For example, while Warner Bros. derived only 5 percent of its properties from foreign sources, the majority of its products were subject to scrutiny for potential foreign offense.[21] The SRC developed relatively standard forms of treatment to defuse the danger inherent in a range of subjects vulnerable to public objection, specifically sex and "adult" themes, crime, and the representation of specific locations and nationalities.

The Sophisticated Subject

In 1930 the MPPDA, with the involvement of representatives of the Catholic Church, formulated a "Code to Maintain Social and Community Values in the Production of Synchronized and Talking Motion Pictures." The Production Code constituted a notional set of guidelines for subsequent motion picture treatments as coordinated by the SRC.[22] The Code, however, by no means covered all the subjects that came under the purview of the SRC. It had little to say about representations of foreigners, foreign nations, politics, or business, all of which Joy and his team tackled under the rubric of "industry policy." On the other hand, the Code did have a marked effect on Hollywood's representation of sex and crime, and it became the public focus of the SRC's activities. Its implementation resulted in a predictable cinematic world of moral certainties in which crime could not, under any circumstances, be seen to pay. Criminals had to suffer the due process of the law, and not even suicide was allowed to intervene to save them from paying their debt to society. For women, sexual transgression resulted in misery and/or death.

The standard history of the Code holds that it was honored more in the breach than the observance until Joseph Breen was installed as its administrator in 1934.[23] However, this is very much a view that has arisen in retrospect. In practice, the Code was a reaffirmation and expansion of the Don'ts and Be Carefuls, which had already actively informed the centralized regulation of motion picture content. Joy saw the application of the Code as a logical extension of aspects of the regulatory framework that he and his assistants had already implemented, although its introduction marked a definite increase in the amount of consultation between the SRC and the studios (see table 3). The extent to which the Code was actively enforced was stepped up during Joy's administration as well as after it. For example, on 8 October 1931 the submission of scripts to the SRC was made compulsory. The Code's introduction led to the augmentation of Joy's staff and strengthened his hand in his negotiations with producers, but it had its most immediate effects less on the affairs of the SRC than on the public relations of the motion picture industry as a whole.[24] The Don'ts and Be Carefuls were three years old; the public declaration of the Production Code provided a fresh opportunity for the MPPDA to advertise its responsible attitude to motion picture content.

Code or no Code, Joy remained committed to securing a place for "adult" material on the screen. So did Lamar Trotti, who would later become a prominent screenwriter. Trotti provided energetic support

Table 3
Studio Relations Committee Contacts with Studios, 1929
and 1930

Contact	1929	1930
Scripts submitted	201	531
Studio consultations	48	1,299
Pictures submitted	323	722

Source: MPPDA memo, 1 May 1931, Production Code
file, reel 9, MPPDA Archive.

Notes: "Scripts submitted" refers to scripts submitted
to the MPPDA for an analysis concerning social values;
"Studio consultations," to studio consultations concerning detailed treatment before and during the preparation
of a story; and "Pictures submitted," to negatives of pictures submitted to the association for review. During this
period the Eastern SRC passed on 26 feature scripts and
109 short subject scripts; it reviewed 26 feature negatives
and 220 short subject negatives.

from his position as a reviewer and MPPDA executive assistant in New
York, before moving to Hollywood in 1929 to assist in the daily operations of the SRC. Joy and Trotti hoped that the appearance of sophisticated themes would provide healthy precedents for subsequent productions, as Joy made clear in a letter to Thalberg concerning *Strangers
May Kiss* (MGM, 1931): "Whenever a sophisticated subject is put on the
screen, we always run the danger of encountering difficulties with the
censors, even when a picture is handled as delicately and subtly as this
one. We are, therefore, unable to predict the difficulties which may be
developed by the censors, but we are hopeful that you will vigorously
oppose any major cuts, not only for the protection of this particular
picture, but for the subsequent effect which such an attitude will
have."[25]

Joy made a personal tour of U.S. and Canadian censor boards from
22 April to 24 May 1930, with a view to strengthening channels of communication and putting the producers' point of view before the
boards.[26] His relationship with the censors remained particularly cordial, as suggested by a letter from Canadian censor Robert Pearson,
written in June 1932:

I will appreciate to the utmost any information that you can send me regarding
pictures that are coming. I feel sure that your interest in my work, as well as
your own candid nature, would not allow you to give me a wrong tip.

A year ago, you wrote me regarding *The Bad Girl,* and after some work upon the picture, as well as a very close check on the advertising, we were able to have the picture presented without any objection, without having it tied up too closely with the book of the same name.[27]

If a picture seemed likely to be controversial, Joy and Trotti regularly provided studios with digests of arguments to use in support of their products when first approaching the boards, explaining the reasons why the SRC had seen fit to pass the movie under the Code.[28]

In the case of *Three on a Match* (Warner Bros., 1932), Joy instructed Vincent Hart of the Eastern SRC to visit the censors in New York, Ohio, Pennsylvania, and Maryland, in order to make special appeals on behalf of the picture. The movie contained a kidnapping sequence, and in the aftermath of the kidnapping and murder of the infant son of Charles Lindbergh, the censor boards were excising all such sequences, on the basis that they would likely "incite to crime." The original request for intervention had come from Darryl Zanuck:

I wish you could get in touch with whoever the New York Censor is now and, in a round-about way, put in a plug for "THREE ON A MATCH" and, as a matter of fact, do this in other spots wherever you can as I am personally of the feeling that this picture is going to be a box-office knockout and if we get by without much censorable grief from it, I am certain it will not do any damage at all. After all, it certainly proves that kidnapping is a very unhealthy occupation from which nothing comes but misery, grief and no reward whatsoever.[29]

Hart, armed with a lengthy letter from Joy explaining the movie's virtues, was able to get the picture passed in all states, although the kidnapping sequence suffered some cuts.

The extent of the SRC's efforts on behalf of *Three on a Match* illustrates Joy's perception of his primary role as being to defend the studios' interests. If controversial material made up the bulk of current source acquisitions, then it was his job and that of his staff not to impede it but to see that it reached the screen in a form that accorded with the Code. Joy tried to persuade both studios and censors to compromise in order to achieve that result. As he explained to Hays when reporting on the first year of the SRC's operation under the Code, "As you know, the popular source material of the year consisted of sophisticated novels, suggestive and ultra-sophisticated plays and realistic underworld stories which called a spade a spade and did not hesitate to fully describe the most gruesome incidents. We have always felt that there is a way of putting the essential theme of any story on the screen provided objectionable details are eliminated and extreme delicacy is used. We therefore urged the producers to consult us con-

stantly the moment it was proposed to produce a story having dangerous possibilities."[30]

Surviving documentation confirms that Joy's consultative work during this period was consistent with this approach. Records of correspondence between the SRC and MGM show that while he generally
tended to recommend the imposition of happy endings, moralistic
warnings, and general moral uplift wherever possible, many of Joy's
specific suggestions were designed to render controversial details
more ambiguous, much like his approach in the period before the introduction of the Code. For example, concerning *A Free Soul* (MGM, 1931)
he reported, "On the script we asked that change be made in that part
of the story which deals with an illicit affair since it is made too plain
and obvious." Similarly, regarding *Inspiration* (MGM, 1931) he noted,
"The situation wherein main character was shown very definitely as
having been the mistress of a number of men too definitely shown.
Suggested that this be toned down and made vague as possible."[31] Joy
may have given such advice even more frequently in correspondence
with other studios, since MGM was notably adept at avoiding censorship intervention.[32]

Joy's approach was at its most explicit in the advice he issued to
Darryl Zanuck concerning *Bought* (Warner Bros., 1931), originally entitled *Virtue's Clothes:*

> We have given a lot of thought to the arguments presented in your letter of
> the 11th inst., over the necessity of the use of Stephanie's seduction in *Virtue's
> Clothes* as her main motivation in breaking from Charles.
>
> If you would grant that merely the slightest suggestion of this seduction
> would be sufficient, so that the audience might if it wishes, *imagine* this to be a
> fact and therefore the reason for her subsequent action or might, if it wishes,
> accept Charles's reaction to Stephanie's confession as the reason for her action,
> we believe the material would not be objectionable under the Code. To grant
> this would be to grant the necessity of omitting the many lines and some of the
> action which directly point to seduction . . . .
>
> Our idea in suggesting this [i.e., the omission of three specified scenes] is to
> so construct the story that *very delicately* it may be inferred, *if one wishes*, that the
> seduction has occurred while Charles and Stephanie were on the edge of the
> cliff in scene 131, after the fade-out on this scene. This will eliminate the impos-
> sible material.[33]

In this memo Joy acknowledges that the sophisticated reading is not
just a matter of knowledge as opposed to ignorance, but it is equally a
matter of choice. An informed viewer may choose the "innocent" reading if, for example, it accords with his or her preferred narrative outcome or perception of a star's persona. Presumably some spectators

chose to indulge in both levels of interpretation alternately, or perhaps both at the same time.[34] While freedom of interpretive response had been a quality inherent in silent movies, with their allusive and often euphemistic intertitles, Joy realized that a more deliberate approach was required to construct such flexibility into the relative fixity of the sound medium.

Joy and Trotti's now-you-see-it, now-you-don't approach to treatment did have its limits. Joy balked at a submission to the SRC in which T. B. Fithian, of Universal, explained that although the proposed production of *Where Are My Children?* would be about abortion, the subject would never be mentioned explicitly. The property had been filmed by Universal before, in 1916, "to favourable reception by both critics and audiences" in the United States.[35] This positive response reflected the comparative ease with which the screen could broach controversial issues when not committed to the spoken word. For the 1931 version, much of the action was to be placed at a clinic that performed unspecified operations on women, and the practice of abortion would, in an "indefinite and subtle manner . . . be gotten over to the sophisticates." Indeed, Fithian's suggestions for subtle treatment seem derived from silent movie technique: we learn about a pregnancy when a husband "finds his wife sewing on some baby clothes," and when a girl asks for an abortion, the movie conveys that "this must be something unusual" entirely by the young doctor's "unspoken reaction, indicating his shattered faith."[36] After some consideration, Joy rejected the proposal on the grounds that abortion, however thoroughly disguised, was an unsuitable subject for commercial motion picture entertainment. The property was continually rejected until 1941, when the abortion ring was transformed into a fertility clinic.

Darryl Zanuck at Warner Bros. took the principle of deniability to its logical conclusion. Instead of directing its use toward censor boards and the more easily offended sections of the public, he tried to use it as a tactic to get around Joy himself. He claimed that the abortion-centered plot of *Alias the Doctor* (Warner Bros., 1932), to which Joy had objected after reading the proposal, had not contained an abortion at all. Zanuck pointed out that the operation was identified as a different medical procedure in the movie: "The trouble, if I may be permitted to say so in this case, is whoever has been handling this script with you is reading between the lines and reading in conditions which cannot possibly prove to be facts." Joy protested that "the audience will believe it has been *fooled* after having been allowed to expect an abortion, it would not regard the medical term as clever, but only as a trick," as indeed he did himself. But to Zanuck this was no problem because, as he told his production staff, "the audience will guess that it is an abortion."[37] "Sophistication" on the screen was becoming a more complex phenomenon all the time.

Although the concept of "delicacy," which involved implication rather than demonstration, ellipsis rather than articulation, was primarily developed in relation to sexual matters, it was also applied more generally in the work of the MPPDA. The notion was brought to bear on a range of other sensitive subjects, from crime and "gruesomeness" to national and ethnic characterization.

Crime

In response to the fears of parents and educators that crime movies could inspire specific acts of imitation by adolescents and other impressionable members of society, the studios frequently resorted to ambiguity and suggestion as a means of depicting criminal behavior in the 1930s. A precedent for such an approach had been established in the Don'ts and Be Carefuls, which had recommended the exercise of "good taste" in the treatment of theft, robbery, safecracking, and the dynamiting of trains, mines, and buildings, "having in mind the effect which a too-detailed description of these may have upon the moron." These restrictions were reproduced in the Code, along with others covering murder, arson, and the use of firearms, with the direction that "methods of crime should not be explicitly presented." In a period of social ferment it was more important than ever that movie crime should be rendered *incapable* of imitation, through the systematic omission of instructive detail.[38] Consequently, the capacity to interpret criminal practices on the screen, like the interpretation of sexual practices, varied according to the prior knowledge and inclinations of individual viewers. In the treatment of *Stolen Heaven* (Paramount, 1931) Trotti advised the studio to shoot a gambling scene "so that the camera is just above the table line, leaving in the hands moving etc." but excluding any details involving the exchange of money.[39] Censorship action encouraged ambiguous treatment. The New York Censor Board, for example, banned any scenes showing roulette wheels or the exchange of money in illegal gambling. The practical methods adopted by censor boards encouraged such evasions: board members typically saw a movie only once and marked items for excision as they went along, resulting in a disproportionate emphasis on concrete visual details.[40]

While movies could be prevented from becoming "textbooks of crime" by the removal of the means of literal imitation, the prevention of the *desire* to imitate criminals, as required by the Code, was less straightforward. Stories with irreproachable moral resolutions were susceptible to subversive interpretations on the strength of the performances they contained, and a mandatory punishment for criminal or unconventional behavior did not necessarily cancel out the appeal of a character's wildness or vitality. For example, the script of *Are These Our Children?* (RKO, 1931), a story about drink and juvenile delinquency with a sympathetic teenage lead, was approved by Jason Joy and John V. Wilson as "a straight, realistic theme, pointing a very strong moral lesson."[41] While the movie's scenes of jazz parties and teenage dissipation may have seemed precautionary to the SRC, the New York Censor Board perceived the movie's inherent attractiveness to teenagers and rejected it. By 1932 Joy had become more alert to the wider "educational" potential of motion pictures, especially their capacity to provide role models for the young. At the end of *Scarface* (Caddo/United Artists, 1932), for example, Tony Camonte was destined to die in a hail of bullets—or by execution, depending on which version of the movie one encounters.[42] Joy still advised Caddo to avoid any implication that "the school boys at the scenes of crime and the girls on the streets comment favorably upon Camonte's appearance."[43]

Contrary to the assumptions of some commentators that the movies of the early 1930s challenged the established institutions of American society, Joy's influence helped to ensure that Hollywood's output was contained within an essentially conservative framework.[44] A letter from Joy to Hays regarding *The Mouthpiece* (Warner Bros., 1932) indicates the range of considerations with which Joy was routinely concerned. It is also revealing with respect to the sections of society that the SRC felt obliged (and not obliged) to protect:

Another big question of the week was to do with a Warners story called *The Mouthpiece*, which in its original form was full of dynamite. It dealt with gangsters, a miscarriage of justice which sent the leading character off on the wrong track, and contained doubtful sex situations. First by attacking the theme itself, we were successful in taking the story altogether out of the gangster category and to substitute dramatic motivation which turned it into proper directions. By the time we had the second script we were in such position as to take up the lesser details and by almost casual suggestions even to correct such a policy matter as the character of a crooked banker, changing him into a stock broker. This latter had some significance as you will see in these precarious economic times when faith in banks is strained. This has been an interesting shaping of basic material which the Code makes possible.[45]

The movie concerned a lawyer, Vincent Day, who was disillusioned with the legal system and cynically manipulated it in order to defend underworld characters whom he knew to be guilty. In its final form,

Day not only recovered his confidence in American justice and underwent moral regeneration but also paid for his transgressions by being gunned down in the final sequence by his former underworld contacts.

Locations

Although it did not usually attract the universal interest that surrounded sexual and criminal matters, the representation of specific locations and/or nationalities was a matter of considerable concern to particular sections of the motion picture audience, both domestic and international. Such representations therefore also concerned the Studio Relations Committee.

The use of locations within the United States could raise the specter of state or municipal censorship. When the Warner Bros. production *The Doorway to Hell* was shown to the MPPDA in May 1930, the Chicago setting was indicated by details such as references to "the South Side" and "the Lake." Joy suggested that all such references be eliminated to obviate problems with the Chicago censors, although he conceded that they were unlikely to pass the movie in any case because it had a gangster theme.[46] Seven months later, when Joy was again looking for a way to placate the Chicago board, he opted for a solution adapted from his principle of deniability. Trotti had prepared a report on the stage play *The Front Page*, which was being considered for picturization by Howard Hughes, warning that the location was definitely identified as Chicago and the mayor in the play was a thinly disguised characterization of Chicago's mayor, William Hale Thompson. Trotti recommended that the text be altered to ensure that Chicago and Chicago politicians were not recognizable. Joy went a step further and reached an agreement with the director, Lewis Milestone, that the opening title of the picture would read, "This is a story of a mythical kingdom."[47] The title was a joke that operated at different levels with different sections of the audience: the "mythical kingdom" was certainly a city in modern America, and a proportion of the audience would have known from the play, a current hit, that it was also Chicago. Milestone, who according to Joy was "anxious to avoid all Code and censor difficulties," proposed slightly burlesquing the action in order to distance it further from any dangerous implication of social criticism.[48]

In the case of *I Am a Fugitive from a Chain Gang* (Warner Bros., 1932), the SRC was worried that the movie would cause resentment in the South, where the chain gang penal system was still in force and where, moreover, it was the subject of intense political debate. There was a particular risk of objection from authorities in Georgia, because the movie was based on actual events that had taken place in that state; it had been adapted from an autobiographical book by Robert E. Burns called *I Am a Fugitive from a Georgia Chain Gang!* Although no part of the country was specifically mentioned in the movie, the high ratio of blacks to whites in the jail scenes definitely located it in the South. The SRC's solution was simple: Joy and his staff advised Zanuck, at Warner Bros., to reverse the number of blacks and whites, in order to cloud the issue of the location of the action.[49]

If it was important for producers to tread carefully in using locations within the United States, the use of foreign locations could prove even more sensitive. It was difficult to ensure that the representation of any nation would be entirely inoffensive, even if the action was removed to the past. As Hays remarked to the SRC, "I note the change of locale of *Tampico* to Northern Africa and while that will no doubt avoid the Mexican angle we must watch that it does not inject, in lieu thereof, a French angle."[50] The obvious solution was to avoid representing any existing political entity at all. The "mythical kingdom" had been available as a smoke screen for Chicago partly because by 1930 it had an established use in the representation of foreign locales.

Fantastic settings, from fairy-tale castles to Arabian Nights cities, had had a prominent place on the nineteenth-century stage, which had reveled in the spectacular and the marvelous. The silent cinema adopted and magnified aspects of this tradition, most elaborately in *The Thief of Bagdad* (Douglas Fairbanks Pictures/United Artists, 1924), which placed a magical narrative in an extravagant and exotic world. "Historical" and biblical epics, such as *Ben-Hur* (MGM, 1925) and *King of Kings* (De Mille Pictures/Producers Distributing Corp., 1927), also effectively belonged to this large-scale version of the "mythical," since they were laid in remote and essentially imaginary lands and were dominated by spectacle. The advent of metropolitan picture palaces in the 1920s, with their extraordinarily ornate and sumptuous fittings, encouraged the conception of the cinema itself as a magical world apart, offering its audiences heightened experiences quite unlike those encountered in their workaday lives.[51] But "mythical kingdoms" could be useful even when they represented comparatively prosaic worlds, inasmuch as they offered producers protection from foreign protests. The economic consequences of offense to Russia may have been relatively small, but the fictional status of states such as Freedonia, Ruritania, or Sylvania gave them the additional advantage of being culturally and historically more versatile while still offering an identifiably European atmosphere.

Theoretically, the mythical kingdom option could render movies po-

The Love Parade (Paramount Famous-Lasky, 1929) contains a mishmash of signifiers of the "foreign," from the architecture and sculpture to the costuming and the company of "Royal Grenadiers." These elements are jumbled together to constitute the imaginary European kingdom of Sylvania.

litically safe for exhibition, without modification, virtually anywhere in the world. Since most motion pictures were not located in purely fantastic settings, however, many "mythical" settings suggested actual locations, by the choice of landscape, dress, customs, or accent. In trying to remove *The Boudoir Diplomat* (Universal, 1930) from the dangerous territories of France and Spain, the company considered placing it in "a mythical kingdom or Russia or some kingdom where it will do no harm."[52] Eventually it was set in "the Kingdom of Luvaria," but Herron still had to warn the studio against calling the kingdom's cities Belgra and Slavia, because of their similarity to Belgrade and Yugoslavia.[53] John V. Wilson thought that Paramount was safe enough with *The Devil and the Deep* (Paramount, 1932), which was laid "mostly in an unidentifiable naval post on the northern coast of Africa." He wrote to Frederick Herron: "The actors speak with a decided British accent, their names are Germanic and their uniforms are nondescript. It is going to be difficult for any country to try to claim the story is that of its own navy. Even if that is done, I doubt very much if there will be any objection because what really happens is due to the insanity of the commander of the submarine."[54] In these cases it was essential that the movie offer its critics no evidence to tie it definitely to an actual geographic location.

The importance of such ambiguity is evident in the example of *Her Man* (Pathé, 1930), in which the safeguard of deniability badly malfunctioned. *Her Man* was a variation of the Frankie and Johnny story, about a prostitute whose life was ruled by her pimp. Originally located on the Barbary Coast of San Francisco in 1905, the script was updated, and in order to avoid American censorship problems Pathé decided to set it substantially in Cuba.[55] Any evidence definitely pointing to the identity of the location was in due course removed, and by the time the movie was reviewed by the SRC's James B. Fisher, he was able to pronounce it reasonably safe: "The police who figure at points during the picture are the only definite characterizations which hint at the Spanish background. There should be no objection on this score however since the setting is never definitely placed. The rest of the characters are all Americans, or else unlabelled." Unfortunately, Fisher had failed to recognize among stock location footage a shot of Morro Castle, a famous Cuban landmark, that figured prominently among back-projections in the movie. It was bad luck for the studio that this picturesque scene was then picked up by its publicity men, who emblazoned it on posters along with the claim that the movie was set in the "scarlet streets of the wickedest pleasure-mad city of the Universe." Understandably, the Cuban embassy immediately issued protests, which were carried extensively in the Latin American press. Herron complained to the SRC that under the circumstances the picture was left "no alibi" and that the bad publicity would give the rest of Latin America the chance to "take a shot at us."[56]

T. S. Dellahanty, the vice president and general manager of Pathé, was contrite. He told Herron that he had ordered the offending shot to be removed from all prints, including, at large expense, those already in circulation. (This undertaking notwithstanding, when a print of the movie from William K. Everson's collection was screened at the National Film Theatre in London on 21 July 1990, it still contained the offending scene.[57]) Dellahanty insisted that the studio had never had the remotest intention of implying that the action took place in Cuba: "There was no intention of laying the story in Havana, as we preferred the mythical island locale and you will note, of course, that no reference to Havana or Cuba was made in any way in the dialogue used in the picture."[58] Herron himself, as the one left to bear the brunt of diplomatic reaction in circumstances like these, was jaundiced about the whole idea of mythical kingdoms. With reference to *The Dictator* (Famous Players–Lasky/Paramount, 1922) and *The Gay Caballero* (Fox, 1932), both of which had offended Latin America, he commented sourly that "although they were placed in mythical kingdoms . . . there was no question of the customs and background used."[59]

Indeed, while it was probably inevitable that fictional locations would be built on recognizable cultural stereotypes, in some cases producers deployed the "mythical kingdom" strategy with a mixture of ingenuousness and cynicism. On viewing *The Gay Caballero,* an official from the Mexican consulate was worried by the impression of Mexico conveyed by the picture. As Joy noted, "It was his opinion that, while the picture was not definitely offensive to Mexico, the general atmospheric impression given by the costumes of the supposed natives in the scenes in which they appeared in large groups was one which the Mexican foreign office has for a long time endeavored to suppress in American pictures through the cooperation of American producers."[60] In a quite startling instance of denying the excessively obvious, Al Rockett at Fox claimed that the peasants in the movie could not legitimately be identified as Mexicans at all, since they were simply represented as belonging to an unspecified non-Anglo ethnic group residing along the U.S.-Mexican border: "With reference to the general atmospheric impression given by the costumes of the natives in the scenes in which they appear in large groups, . . . these scenes were not laid in Mexico but on the American border and the nationality of the people is not definitely established. This was done deliberately so as not to offend the Mexican government."[61]

The problems associated with Latin American locations were partly caused by the failure of the studios to differentiate between the political and cultural entities that made up the region. In 1930 the Chilean consul expressed the hope that the Code would lead the industry to respect the integrity of different regional identities and cease to allow "a few backward, tropical countries" to act as the representatives of South America.[62] Notwithstanding a certain animosity between Mexico and Cuba, however, MGM produced the musical *The Cuban Love Song* (MGM, 1931) starring Lupe Velez as an attractive Cuban peanut vendor with a pronounced Mexican accent. According to Herron, words such as *cochina* that were used in the movie were also typical of Mexico, and thoroughly atypical of Cuba. As a result of this mutual insult, the Latin American consuls passed a unanimous resolution at one of their regular Pan-American meetings condemning the industry for the wrongful portrayal of their nationals. Herron did not consider that the mixture of cultural identities was the movie's worst problem:

Many of the street scenes are much more Mexican than Cuban, however, I think the whole thing would have been passed over if it had not been for the one scene of the marines in the police station. You will always have to consider that the American marines in Latin America are unpopular with the masses; they are the symbol of the so-called American despotism. You know the marines well enough to know that wherever they are they do run riot. These points just have to be considered if our people expect to keep their Latin American markets.[63]

It is ironic that the attempts by Herron and the SRC to keep overt representations of "American despotism" from the screen, encouraged by Latin American governments, actually aided Hollywood in maintaining its cultural hegemony in Latin America. One Cuban journalist commented, "Cuba's population cannot see pictures other than the American and is therefore under the exclusive influence of Hollywood. Hollywood plays a great and two-edged part in the imperialistic scheme."[64] This was undoubtedly true, but Hollywood's approach was "two-edged" in a way the journalist might not have intended. The industry was only intent on appeasing its foreign territories in order to occupy them.

Foreigners

The representation of different ethnic types was a matter at least as sensitive as the representation of locations. With varying degrees of assistance from studio executives, Joy and Herron attempted to keep offensive characterizations out of the movies. Within the United States, the vocal and powerful Italian community required especially sensitive treatment at this time because a spate of movies made in the production season of 1930–31, inspired by the exploits of Al Capone, had featured Italian American gangsters. *Scarface* was the most notorious of these. Despite the insertion of a speech by an upright and community-minded Italian American character which condemned the activities of the gangsters, the movie still led to protests from community groups and the Italian embassy. Hays wrote to the ambassador explaining that the movie was an anachronism, having been held up in production for more than two years, and that current practice was "to eliminate any reference in crime pictures to individuals with names that could be connected with any foreign country."[65]

An inevitable consequence of this tactic, if it were to be applied with any degree of consistency, was the restriction of the world of the movies to Anglo-American characters, especially where villainy was concerned. Herron observed this tendency as early as 1930, and he was

Richard Barthelmess (middle) might not have been entirely convincing as a Mexican in *The Lash* (First National, 1930), but if an American in disguise was the hero of the movie, Americans were also the villains. In the face of diplomatic sensitivities surrounding ethnically marked characterizations, First National demonized American westerners instead. Land commissioner Peter Harkness (Fred Kohler, left) was depicted as an unscrupulous, rapacious oppressor of the Mexican natives.

afraid it would occasion a new kind of diplomatic backlash. *The Lash* (First National, 1930), starring Richard Barthelmess, seemed to typify the problem. The movie was a "western in costume, but with the costumes of the Spanish and Mexican era before 1850." It depicted Barthelmess as a "Spanish Robin Hood." According to *Variety*, "After the conquest of Lower California by the Americans, the Americans are disclosed as cheating and abusing the natives, stealing their lands through crooked land commissioners, and beating their prisoners."[66] Herron wrote:

I was so mad after I saw it that I saw red for days. If the picture had been made abroad it would never have been allowed distribution in this country and would probably have been objected to in every place in the world where it was shown by American representatives, and I hate to think of the loss of prestige we will experience in Washington if the picture is shown there and seen by some of our friends in the State Department. I feel I am a lot to blame on pictures of this type because of the continual harping I have been going through in telling people to lay off the foreign villains and make the villains American, but I didn't know they would go quite as far as this.[67]

An alternative solution to confining ethnic difference to the roles of heroes or victims—and a solution that seems to have appealed to the SRC—was to let characters occasionally remain foreign, but in an unattributable sense. Joy advised that excitable characters in both *As You Desire Me* (MGM, 1932) and *So This Is Africa* (Columbia, 1933) be rendered as "not too obviously Italian."[68] His successor, James Wingate, issued the same suggestion in relation to a criminal in *The Headline Shooter* (RKO, 1933), and when advising on *Our Betters* (RKO, 1933), he recommended that, since the character of Pepi was likely to cause objection in South American countries, "it would be wise to avoid difficulties in this regard by omitting any references in the dialogue that label him as anything more definite than a 'foreigner.' "[69] The effect was to remove these generic foreigners from the geopolitical sphere altogether and to give them citizenship of Hollywood's mythical kingdoms. Perhaps the neatest solution of all lay in films like *Dracula* (Universal, 1931), *Frankenstein* (Universal, 1931), and *Murders in the Rue Morgue* (Universal, 1932). As James B. Fisher reported in assessing *Dracula*'s foreign angle, "Dracula is not really a human being so he cannot conceivably cause any trouble."[70]

The End of the Beginning for the Production Code

From the beginning of his association with the Committee on Public Relations, Jason Joy had pinned his faith on reforming the movies through box office pressure, trusting in the good taste of the public and the good faith of the producers. Although the Code machinery seemed to offer a golden opportunity for the perfection of the art of self-regulation, Joy was to suffer a measure of disillusionment in the first year of its operation. Not all the studios were in sympathy with the aims and methods of the SRC. From May 1930 to April 1931 two-thirds of the industry's output was not submitted during production for discussion and advice, and although most of these movies were innocuous, some were not. Consultation with the SRC during script development was optional at this time, but submission of the finished films was compulsory under an industry-wide agreement on "uniform interpretation" of the Code's regulations. In the first six months of the Code's operation, Warner Bros. submitted few scripts and fewer finished products, and the company was only brought into line through intervention by Hays in October.[71] Irving Thalberg at MGM sympathized with Joy's aims and approach, but because he prided himself on his ability to handle difficult subjects with taste and sensitivity, he resented being restrained by rules that he felt were more appropriate for some of his more heavy-handed competitors.[72] Paramount entered into the spirit of the Code wholeheartedly—a situation that was to change with the arrival of Emanuel Cohen as head of production in 1932—and Fox usually managed to stay out of trouble, but lapses occurred across the whole industry with disappointing frequency.

According to Carl Milliken, the pictures which caused the most trouble during the first year of the Code's operation were diverse in origin and in kind. The most problematic were *Lonely Wives* (Pathé/ RKO Pathé, 1931), which made light of sexual infidelity; *Many a Slip* (Universal, 1931), which found comedy in pregnancy and divorce; and *The Lady Refuses* (RKO, 1931), a melodrama about prostitution and self-sacrifice. Nearly as bad were *Millie* (RKO, 1931), a drama about infidelity; *Her Man* (Pathé, 1930), which ran into the foreign difficulties described above as well as problems surrounding its depiction of prostitution; and *Illicit* (Warner Bros., 1931), a drama involving the themes of marital infidelity and "free love." In addition, *Doorway to Hell* (Warner Bros., 1930) caused objection by characterizing a gangster as a hero, *Hell's Angels* (Caddo/United Artists, 1930) brought protests about its sexual elements, and *Whoopee!* (Samuel Goldwyn/ United Artists, 1930) gave rise to complaints about excessive nudity.[73]

Joy, however, persisted in seeing himself not as a censor but as a mediator. He articulated his position in a letter in late 1931, ironically enough addressed to Joseph Breen, a future head of the Code machinery who would bring to the job a very different outlook:

I am quite concerned about [complaints received from the New York Censor Board] although I cannot say I am exactly surprised. The list of sex pictures we made up while you and the General [Hays] were here showed conclusively that we were in for trouble because of the *number* of such stories. With crime practically denied them, with box office figures down, with high pressure methods being employed back home to spur the studios on to get a little more cash, it was almost inevitable that sex, as the nearest thing at hand and pretty generally sure fire, should be seized on. It was.

Until a short time ago, the *number* of such pictures was not a thing which we could very well combat. We were limited to the individual picture under the Code machinery, judging each in its turn. Now we have done something to rectify them by being ordered to take up with the executive committee, through Mr. [Fred] Beetson, the matter of too many of any type of picture. In this way, we hope to be able to call a halt and keep them from piling up. I am not optimistic enough to think we will ever get to the place where there will be no sex pictures. Nor do I know that would be a good thing. Sex has a legitimate use in drama as one of the most interesting factors in life. It is only by overdoing it that we get in trouble.[74]

The decision to stagger the release of pictures with a single theme to avoid having the public exposed to "too many of any type of picture" was initially taken in 1931 with respect to gangster movies. Hays returned to the tactic on several occasions.[75]

Joy's principal strategy remained his promotion of oblique and ambiguous treatments of illicit subjects, designed to encourage the kind of "genteel and delicate" treatment that in his view rendered such material unobjectionable.[76] However, the public relations problems that confronted him were not confined to the content of the movies themselves. They also stemmed from the advertising and promotion that surrounded the films. Indeed, the development of strategies of ambiguity in movies' narrative techniques had the effect of shifting some of the burden of explication to the advertising men, with posters and newspaper advertisements providing the context for the audience's imaginative elaboration of the action on the screen. Those sections of the public which objected to the movies on moral grounds were nevertheless confronted with the advertising, which, despite the introduction of a separate Advertising Code in June 1930, seemed to many to be growing more offensive.[77]

The MPPDA was faced with a barrage of oddly contradictory complaints: first from those critics who complained that the advertising was salacious, and second from the picture-going public, who objected to the fact that the movies themselves failed to live up to the promise of the posters. As one Philadelphia newspaper put it: "What is needed is a ban on the growing tendency toward the use of misleading, lurid, suggestive and sometimes salacious posters that frequently misrepresent the plot and purpose of a film and show and make the picture appear far worse in imagination than it is in reality."[78] Catholics in particular were unimpressed by the quality of both the advertising and the entertainment on the screen, and often disapproved of the appearance of the "sophisticated" subject, no matter how it was treated. With the social conditions created by the Depression worsening, the industry came under the increasing threat of a conservative moral backlash. In September 1932 both Joy and Hays worried that 24 out of 111 pictures in production dealt with illicit sexual relations.[79] The approach to sophisticated subject matter that had evolved under Joy's administration no longer seemed to offer sufficient protection in the prevailing cultural climate, and in October 1932 Joy left the MPPDA to work as an SRC contact at Fox.[80]

James Wingate must have seemed a good choice to succeed Joy at the SRC because he was recruited directly from his position as head of the New York Censor Board. Not only could he be expected to have a thorough knowledge of the board's requirements at a time when it was setting the censorship standard for most of the country, but he was also in a unique position to command a sympathetic hearing for the MPPDA in negotiations with his friends on the board. Wingate was known to differ with Joy and Trotti on the matter of sophisticated subjects, which under the circumstances must have especially recommended him to Hays.[81] However, Wingate was never a great success at the SRC. He took on the job at an especially difficult time, when the industry was under extraordinary public relations pressure and when censorship boards were tightening their standards all over the country, particularly where sexual matters were concerned.[82]

The situation was made worse in early 1933 with the publication of the Payne Fund Studies, the widely publicized result of a five-year research program investigating the effects of motion pictures on youth, which seemed to confirm the movies' influence on morals and behavior.[83] Under these circumstances Wingate could not predict the fate of pictures at the hands of censors and the public as accurately as might have been expected, and in some cases he made unaccountable errors of judgment. An example was Columbia's *So This Is Africa*, which he passed for release during his first month on the job. The movie was widely considered untenable by state censorship boards because of its wisecracks, general vulgarity, and sexual innuendo. The MPPDA's lawyer, Charles Pettijohn, pleaded for it to be withheld in Nebraska while a state censorship bill was pending. Eventually the film was withdrawn and recut under the supervision of Hays himself. Other movies that ran into trouble during Wingate's administration included the drama *Fast Workers* (MGM, 1933), which contained "vulgar and offensive" sexual elements, and *Love, Honor, and Oh, Baby!* also known as *Sue Me* (Universal, 1933), a comedy about sexual entrapment to which censors and public alike objected. Paramount's adaptation of William Faulkner's notorious novel *Sanctuary* as *The Story of Temple Drake* (Paramount, 1933) was not markedly censorable in itself, but it did little to convince the public that the trend of motion pictures was "upward."

At base, the industry's crisis was inseparable from the broader social and economic malaise that afflicted the country. When President Franklin D. Roosevelt closed the banks on 6 March 1933, Hays responded by calling an extraordinary meeting of the MPPDA Board of Directors to impress upon them the vulnerability of their business. The general mood was reflected in a letter from Wingate to Hays, written a few days later: "During the past few weeks we have just witnessed the most critical business and economic period that I can recall. The public and organized minorities have become more keenly critical and more expressive. Attention is turned from building up attendance upon good pictures generally to expressing what is wrong not only with pictures but with everything that pertains to pictures. In other words, this is a moment of hysterical criticism."[84] Wingate insisted that overall the quality of movies had not declined, and indeed it is interesting to note that the adoption of subjects from the stage, which had been the focus of such concern in 1930, had fallen off significantly by 1933. According to Gustafson, only eight plays were acquired that year at Warner Bros., as opposed to thirty-five in 1930.[85]

Wingate observed, however, that critics and possibly audiences tended to express their disapprobation particularly stridently in times of economic crisis. Producers, he thought, were also more likely to be tempted to make the occasional low-toned movie for ready cash without considering the long-term consequences. In his opinion the industry could best meet its critics by exercising more care in its choice of material, and by a new approach to the method of treatment: "[Producers should refrain] from so directing a picture that the immoral and salacious may be inferred although not technically expressed, either in dialogue or portrayal. It is difficult, under the powers granted us by the Code and its interpretation, to delete an unexpressed thought although we may be conscious that portions of the audience will think that particular thought."[86] Wingate clearly recognized that the technique of communicating the "unexpressed thought," having been brought to a fine art under Joy's regime, would not easily be unlearned, either by producers or audiences. His problem, and one that would soon be inherited by Joseph Breen, was how to put the cinematic genie back into the bottle.

5

Why Is Mr. Brown Eating Spaghetti?

Content Regulation and the Production
Code Administration

The relationship between the industry and its consumers, both local
and international, was a dynamic one. Just as the studios and their
regulatory agencies became more practiced at anticipating and avoiding public relations problems, so some groups, most notably the Catholic Legion of Decency, developed considerable expertise in applying
pressure on the industry through the channels offered by the MPPDA.
The Legion was the most visible sign of a domestic social climate growing increasingly hostile to the movies. The industry's response to this
climate took the form of a reconstitution of the Studio Relations Committee. Its central function in overseeing movie content was affirmed,
its machinery of enforcement was strengthened, and it was renamed
the Production Code Administration.

In this more rigorous environment the thematic and stylistic tendencies that had been established since 1930 were rendered more emphatic. Narrative strategies that had been merely ambiguous became
increasingly cryptic, and subjects known to be "sensitive" were
hedged about with elaborate demonstrations of their innocuousness.
The outcome was a highly codified and conventionalized cinema in
which audiences, practiced at consuming narratives somewhat arbitrarily contained within the strictures of the Code, were able to exercise
considerable freedom in interpreting the condensed images on the

screen. The visual and narrative incoherence that often arose from the effacement and displacement of sensitive subjects encouraged audiences to become active interpreters, obliging them to make their own sense of contradictory cinematic evidence.

It was not only in the domestic sphere that Hollywood's consumers were developing more sophisticated methods of applying pressure on the MPPDA. In the international arena, economic and diplomatic arm-twisting by foreign governments developed into a fine art during the 1930s. International concerns were typically expressed through diplomatic channels to the MPPDA's Foreign Department in New York, but they were ultimately directed to the association's agencies on the West Coast, where they were integrated into strategies of self-regulation devised in response to domestic public relations pressures. Several countries developed particularly effective methods of influencing production, ultimately affecting aspects of Hollywood's ideological expression in the second half of the decade. Britain was Hollywood's most important customer, and its concerns were therefore routinely taken into account by producers. But at the same time, other much smaller markets were able to make their influence felt on the production floor by bringing diplomatic pressure to bear on the American industry.

Emergency Measures

At the MPPDA's crisis meeting following the closing of the banks on 6 March 1933, the Board of Directors issued a statement reaffirming their commitment to the Production Code. Hays recognized that this reaffirmation had to amount to more than an empty gesture if the industry was to escape governmental intervention in its affairs. Federal regulation, of both business practices and movie content, still posed the greatest threat. In addition, numerous other censorship bills were pending all over the country, at municipal and state levels, and legislative and civic bodies were determined to pass these bills into law. It was imperative that the industry be seen to change direction.

The urgency of the situation was communicated to the West Coast. At Universal, for example, Harry Zehner, assistant to Carl Laemmle and later a staff member at the MPPDA, sent a memo to producer Martin Murphy to inform him of the import of the meeting:

[Hays] informed the producers that there was now a new order of things in connection with the Code and censorship and that Dr. Wingate and his force had received instructions from him to be more strict than ever in the enforcement of the Code.

There is no use referring to pictures made by other companies, such as *She Done Him Wrong, Picture Snatcher* etc., and say, "See what they got away with—we can do the same." There is a "new deal" in censorship, so far as the Hays association is concerned, and it means they are going to be more rigid with the enforcement of the Code. This attitude is already evident in the letters we are now receiving from them on scripts. Prior to this time, we were told, "it is recommended, etc.," but recent letters definitively state, "it is inadmissible, etc." or something equally definite.[1]

Zehner stressed that Code requirements should be kept in mind from the drafting of the first script onward, so that the "feel" of the final cut would not be impaired by late alterations. He described Hays's impatience with the producers: "He further stated if his pleas at this meeting failed to attain the desired result he personally was going to the Press of the country to state the case and have the matter ruled on in legislation which *he* would instigate."[2]

In view of Hays's very public leadership of the MPPDA, his attitude was not surprising. If industry self-regulation ended in a shambles, after ten years of effort, it would mean the end of his credibility in public life. His reputation had already suffered as a result of his unconvincing performance before a congressional committee investigating the Teapot Dome scandal in 1928: he had admitted illegally accepting campaign contributions from Harry Sinclair, the figure at the center of the scandal, when he chaired the Republican National Committee during the election of 1920. Furthermore, much of his work on promoting innovative business practices had been undone in a series of 1930 court decisions that had ruled against his industry-wide arbitration scheme. Now the concept of industry regulation of movie content was coming under attack, and as publisher Martin Quigley had warned him in August 1932, "Many of the persons immediately responsible for the wrong things being done are not going to suffer in prestige or reputation, because as far as the public is concerned they have none of either to lose. In the event of a public revulsion, you will be the first and principal victim. Even now, you must be seeing from time to time in newspapers and magazines the often repeated questions, 'What about this, Mr. Hays?' and 'What is Hays going to do about this?' etc."[3]

Hays's threat to take independent action in response to the criticism directed toward both the industry and his personal position begs the question of whether he himself may have solicited the intercession of forces external to the industry to compel producers to comply with the terms of the Code. In any case, if at this point the industry required a dramatic public act of propitiation and definite evidence of a reformed attitude, then the opportunity presented itself in the nick of time as a result of the intervention of the Catholic Church. In the summer of 1933 a group of Jesuits who were in contact with both Quigley and Breen began to develop proposals for a drive to boycott those pictures which in their opinion did not live up to the spirit and letter of the Code, and to blacklist those theaters which exhibited them.[4] In October the Apostolic delegate to the United States, the Most Reverend Amleto Giovanni Cicognani, addressed the Charities Convention in New York, denouncing the influence of the cinema. In November the annual meeting of American bishops appointed a committee on motion pictures. By April 1934 a nationwide Legion of Decency, with its headquarters in New York, had begun recruiting members.[5] Within a few months millions of Catholics had joined up, signing a pledge to boycott films that were listed as offensive within their diocese. Protestant and Jewish leaders voiced widespread support for the campaign.

By targeting the box office, the Legion of Decency took the message for movie reform to the producers in a way that they could not ignore. The Legion's campaign included a total boycott by Catholics in Philadelphia, which caused a reported 40 percent drop in receipts there.[6] Lest this be construed as a fundamentally hostile attack on the industry, however, it is worth noting that the Catholics' action was designed to uphold the industrial status quo. They only demanded that the Code—in which, after all, they had an authorial interest—should be interpreted according to their own lights. The industry had long had constructive contact with Catholic organizations, particularly the International Federation of Catholic Alumnae. The Legion now aimed its criticism not at the vulnerable business practices of the industry, but at the essentially negotiable area of movie content. The MPPDA's secretary, Carl Milliken, subsequently remarked that "one of the reasons for the influence of the Legion of Decency movement on the public and therefore on the industry, was the fact that its leaders wisely refused to be beguiled into attacks upon the trade practices and criticism of the machinery of the industry. They properly concentrated their attention upon the moral and social values in motion pictures."[7]

The extent to which Hays was actually implicated in the formulation of the Catholic action, if at all, remains a moot point. Leonard Leff and Jerold Simmons maintain that Joseph Breen was its prime instigator at the MPPDA and that Hays effectively relinquished control to Breen over matters concerning production, being "physically and perhaps temperamentally too weak to dominate the producers."[8] This assessment of Hays's position, however, seems untenable in view of the evidence offered by the MPPDA's archives, which reveal him as the central figure of authority in the association's machinery and the prime architect of its self-regulatory policy, of which content regulation was only a part. What is certain is that the pressure exerted by the boycotts made it possible for him to institute a new, more powerful order in the administration of the Code. The conspicuous guardianship of the Catholics also gave the industry the kind of moral credibility that had eluded it in the past.[9]

Breen

When the Studio Relations Committee was reconstituted as the Production Code Administration, the personnel of the office and its powers of enforcement were again expanded. All the studios were instructed to appoint a special contact to work with the PCA to interpret the requirements of the Code to production staff, following the precedents of Joy at Fox, Zehner at Universal, John Hammell at Paramount, and Al Block at MGM. In a characteristic restraint of trade, the MPPDA agreed that none of its member companies would release, distribute, or exhibit any picture unless it had been approved by the PCA and bore its seal. Any company infringing this agreement was liable to a penalty of twenty-five thousand dollars. Formerly, a studio wishing to appeal against the decision of the SRC had been able to take its case to a jury composed of a panel of three West Coast studio executives, which usually—though not always—viewed such appeals sympathetically.[10] Now appeals had to be carried directly to the Board of Directors of the MPPDA.

The PCA's director was Joseph I. Breen, a Catholic and former newspaperman who had been the press relations officer for the Eucharistic Congress in Chicago in 1926. After working in publishing in New York, he moved to the MPPDA, where Hays assigned him to press relations in Hollywood. In August 1933 he joined Wingate at the SRC, as indeed did Colonel Joy, who agreed to a temporary return from his position at Fox to help the committee weather its crisis. When Wingate went "on vacation" in November, Breen took over the office, and he was officially installed as its head in mid-1934.

Except for Lea Jacobs and Richard Maltby, the historians of the Production Code Administration have represented Breen's regime as a radical departure from that established by Joy.[11] While it is true that the mechanisms of self-regulation were strengthened considerably in 1934, it should be remembered that this was part of an evolving process of supervision that had been tightening since at least 1922. Breen himself was far from having perfected the system when he finally left the job in 1954. Despite the enthusiasm of his apologists—Raymond Moley hailed him as "the John the Baptist of the Code Administration"—he never managed to receive 100 percent cooperation from the studios, or to eliminate the demand for regional censorship within the United States or abroad.[12] In much of his work, Breen maintained or extended regulatory mechanisms established by Joy. The mythical list of arbitrary prohibitions associated with his regime—so many inches of cleavage, so many inches between beds—never existed.[13] Despite a comparatively pugnacious personal style, Breen followed censorship precedents, as Joy had done. However, a new element of economic pragmatism was evident in his negotiations with producers, as can be seen in the correspondence relating to MGM's production of *Outcast Lady* (1934), a new adaptation of Michael Arlen's book *The Green Hat*.

Originally, in addition to the implication of venereal disease that had exercised the ingenuity of the SRC during the production of the previous adaptation (*A Woman of Affairs*, 1928), the script of *Outcast Lady* contained an extramarital affair followed by an illegitimate birth. Irving Thalberg argued that the birth was essential to the drama of the movie, but he eventually agreed to prepare a rough cut in which all reference to the baby was removed. Geoffrey Shurlock, Islin Auster, and Wingate, who was still employed at the PCA, reviewed this version and approved it on the following grounds: "With this element out, the story now tells of two clean straightforward characters who are prevented by circumstances from marrying when they want to. Throughout the story they refrain from giving in to their passion for each other; and their sudden decision at the end of the story to run away and fight convention is of course cancelled out by the girl's suicide." When Thalberg protested about the comparative feebleness of the new version, Auster and Wingate defended it on the grounds that it would demonstrate the industry's effort to be inoffensive to "the vast majority of mixed audiences everywhere."[14]

For his part, Breen conceded that the changes would indeed affect the dramatic impact of the story, but he felt that this price was worth paying. He told Thalberg:

You are, of course, as fully conversant as I am with the fact that the recent criticism of pictures is directed as much against this element [i.e., illicit sex and illegitimacy of children] as against any other one factor. It would therefore seem important, in all discussions of this subject, that we should keep in mind not only the dramatic value of this factor to any particular story, but also the fact that we have to deal with the definite wave of public reaction against stories of this type—a public reaction which has gone beyond mere written protests, and is making itself actively felt at the box office.[15]

Thalberg's arguments proved fruitless against Breen's insistence that, by jettisoning the "offensive" elements of the script, MGM could improve Hollywood's institutional image, reduce consumer resistance, and ultimately benefit the whole industry. In the meantime the baby was thrown out, and producers like Thalberg were left to seek new ways of cultivating the "sophistication" of the screen.

On the other hand, while the popular press and the MPPDA itself represented Breen's regime as having a brief to clean up the "morals" of the screen, strongly sexualized "romantic" subjects remained, in practice, a mainstay of motion picture entertainment. Although homosexuality ("sex perversion"), venereal disease, and white slavery could not be shown under any circumstances, the Code specifically allowed various other sexual themes, including adultery, "scenes of passion," seduction, and even rape, with two provisos. First, the sexual behavior in question had to be essential to the plot. The general stricture that the sympathy of the audience should never be thrown to the side of "wrong-doing" led logically to the presumption that illicit or unconventional sexual behavior should only be shown in order to be condemned. One of Breen's objections to *Outcast Lady*'s illegitimate baby was that it was not sufficiently central to the plot: the rest of the movie did not hinge on the dire consequences, for its mother, of its birth.[16] Prostitution appeared on the screen relatively frequently, always with miserable consequences for the woman concerned. A concept of "compensating moral values," first suggested by Irving Thalberg in 1930, helped to keep a place on the screen for "adult themes," albeit expressed within a closely circumscribed moral universe.

Second, the Code required that sexual themes should not be shown explicitly. Rape and seduction, for example, could "never be more than suggested." This stricture, which was consistent with strategies for sexual representation that had been established under Joy's regime, created new problems for Breen, who tended to equate suggestiveness with salaciousness. What form of nonexplicit treatment of seduction or scenes of passion could be guaranteed not to "stimulate the lower and baser element"? How could adultery or rape be represented at all without causing offense? In practice Breen settled for a more cryptic version of Joy's approach. Whereas Joy had relegated sexuality to the subtext of the action, Breen tried to submerge it even further. As he wrote to H. N. Swanson at RKO upon reading the studio's scenario of *The Gay Divorce* (released as *The Gay Divorcee*, 1934), "If you should decide to attempt an emasculated version of the story, we will be glad to discuss it with you further."[17]

The consequences of his approach are demonstrated by the history of *Dr. Monica* (Warner Bros., 1934), which starred Kay Francis. The original script contained adultery, a pregnant unmarried woman, attempted abortion, and several clinical discussions about infertility. Breen complained to Jack Warner that he could not recall any picture which "combined so many difficult elements into one story."[18] Nevertheless, Warners persisted with the adaptation. The studio proposed that Monica should be a successful gynecologist, herself unable to conceive children. She discovers that her unmarried friend Mary is pregnant and promises to look after her until the baby is born. On the night of the birth, she is shocked to discover that the father of Mary's baby is her own husband. The situation is resolved when Mary commits suicide, and Monica and her husband, now reconciled, decide to adopt the baby.

The studio and the PCA faced the difficulty of getting across the facts of Mary's pregnancy without being too blatant about it. Warners tried giving Mary a fainting spell, but this was such a well-established convention that it was considered to be insufficiently subtle. As Breen told Warner, "This action of Mary fainting at the piano will very likely be interpreted by censor boards as an indication of her pregnancy, as has proven to be the case in numerous previous pictures. If this interpretation is given, it will probably be cut."[19] The studio tried hinting about the pregnancy in dialogue, but this was not permissible either:

In the first bedroom scene between Monica and Mary, you will delete the following lines:
    "Just what do you mean?"
    "You know!"[20]

In the end the fainting scene was kept in, although Mary claims that she fainted with shock at discovering that Monica's husband was about to leave for Europe. In any case, the studio and the PCA were probably right in assuming that any direct reference to the pregnancy would have been unnecessary for audiences to infer its existence. In a "woman's picture" of this type, especially one starring Kay Francis, there would have been a generic expectation of something of the kind, which the slightest indication would have been enough to confirm.[21] More demanding of the audience's interpretive skill is the movie's residual reference to the subject of abortion. Mary indulges in all the excessive behavior characteristic of young women on the screen who are anxious to dispose of their unborn babies: hard drinking, reckless horse riding, and so on. Deniability is assured by the fact that when she embarks on this campaign of self-abuse the audience knows she is preg-

nant, but she does not: Monica breaks the news to her in a scene immediately *following* a particularly heavy fall. Mary also tells her maid that
she is leaving town for the country and does not know when she will be
back—a standard indicator of pregnancy and possibly abortion—
several scenes before she discovers her condition herself. While all this
makes no sense whatsoever in the plot, it makes the theme of attempted abortion available to any section of the audience prepared ret-
rospectively to reconstruct the chronology of the action.[22] Others may
choose to attribute Mary's behavior, from her desire for country soli-
tude to her suicidal horsemanship, to her unhappiness at being separated from her married lover.

In some ways, the prevalence of censorship at both regional and
international levels provided the industry with a scapegoat for the kind
of textual incoherence that characterized *Dr. Monica*. As one American
observer remarked in relation to another absent abortion attempt, "The
impression of abortion . . . did not strike me too definitely: all I remem-
ber is a vague suggestion of something that might have been plus the
feeling that something was missing or had been cut out, and so it was
our censor board that was responsible."[23] Both *Dr. Monica* and *Outcast
Lady*, however, were produced in the transitional period following
Wingate's tenure at the SRC and largely before the official constitution
of the PCA. As the decade wore on, the interventions of Breen and his
staff became less clumsy and less overt. Not only did they gather expertise themselves, but the studios more successfully anticipated and accommodated their requirements.

Breen's approach to treatment, like Joy's, threw the responsibility
for interpretation squarely onto the audience, but Breen required viewers to work harder in the construction and elaboration of the action
than Joy had done. In the process Breen necessarily handed audiences
a wider range of imaginative options. The harder the industry worked
officially to regulate content, the less control it exercised over the activity and experience of its consumers. Hays himself recognized this in
correspondence with J. Robert Rubin of MGM concerning the handling
of an abortion sequence in *Men in White* (MGM, 1934):

A long session was had on the 28th between Messrs. Mannix, Pelton and Bell
with Mr. Breen and they agreed to eliminate the definite suggestion of abortion. The cause of the girl's illness in the picture will have to be guessed at; the
lines seem to suggest any one of a dozen things and an impression may be
given that her illness may be caused by an abortion. It is believed that "ninety-
five percent of the audience who see the picture will have to guess at what
causes the tragedy. Some will think she tried to commit suicide, the others—
none can tell."[24]

It seems likely that the subterranean nature of the "illicit" subjects in these melodramas added to their powerful attraction. The overt reactions denied to the characters on the screen could find expression in their audiences, whose personal investment in the action was only limited by their experience, imagination, and desire. With audiences accustomed to reading the action on the screen freely, if not perversely, even the moral outcome of the action was not necessarily assured. The Code's relentless imposition of moral outcomes may have been itself sufficiently clichéd to give the audience a choice as to whether to accept a movie's "happy ending" at face value or to read through it, to an ironic subtextual outcome that defied the control of the PCA.

As had been the case under the SRC, the technique employed to cloak controversial sexual themes in obscurity was extended to the treatment of other potentially offensive aspects of movie content. In order that *Marked Woman* (Warner Bros., 1937) should escape criticism or censorship on the grounds of brutality, Breen suggested that Jack Warner "further confuse" a shot in which a little girl was violently struck.[25] For the same reasons he felt that some shots required modification in *The Adventures of Robin Hood* (Warner Bros., 1938): "We suggest that you trim all these scenes of torture, hanging, men pierced with arrows, etc., as impressionistically as possible, avoiding any specific details or close-up shots that might be offensive."[26]

The Code directed that gruesomeness should be treated "within the careful limits of good taste" but specifically relegated some criminal subjects—brutal killings and the use of firearms—to nonexplicit representation. In practice this general stricture was carried much further, as shown by the advice from Breen to Warner in relation to *G-Men* (Warner Bros., 1935):

There should be no details of crime shown at any time. The action of the gangsters entering the bank, holding up the clerk and bashing him over the head with the revolver; slapping the girl; getting the money and running away; as well as the use of machine guns either by actual display or by inference from the sound track will have to be entirely deleted. We suggest that you indulge yourselves in this connection in a series of Vorkapich shots [i.e., a "Hollywood montage" sequence] merely suggesting the hold-up. . . . There should be no definite details of the hold-up at any time. Not only are the detailed methods of crime forbidden by our Code, but invariably they are deleted by censor boards everywhere—both in this country and abroad.[27]

Breen was overstating the case, as was his habit, but the general trend of the treatment toward minimalism is clear. In addition, agents of law enforcement were not allowed to be shown dying at the hands of criminals, and a peculiar convention also prevented the depiction of a shooting where the gunman and his victim were shown in the same frame. These guidelines were introduced in order to avoid setting a bad example to impressionable and criminal elements, although it is possible that, by making violent criminal acts less explicit—and certainly less repulsive—they may have actually lowered public resistance to the spectacle of armed criminality on the streets of American cities.[28]

The guidelines also made it more difficult for the studios to characterize their criminals as utterly murderous, which, from the point of view of the studios, eroded some of the appeal of their criminal subjects. Breen consistently attempted to modify the established iconography of crime pictures and to discourage the appearance of the "hard-looking, foul-speaking" type of gangster. Instead, he tried to promote a new kind of criminal who was soft-spoken and had the appearance of a gentleman: "[I]nstead of showing an eagerness to kill, he is eager to avoid killing, preferring to use his wits to gain his ends rather than to use weapons, to resort to scheming rather than violence."[29] Under these conditions it was comparatively difficult to ensure that criminals would not be viewed sympathetically, especially when they were inevitably doomed to be shot, executed, or incarcerated before the end of the picture. In 1935 the studios arrived at a typically ingenious compromise: they began to exploit "G-man" themes, in which an undercover policeman with a cinematic license to kill infiltrated the underworld and, in more ways than one, assumed the role of a mobster.[30]

The PCA had a policy of not approving stories that dealt with ethnic bigotry, on the basis that such treatments were "provocative and inflammatory." When Warner Bros. decided to make a topical story based on the Black Legion, a secretive midwestern organization modeled after the Ku Klux Klan, Breen reacted cautiously, but he eventually agreed that producer Robert Lord should prepare a movie in which he would "treat the subject as broadly and strongly as he wished, so that we might test out the limit of the acceptability of the treatment of such subjects as racial and religious prejudices." In the end it was not difficult for Breen and Lord to agree on a script designed as a narrative exposé of organizations that proclaimed their "Americanism" but were really violently opposed to "foreigners." The iconography in *Black Legion* (Warner Bros., 1937) and its advertising, showing fearsome hooded aggressors, strongly evoked the racial violence that characterized the Klan, but the targets of the attacks in the movie—as of the historical Black Legion itself—were Eastern European immigrants. The PCA would have perceived a story featuring the persecution of African Americans as "inflammatory" to the point of being unthinkable, and

The artwork of *Black Legion* (Warner Bros., 1937) may invoke the imagery of the Ku Klux Klan, but southern interracial conflict was too sensitive an issue for Hollywood to touch. The victims of ethnic oppression in the movie were Eastern European immigrants.

indeed, such subjects were simply not on the studios' agenda. *They Won't Forget* (Warner Bros., 1937) trod dangerous ground by featuring a southern lynching, but the victim was a white northerner, as was the intended victim of an attempted lynching in *Fury* (MGM, 1936).

Both the MPPDA and the studios usually considered stories featuring African Americans in any central capacity—certainly any capacity implying social equality—as too sensitive.[31] Sequences showing the "mingling" of blacks and whites often led to protests in southern states and could lead to the movies' distribution being curtailed in parts of the South.[32] In 1927 Hays had cabled First National about the inherent problems in *The Love Mart* (First National, 1927), which featured a white woman, mistakenly thought to have black ancestry, who was sold into slavery: "Inadvisable always to show white women in scenes with Negroes where there is any inference of miscegenation or social relationship."[33] Sure enough, the picture was rejected in Virginia, although it was later passed in reconstructed form.

The same problem occurred in reverse in relation to *Imitation of Life* (Universal, 1934), in which one of the characters, though of black ancestry, tried to pass as white. The PCA was concerned that her light skin indicated a miscegenational relationship among her forebears, but Universal assured Breen that the studio "would definitely establish that her white skin was due to a rare but scientific fact that such a child might come of a line of definitely Negro strain."[34] In trying to decide how to treat the property, the PCA consulted its case files on the subject of miscegenation, but staff member Islin Auster had to report to Breen that "I am afraid there is very little here of assistance to us, but I should say the reason for that is that the subject has always been taboo, and that there has been no opportunity to collect evidence referring to it."[35] Hays hoped that the studio could be dissuaded from making *Imitation of Life* at all. He wrote to Robert Cochrane at Universal, "Even though the story has powerful possibilities and might technically possibly be brought within the Code, it deals with persons and situations (lynching scene, pretending to be white when black, etc.) which would cause criticism or prevent exhibition in the Southern states and possibly in some of the border states, as well as many English colonies. The prohibition would also extend to large Northern cities which have a substantial percentage of Negro population. It is believed the story could not be accepted by Southerners and is sure to draw fire there."[36] The studio proceeded with the project, minus the lynching scene, which had shown the persecution of a young black man who approached a white woman in the mistaken belief that she had encouraged him. In the event, any fears concerning the loss of the southern market proved unfounded. The studio kept a close eye on the movie's progress and found that it generally performed better in the southern states than two of Universal's other prominent productions released about the same time, *Only Yesterday* (1933) and *Little Man, What Now?* (1934).[37]

The timidity that characterized the industry in treating African American subjects was occasionally exacerbated by other commercial pressures arising from community prejudice. For example, in 1936 Breen received the following complaint from Nebraska:

> We wish to call your attention to the fact that the raising of Silver Foxes is now a large industry in the United States and that thousands of people depend upon the successful marketing of Silver Fox pelts for their very bread, butter and existence.
>
> We wish to further call your attention to the picture *Bullets or Ballots?* in which a negro woman appeared several times in the film wearing a double Silver Fox Scarf. We have no prejudice, as far as colored people are concerned, but you must realize the feeling of the white people of the South. We are carrying on a nation wide advertising campaign costing thousands of dollars and we depend upon St. Louis, Atlanta, and New Orleans and all of the Southern cities for the absorption of a certain percent of these Silver Fox Scarves. Now, when the Southern women see a colored woman wearing these Silver Foxes, they drop them like poison. As far as colored women are concerned, we doubt if a dozen of them can, or do wear Silver Foxes, but just one in a picture as popular as *Bullets or Ballots* will do tremendous damage to our industry. We doubt if it makes one ounce of difference to this colored woman whether she wears the Silver Foxes or not, and it certainly would not detract one bit from the picture if the Silver Foxes were not shown on the colored woman.
>
> Many of your white stars do wear Silver Foxes in your pictures and we do think that is wonderful advertising and profitable for us, and which is very much appreciated.[38]

Whether this particular letter would have had much influence on industry policy is doubtful, but it would have contributed to the wider set of pressures that helped to keep African American characters off the screen except in patently subordinate roles.[39]

Playing to the Foreign Field

Along with his general tightening of regulatory procedures, Breen attempted to exert more control over products sent to the foreign market. Under the SRC, material cut out of prints by American censors for national distribution frequently remained intact in prints and negatives destined for foreign release. As a result, the movies often ran into trouble over the same controversial material twice, on the domestic and on the international fronts. For example, *Sunny Side Up* (Fox, 1929) contained an "esquimau dance" performed to the song "Turn on the Heat" which ran into trouble with censors all over the United States and had to be removed before the movie could be exhibited nationally. When the picture went abroad, it was sent uncut, to markets including Britain and Australia, where censorship of this type of sequence was known to be more stringent than it was domestically. Colonel Herron, pointing out that the picture would have fared better if it had been cut by "an artist in Hollywood rather than by a butcher in Australia," suggested to Joy that the supervision of foreign versions ultimately rested with the SRC, since the foreign departments of most of the production companies seemed to have little control over content.[40]

The issue of the status of international versions had been complicated by the production of culturally specific foreign-language versions, as described in chapter 3. However, in October 1934, three months after the establishment of the PCA under Breen, production executives agreed not to use "reinstated shots or different versions for other countries."[41] In practice, this agreement was more a rhetorical gesture in recognition of Breen's new regime than a literal statement of intent. Such a policy would have been impossible to implement, partly because some foreign-language pictures were still being produced specifically for distribution abroad—about a dozen a year in the mid-1930s, mostly in Spanish.[42] More routinely, protection shots played an important part in the preparation of versions for sensitive foreign markets, especially the British territories, and although they were intended to reduce censorship action, the prints containing them technically constituted "different versions." It was probably inevitable that the studios would fail scrupulously to edit their international prints to the American standard, especially if the movies had already earned their seals, and evidence in the censorship records indicates that unexpurgated versions continued to go overseas up to the end of the decade.[43]

The application of the Production Code to foreign-language versions also continued to diverge somewhat from its application to movies intended primarily for American release. Breen judged the Spanish-language picture *The Downfall* (Paramount, 1934) to be "realistically sordid" and admitted that it would not have been passed if it had been intended for exhibition in the United States. Since it was produced for what he saw as the more "realistically-minded" Latin American audience, however, he decided that it could be released without danger of offense.[44] Whether or not such a divergence of aesthetic appreciation actually existed between North and Latin America, the observance of the Code under Breen meant that movies distributed in the United States and Canada increasingly had to conform to more stringent guidelines, especially in the areas of morals and sexual behavior, than they did in Hollywood's major markets overseas, with the probable exception of Australia.

The differences between American and British censorship can be gauged from the changes required on the British and Dominions picture *Escape Me Never* to make it fit for American distribution by United Artists in 1934. After discussions with Vincent Hart, who previewed foreign movies at the Eastern PCA, United Artists told the studio that it would have to insert a protection shot "making the child legitimate." Hart also insisted that it must be "definitely and affirmatively established" that the central couple did not live together before marriage.[45]

In effect the Production Code Administration exerted two conflicting pressures on foreign versions. On the one hand, in line with its general insistence on stringent regulation, it tried to exert as much control as possible over what was sent overseas; in particular, it resolved to apply the strictest standards of supervision to sequences depicting the American way of life.[46] On the other hand, the Code had been designed primarily to meet a *domestic* public relations emergency. By trying to insist that all the industry's product should conform to its guidelines, including movies for foreign distribution which were likely to be exhibited alongside more frank and explicit modes of representation, the PCA increased the incentive for producers to evade its strictures and to adopt a combative rather than a cooperative stance.

The Code did not have much to say on the subject of foreign relations, requiring only that "[t]he history, institutions, prominent people and citizenry of other nations shall be represented fairly." In 1937 Olga Martin claimed that the PCA interpreted *fairly* somewhat legalistically. She warned scriptwriters to be aware of the necessity of balanced representation, which was a kind of variation on the theme of compensating moral values: "Do not portray the characters of the story, if they are villains, as of any specific racial or national type unless you have a sympathetic character in the story of the same nationality."[47] A precedent for this kind of treatment had been established as early as 1930, in *East Is West* (Universal, 1930), in which the studio promised to write in a Chinese hero for every Chinese "heavy." In this case the tactic was not a great success, since the film was still banned in several countries.[48]

The SRC advised the studios to avoid declaring the national origins of their villains and sometimes to take steps to render them unrecognizable. By 1934 Cline M. Koon could write, "The foreign villain—even the naturalized villain—is disappearing from the motion picture."[49] Under Breen, in line with the general trend toward greater obfuscation in the handling of sensitive subjects, the treatment of foreign locations and of characters' cultural identities became even more coy and contradictory—a trend encouraged by the increasing sophistication of foreign nations in applying pressure through the PCA's regulatory mechanisms.

In 1937 Italy took exception to the comic Italian musician in *Top Hat* and the ineffective professional co-respondent in *The Gay Divorcee* and banned both films. Herron was told that no films featuring Italians or characters bearing Italian names could be distributed in Italy unless those characters were completely sympathetic. In fact, this stance had characterized the Italian position for some time. *Star of Midnight* (RKO, 1935) had been banned in Italy on the strength of a reference to a Chicago gangster called Moroni, although the studio claimed that the villain was actually an Irishman named Maroney. The point was moot, since the character never appeared onscreen.[50] Breen began to feel that things were getting out of hand, and he protested to Hays:

I take it, from the correspondence with Ted Herron, that we are not to use Italian names, even in comedy situations. If this be true, then it establishes a further step in the general mass of restrictions, which are rapidly crowding in on us.

Heretofore, we have had to be careful not to identify the race or nationality of criminals or heavies; now we shall have to go a step farther and not identify comedy characters with any specific nation, or race, of people.

This is all very much to be regretted. It suggests enormous difficulty for our producers, because, once we establish this kind of rule for the Italians, it is only a mere matter of a few months before we shall have to do the same thing for the Chinese, Japs, Spaniards, Russians, Germans, French, Czechs and Poles.[51]

By the late 1930s the repression of nationality, like the repression of sexuality, resulted in representational strategies that sometimes challenged the interpretive skill of the viewer. An example is the characterization Nick Brown, a gangster in *The Roaring Twenties* (Warner Bros., 1939). The audience is introduced to him in a sequence placed in a Chicago café that begins with a close-up of a plate of spaghetti, which Brown eats throughout the sequence. He does not have an Italian name; he does not look noticeably Italian (he is played by Paul Kelly); he does not speak with an Italian accent; and no one mentions the Mafia, although we learn that Brown is part of a "syndicate that's running all the high-class [bootleg] merchandise that's being sold in this country." Mr. Brown just happens to be eating spaghetti, and Eddie Bartlett (James Cagney) makes reference to this culinary partiality in the only other sequence in which Brown appears.

A gangster enjoys his favorite dish in *The Roaring Twenties* (Warner Bros., 1939). On the evidence of this characterization, how Italian is Mr. Brown?

The Italians and the Irish were particularly well placed to protest to Hollywood because of their large and vocal constituencies within the United States, who channeled complaints through the Italian embassy and the Catholic Church. The Greek community was also influential, partly because Greek organizations were quick to contact Hays if they felt that they had been slighted in the movies, and partly because a large number of exhibitors were of Greek origin.[52] The most prominent of these exhibitors was Spyros Skouras, who built up a series of cinema chains before becoming president of 20th Century–Fox in 1942. Most other nationalities, with smaller or less well-organized domestic representation, depended on economic and/or diplomatic pressure to influence their portrayal on the screen.

The British Influence

Globally the industry's most influential customer, excluding the United States itself, was Great Britain. Despite its relatively stringent quota restrictions, Britain provided 30 percent of the American industry's foreign gross and was indispensable to every producer.[53] The income derived from England alone had passed thirty million dollars per year by 1936.[54] The British Empire constituted the overwhelming proportion of the foreign "English version" territories, which contributed approximately half of Hollywood's foreign income. For bookkeeping purposes, some companies classified this area as a single unit, as opposed to the "foreign-language version territory," which comprised all markets supplied with subtitled or dubbed prints.[55]

During World War I American producers came under pressure to paint a favorable picture of the British for reasons that had less to do with the motion picture trade than with upholding the American public's commitment to the war. D. W. Griffith complained that he had been discouraged from making a film about American history because "the English and their sympathizers" would not take kindly to a depiction of the events of the American Revolution.[56] Indeed, when producer Robert Goldstein exhibited his American Revolution movie *The Spirit of '76* (Continental Producing Company/States Rights) at Clune's Auditorium Theater in Los Angeles in 1917, the movie was confiscated, and he was indicted for "subversion." Goldstein eventually served three years of a ten-year sentence for showing it. The movie incorporated a sequence showing British soldiers brutally massacring civilians in the Wyoming Valley—a sequence which Goldstein had not included when offering a preview of the film to "diverse local and government representatives"—and the producer was convicted on the grounds that "[i]t seems but reasonable to say that the exhibition of such a picture is calculated to arouse antagonism and to raise hatred in the minds of some who see it against the ally of the United States, and as a probable effect to put obstruction in the way of the necessary co-operation between the allied countries against the enemy, and to undermine an undivided sentiment for the United States and to encourage disloyalty and refusal of duty or insubordination among the military and naval forces."[57]

After the war the British influence on American pictures arose mainly from market strength, and as Hollywood's regulatory mechanisms became more refined throughout the 1920s and 1930s, so British sensibilities increasingly informed production. In 1923 an English distributor complained vaguely to Hays about "little domesticities and characteristics of an obvious alien nature" in Hollywood's depiction of the British, including characters eating grapefruit for breakfast and shaking hands with their gloves on.[58] By 1932 the SRC customarily recommended that studios get specialist advice concerning matters of British protocol. For example, the SRC was nervous about the British response to *Our Betters* (RKO, 1933), in which Constance Bennett plays a woman who commits a breach of tradition at a royal court presentation by wearing a black dress instead of a white one. Wingate recommended that the studio consult a "responsible individual" who would know about the possible reactions to such a gaffe.[59] The British consulate eventually became the arbiter of such matters, and the opinion of its staff was sought on such productions as *Bombay Mail* (Universal, 1934) and *British Agent* (Warner Bros., 1934), although Herron was of the opinion that they were "too busy with their social careers to bother about helping business matters in any way."[60]

The acid test was whether the pictures were passed by the British Board of Film Censors (BBFC) in London. Although the board did not enjoy governmental status, pictures were rarely distributed in Britain without its approval, and Britain's possessions and colonies closely followed its lead. Its provisions were consistently taken into account in the production of Hollywood movies. By the mid-1930s the studios had developed a system whereby particularly sensitive scripts could be developed in close consultation with the board, as was the case with *The Last Days of Pompeii* (RKO, 1935) (see chapter 6). Olga Martin specifically cautioned prospective scriptwriters to keep their stories within the bounds demanded by the board.[61] The need for caution was the greater because the British government, having introduced its Cinematograph Films Act in 1927, had shown itself sympathetic to the British industry's appeals for protection. In 1936 it set up the Moyne Committee to consider revisions to the Cinematograph Films Act that would enable it to operate more positively in Britain's favor. As Sarah Street has shown, relations between the British government and the American industry were on an especially delicate footing until a new act was passed in 1938.[62]

British requirements were sometimes idiosyncratic. Jack Vizzard maintains that the British insisted on twin rather than double beds in all circumstances. This stipulation was not required by American censors but was usually accepted for the sake of British distribution.[63] The British also had inflexible requirements concerning the representation of Christian ceremonies. Certain parts of church services were invariably deleted, no matter how respectfully they were treated. These included the Lord's Prayer, the sacramental elements of Communion and absolution, and the blessing "In the name of the Father, the Son, and the Holy Ghost." Any ceremony taking place in a church had to be treated in a reverent manner, although comedy was allowed to pass in civil marriages, such as those in *It Happened One Night* (Columbia, 1934) and *The*

Bride Comes Home (Paramount, 1935). In biblical pictures the material figure of Christ could not be represented on the screen. Even though such strictures were sometimes inconvenient, producers accepted them amicably enough, because they were uniformly applied and could therefore be accommodated in production, either by eliminating the relevant material from scripts or by providing protection shots for prints to be distributed in British territories.

Gruesome scenes also had to be treated with an eye to the British market, especially "harrowing scenes of illness and ultra-realistic surgery."[64] The regulations governing such scenes tightened in 1937 with the installation of Lord Tyrell as the new chairman of the BBFC. Perhaps he wanted to make his mark in the job, as Warner Bros.' London distributor claimed, or perhaps he was just squeamish, but his ban on surgery caused the British distribution of several American movies—including Warner Bros.' high-minded production of *The Green Light* (1937)—to be held up until changes could be effected.[65] The censors eliminated most of *The Green Light*'s important operating theater sequence, including the following dialogue:

Endicott: Dr. Paige—hemorrhage—sponge! Clamp! Clamp!
Paige: I can't. The artery's cut too short.
Assistant: Adrenalin—quick![66]

The board's sensitivity about surgical procedures was matched by its concern about cruelty to animals, and sequences depicting their maltreatment were always cut. *The Charge of the Light Brigade* (Warner Bros., 1936), for example, caused particular controversy in Britain, not, as the studio had feared, because of its flagrant disregard for historical accuracy, but because three horses were killed during the shooting of the Charge.

Insanity was also a danger area. Olga Martin warned that in Britain "*any* suggestion of insanity is always *entirely eliminated.*"[67] This caused some concern among PCA officials when they read the script of *His Girl Friday* (Columbia, 1940), featuring the crazy Earl Williams. "If the British Board gets the impression, in looking at your picture, that we get in reading the script," Breen told Howard Hawks, "it is almost certain that your picture will be rejected, in toto, so far as the English market is concerned."[68] Hawks, Breen, and Sam Briskin had a conference about the problem and decided that the story required Williams to be neither seriously nor permanently deranged: "[T]he character of Earl will not be played as an insane man, but rather as a confused soul, and a line will be inserted, somewhere, suggesting he was mentally unbalanced at the time he shot the police officer."[69] Subsequent versions of the script portrayed Earl as extremely confused, certainly; several characters stressed that he was also "goofy" because of a lack of food.

Movies featuring aspects of the conflict between Britain and Ireland constituted obvious targets for the British censors, and for this reason Breen tried to dissuade producers from using this subject at all. In the case of *The Key* (Warner Bros., 1934), which was essentially a love story with the Irish rebellion used as a backdrop, he thought the movie would be politically innocuous enough not to offend either Britain or Ireland, but it suffered a huge number of deletions at the hands of the British board. Many phrases were cut out simply because they contained the words *Irish* or *English*. Anything pointing to the movie's historical context and any mention of revolution or political resistance were removed. *The Informer* (RKO, 1935) met an almost identical fate during its British distribution. When RKO decided to make a movie version of Sean O'Casey's play *The Plough and the Stars* (RKO, 1937), Breen sent the studio a copy of the censorship record of *The Key*. Herron recommended that the RKO producers study a print of the movie and "find out just how it was treated and what they were able to get away with."[70] Breen was principally worried about the reaction of Irish Americans to what he saw as basically negative characterizations, but he was also very conscious of the potential for trouble from the British. RKO took the precaution of seeking the advice of British censors while the picture was still in production, but even so the movie suffered the excision of three complete sequences when it was released in Britain. As Breen commented to B. B. Kahane of RKO, "Lord Tyrell's Board has not been favorably disposed towards motion pictures showing, or suggesting, revolution within the British Empire."[71]

The British market also affected the representation of wider areas of colonial influence. The British were concerned about maintaining prestige in their colonial possessions, and this was reflected in the censorship provisions they imposed throughout the Empire. In 1928 the Hong Kong censor had told the American consul general that upholding British prestige was central to his activity in "a small settlement of white men on the fringe of a huge Empire of Asiatics." According to a report from a United Artists agent in Hong Kong, subjects banned by the censor included depictions of "white women in indecorous garb or positions or situations which would tend to discredit our womenfolk with the Chinese," and armed conflict between Chinese and whites.[72] These restrictions prevailed throughout Britain's colonies. Alongside provisions banning scenes of obeah and witchcraft, the Trinidad government's Principles of Censorship included bans on the "improper use of the names or descriptions of British institutions" and "scenes intended to ridicule or criticise unfairly British social life." The principles also prohibited the following subjects:

Propaganda against the Monarchy, Royal dynasties or any other method or form of constitutional government.

White men in a state of degradation amidst native surroundings, or using violence towards natives, especially Chinese, negroes and Indians.

Equivocal situations between men of one race and girls of another race.

Any picture likely to be provocative to British sentiment.[73]

Within Britain itself, the Board of Film Censors banned pictures depicting the degradation of white men in Far Eastern and native surroundings.[74]

Such provisions inevitably filtered back to American producers via box office receipts and the MPPDA. Jason Joy warned the studios that the British would not permit "the portrayal of the white man and woman (the conqueror and governing race) in a way that might degrade him or her in the eyes of the native, nor will they permit anything in films tending to incite the natives against the governing race or to commit crime."[75] *The Green Goddess* (Warner Bros., 1930) was a case in point. The movie depicted the fate of a small group of British travelers marooned by a plane crash in a remote mountainous area of southern Asia. George Arliss played a turbaned raja, highly educated but essentially barbaric, who was determined to make the party atone for "centuries of subjugation and exaction." He told them, "Asia has a long score against you swaggering lords of creation." At the same time, he had undisguised sexual designs on the heroine. Although the movie was widely acclaimed in the United States, especially for Arliss' performance, it was considered very dangerous by the British, who extracted a guarantee from the company not to distribute it in their territories in the Near and Far East.[76]

In the light of this reaction, Herron was understandably less than enthusiastic when T. B. Fithian of Universal sought the advice of the MPPDA about a similar property, *East of Borneo*, also known as *The White Captive* (Universal, 1931):

The attempted seduction of a white woman by the rajah in this picture would cause severe criticism of the picture in the Near and Far East and British possessions.

In addition to this, all pictures that have gone into the British possessions which have shown harsh treatment of white women have been chopped to pieces. The British colonies claim that they can't control the natives if they allow pictures to be shown in which white women are anything but at their best.[77]

As far as the British were concerned, protagonist George Arliss' obviously non-Asiatic ethnicity did nothing to defuse the sensitivity of *The Green Goddess* (Warner Bros., 1930) as a comment on their colonial relations. They extracted a promise from Warner Bros. not to distribute the movie in British territories in the Near and Far East.

Considering the preoccupation with heterosexual relations in American movies, it is not surprising that colonial attitudes most commonly found expression in the movies through the politics of sexual dominance.[78] *The Bitter Tea of General Yen* (Columbia, 1932) ran into trouble in the British territories for its depiction of an attempted seduction of a white woman, this time by a Chinese general. The logical response, which soon came into force under the PCA, was the banning of interracial affairs in every context except that of the politically innocuous Pacific Ocean. Olga Martin stressed the inadmissibility of miscegenation but explained that "the union of a member of the Polynesians and allied races of the Island groups with a member of the white race is not ordinarily considered a miscegenetic relationship."[79]

Although the filmic examples cited above predated Breen's regime at the PCA, they entered the case files and set the standard for the treatment of similar subject matter until the end of the 1930s. The British influence in general, and its impact in the area of colonial relations in particular, had far-reaching implications for Hollywood's expressed ideology throughout the Classical era. Just as the depiction of race relations within the United States could only take place within limits determined by the southern American states, so the industry was bound to tacit, if not active, compliance with British notions of global white supremacy. Details of representation that were contrary to British requirements could be covered by protection shots, but the central themes of the movies needed to be consonant with an imperialist outlook. The fact that British Empire versions did not undergo subtitling or dubbing put extra pressure on American filmmakers to produce acceptable versions in the studio.[80]

If Hollywood's dealings with its multifaceted market, both domestic and foreign, largely involved meeting the requirements of the agents of social control, this was never revealed more clearly than in its relationship with territories under colonial rule. Providing films suitable for a particular territory meant pitching the movies to the ideology of the governing class, while still supplying the entertainment values that would appeal to audiences. The situation was complicated by the fact that, as Joy had found in relation to crime movies, performance could sometimes defeat ideological statement. The American assistant trade commissioner in South Africa noted something of the kind in his 1931 report: "[T]he native population of the Union, which far exceeds the white or European, must always be kept in hand and . . . a careful censorship must be maintained. It has been found, for instance, that American western pictures, with their intense activities, appeal particularly to the natives, but this kind, on the other hand, excites the audience and is considered a potential source of trouble."[81] While the movie diet of the black population may have caused the South African government concern, it probably did not trouble the distributors much. The movies only reached black audiences in late "subsequent-runs," by which time their earning power was all but exhausted. With most movie revenues being earned during the first runs at key metropolitan centers, there were economic as well as diplomatic reasons for accommodating the sensibilities of the affluent and predominantly urban colonial classes.

Distribution and exhibition also tended to favor the ruling classes, in that the language used in the distributed versions was that spoken by the colonizers. Movies preferred by many colonized populations— action stories, including westerns and underworld stories—were those least dependent on language for their comprehension. At the same time, their graphic and visceral qualities, such as those alleged to appeal to the South African blacks, made them the ones most likely to be heavily censored. For example, in 1931 the American consul in Madagascar reported that the native people loved "films of adventure, especially wild-west dramas, stories of the underworld, and in general those in which fighting of all descriptions, automobile and other acrobatics, and similar scenes abound," but unfortunately for them, "such films are the very types, particularly those showing criminal methods, which are most likely to be severely clipped or refused exhibition altogether under local censorship laws."[82] While it is possible that the consul's assessment of the natives' preferences may have derived from stereotyped racial assumptions as much as from empirical observation, he was probably correct in assuming that the state was not greatly interested in catering to their cinematic tastes.

International Relations

A market did not have to rival the British Empire in size to exercise an influence on Hollywood's output. Creatively applied diplomatic pressure could be as persuasive as economic muscle. At the same time as Hollywood was trying to smooth its access to the foreign market by tailoring its products to foreign requirements, several of its customer nations were learning how to use its system of self-regulation in their own interests—sometimes in their own self-defense—by applying pressure through a network of diplomatic channels.

Virtually all censorship charters around the world contained clauses prohibiting the exhibition of motion pictures likely to offend friendly countries, but the French were the first to realize that they could turn this around and insist that other nations ban movies offensive to French sensibilities. French diplomatic intervention stopped the circulation of *Beau Geste* (Famous Players–Lasky/Paramount, 1926) in Italy in August 1928. The French ambassador in Romania also asked that its exhibition be stopped, alleging that it would be a bad influence on the French military. The Romanian government, "being anxious not to disturb the good relations between the two countries," eventually complied with the request, and the film was "confiscated."[83]

In view of these actions, Herron worried about possible reprisals when Fox brought out their Foreign Legion comedy *Plastered in Paris* just one month later: "I have taken this matter up with the Fox office here and they assure me that the film won't be sent to France, but of course, that is not the question. I know it won't be sent to France because it would be impossible to release it there. It is the trouble that will result from its being distributed in this country or any other place in the world that I'm worried about."[84] *Du Barry, Woman of Passion* (Art Cinema Corp./United Artists, 1930) was the subject of intense SRC scrutiny for the same reasons: Herron and Joy feared that French diplomatic intervention would prevent the exhibition of the picture throughout the foreign field and would "greatly embarrass the exhibition of it in this country."[85] The French already wielded power in Hollywood disproportionate to their contribution to foreign income because of the sensitivity of their quota negotiations. They also had their own colonial possessions, so they, like the British, the Portuguese, and the Dutch, exercised control of markets beyond the borders of their home country. Their enlistment of other foreign nations to bring pressure on their behalf further enhanced their influence.

China was not far behind France in calling on its allies and trading partners for support. Like Mexico, China had been sufficiently insulted by Hollywood's characterizations of its citizens to be suspicious of Hays's claim that movies were agents of international amity. Hollywood's propensity to represent Chinese characters as vulgar stereotypes, combined with its historical preference for Chinese villains and the exacerbating factor of Britain's representational influence, gave Chinese diplomats in the United States sufficient cause to be on their guard. An internal Warner Bros. memo from Hal Wallis to William Koenig about a sequence in *Footlight Parade* (Warner Bros., 1933) suggests that their suspicions had some foundation: "I would hesitate to show the 'SHANGHAI LIL' number to the Chinese Consul in view of the fact that we do just exactly what he thinks we are doing. It would probably be difficult to make him understand that this is a musical comedy and that we have musical comedy license on such matters. I think we are better off in not looking for trouble. Tell him that the sequence is not yet ready to be shown."[86]

In 1930 the Chinese government banned Harold Lloyd's first talkie, *Welcome Danger* (Harold Lloyd/Paramount Famous-Lasky, 1929), after its portrayal of the residents of San Francisco's Chinatown as kidnappers, gamblers, and opium smugglers led to a riot at the Grand Theatre of Shanghai.[87] Chinese diplomatic officers began campaigning vigorously in other countries, resulting in several more cases of the film's rejection. The SRC maintained special vigilance during the preparation of *East Is West* (Universal, 1930), which also involved villainy in Chinatown. Although Joy was satisfied that "the Chinese point of view has been so carefully considered that we cannot conceive of any objection from that direction," the movie was banned in British Columbia, where the censors cited business and political connections with China as the reasons for their action.[88] Cuba also ordered the movie's withdrawal after protests from the Chinese consul general in

About *Footlight Parade* (Warner Bros., 1933), a Warner Bros. official remarked, "I would hesitate to show the 'SHANGHAI LIL' number to the Chinese Consul in view of the fact that we do just exactly what he thinks we are doing."

Havana. The Chinese objections arose out of a slave market sequence set in China, in which the heroine was rescued by the American hero. Herron urged Joy to take action over such sequences while the movies were still in production:

> As I have said many times before, it's not a question of whether we should or shouldn't do these things, but it's a question of box office receipts. Universal is losing a lot of money because this film is being banned in different places of the world. It would have been much to their advantage to have given a little more time and thought to this scene before the picture was made.
>
> These diplomatic and consular representatives in a good many places of the world have very direct contacts with the foreign offices, and are able to stop the showing of pictures that they object to. Even if we can go over their heads and have these pictures passed, which sometimes happens, it requires a tremendous lot of hard work and labor.[89]

Although China's contribution to the American companies' foreign revenue was minuscule, its cultivation of diplomatic channels of protest had a significant impact on the industry. In 1937 Herron asserted that "it is a deep dent in the box office receipts for world circulation of any picture that runs counter to the ideas of the Chinese."[90]

The influence of the Chinese in the 1930s could not be equated to that of the British, who generated at least thirty times as much revenue. As a last resort, studios could cut their losses and withhold offensive products from areas where the Chinese held diplomatic sway. Nevertheless, the Chinese managed to make PCA and studio executives acutely aware of their presence, partly through maintaining a highly reactive position. Paramount was banned twice from doing business in China, once as a result of *Shanghai Express* (Paramount, 1932) and once as a result of *The General Died at Dawn* (Paramount, 1936). In both cases the company was only readmitted after U.S. diplomatic intervention.

Ironically, the guarantee of inoffensive characterizations had become such a recognized factor in negotiating American access to markets that in 1938 the American industry was able to turn the tables when Japan threatened to reduce its intake of films drastically. The American negotiators warned the Japanese that if they did not constitute a reasonably lucrative market they might find themselves singled out to wear the black hats in American movies:

In these interviews with the Japanese authorities and representatives of the American Motion Picture Association, the former were permitted to sense a certain danger which might accompany the exclusion of American films. Almost every plot must have a villain, and the American producers find it difficult to discover a suitable nationality for such villains, encountering violent opposition from any country of which the villain happens to be a national—an opposition which sometimes results in the exclusion or boycott of films with consequent financial losses—so that for the present a disproportionately large percentage of movie villains and characters arousing feelings of resentment are American. The same attitude of opposition is shown by foreign nations toward uncomplimentary news reels. Should the producing companies decide that some one country is determined to rule them out entirely so that resentment as to villains from that particular country would not diminish the financial returns of their films, they might consider it an opportunity.[91]

Similar considerations may have had some influence on the studios' willingness to make "preparedness" and anti-Nazi films before World War II. In 1937 all aspects of the German film industry were placed under governmental control. Quota restrictions applied throughout the German territories in 1938 were so severe that they "virtually shut out" American films. On 1 January 1939 Italy placed the distribution of motion pictures in the hands of a government monopoly and an-

nounced trade conditions so onerous that the MPPDA declared that
the Americans would withdraw from the market altogether. Consequently, American producers ceased to be so inhibited about making
movies that impugned the motives and characters of their formerly
cosseted customers. In working on the script for *Juárez* (Warner Bros.,
1939), Wolfgang Reinhardt frankly intended that "every child must be
able to realize that Napoleon, in his Mexican adventure, is none other
than Mussolini plus Hitler in their Spanish adventure."[92] When Jack
Warner wrote to producer Bryan Foy in 1939 to warn him about the
dangers inherent in offending the Chinese, the Mexicans, and especially the French, he added, "If we don't do business in Italy and Germany, that is another story, as they can't very well blackball us."[93]

Meanwhile, as nations increasingly adopted diplomatic alliances to
restrict specific films, a series of permanent and formalized agreements began to emerge. Spain and Latin America had moved in this
direction in 1930, with the convening of a Hispano-American Motion
Picture Congress in Madrid. The congress was primarily intended to
promote Spanish-American production and distribution, but one of
its resolutions was mutually to prohibit films which misinterpreted
local or national customs.[94] In 1935 Spain and El Salvador were the
first countries to agree formally not to circulate or exhibit movies
disparaging to either party or to any other of the Hispanic American
countries.[95] Production companies guilty of repeated offenses would
be mutually banned. This treaty formed a precedent, and before the
military coup that initiated the hostilities of the Spanish Civil War in
September 1936, Spain had struck similar agreements with Nicaragua,
Peru, and Chile.[96] In 1937 the Italians arranged alliances with the
Germans, the Chinese, and the Turks, while Chile signed an agreement with Costa Rica.[97] By 1938 these agreements had become so
widespread that the chief of the Motion Picture Division of the U.S.
Department of Commerce considered it a matter for comment that
Australia had not entered into any such formal arrangement.[98] Hollywood had had close relations with the State Department and intimate
relations with the Department of Commerce since 1926. Twelve years
later, not only were movies themselves objects of diplomatic currency,
but a mutual agreement to restrict them had become a recognized
term in the wider language of diplomacy.

The late 1930s saw the Classical Hollywood cinema achieve its most
highly developed form. The mechanisms of self-regulation that
helped to maintain the consistency of its vision, despite the diversity
of its forms, were well established, and institutions both inside and
outside the industry had learned how best to take advantage of the

PCA's mediating role. If Hollywood's particular vision was often marked by contradiction and incoherence, this was principally a consequence of the industry's two most devout ambitions: to please all of the people, everywhere, all—or at least most—of the time, and to displease as few people—or at least as few people who mattered—as possible.

6

Diplomatic Representations

Accommodating the Foreign Market

Pressures arising from the domestic American market, particularly matters affecting the representation of sex and crime, necessarily featured prominently in the production policies of all the major studios in Hollywood. However, the extent to which international demands featured in a movie's progress to the screen differed somewhat, depending on the size of its budget, its expected range of distribution, its thematic concerns, and the status of its source material. In this chapter I shall address the specific outcomes of such pressures in instances where the demands of global distribution affected the production histories of movies. *The Last Days of Pompeii* (RKO, 1935) exemplifies a successful case of negotiation between a foreign censor board—the British Board of Film Censors (BBFC)—and a production company, undertaken in order to maximize profits in an important overseas market. The producers of *Woman Trap* (Paramount, 1936) tried to ameliorate the potential offense inherent in the use of a stereotypical Bad Man character and Mexican locations by introducing a series of compensating elements into the movie's narrative. *West of Shanghai* (Warner Bros., 1937) demonstrates the point at which efforts to please a small foreign market, in this case China, were abandoned by the production company as uneconomic. During the production of *Devil's Island* (Warner Bros., 1939), the same company was at war with itself, with its distribution branch trying to block the actions of its producers in Hollywood in order to avoid antagonizing France. *Idiot's Delight* (MGM, 1939), which encountered problems in Italy, illustrates the ways in which external political events could frustrate even the most careful efforts by producers to give their products the best chance for full distribution in the foreign field.

Despite the disparate ways in which these cases were handled by their producing companies, stemming from the studios' different levels of economic dependence on the foreign market, it is notable that the industry's approach to international distribution involved negative, rather than positive, forms of accommodation. In the international as well as in the domestic sphere, the studios recognized the necessity of avoiding diplomatic hazards, and to differing extents they were prepared to modify, obfuscate, and eliminate movie content in order to stay out of trouble. In general, however, they were not interested in devising ways of making their products more positively attractive to audiences overseas. Even the careful preparation of *The Last Days of Pompeii*, which had an unusually high dependence on foreign returns, was characterized by a cautious and reductive approach, essentially designed to minimize international offense rather than to maximize international appeal.

Catering to the Foreign Market

The specific requirements of foreign markets, mediated by the SRC and PCA, helped to define the parameters within which the content of Hollywood movies could be elaborated. The higher the budget of the movie, the more comprehensively the foreign market needed to be taken into account. Smaller films did not have to be shown everywhere to recoup their production costs and consequently had to make fewer concessions to foreign sensibilities. Luigi Luraschi, who handled the preparation of foreign versions for Paramount from 1933, has made the distinction: "The 'A' picture was a high-budget picture that was supposed to appeal everywhere, and the 'B' picture was a small local picture with a small budget that could cover itself in the U.S. In other words, we made a lot of cheap westerns that never saw the light of day abroad. Maybe they did later on, but we didn't count on it. But the 'A' picture had to appeal everywhere, because we needed the whole market, the whole world."[1] According to Warner Bros.' foreign manager Sam Morris, the only countries to be sent the majority of Warners' output in 1937 were Great Britain and Australia. The rest of the world received on average twenty pictures, about two-fifths of Warners' regular output, and Morris thought this situation was typical of the foreign business conducted by the major studios.[2]

Beyond the broad principle of recouping costs on expensive productions in the maximum number of markets, selecting pictures for foreign distribution was a vexed issue. A theme running through the market reports compiled by the U.S. Department of Commerce throughout the 1920s and 1930s was the need for more careful selection procedures to be applied to avoid the exhibition of inappropriate subjects. The Motion Picture Division helpfully provided detailed reports of the pictures that were best received in each country. Unfortunately, this recordkeeping did little more than confirm a diverse and perplexing range of tastes. For example, in 1930 Mexican audiences favored dramas of the super-rich, Guatemalans craved spectacular pictures and weepies, British Hondurans preferred westerns and love stories, Panamanians wanted historical and costume dramas, and Haitians favored comedies and melodramas. Honduras exhibited a marked regional difference, with audiences in the north desiring action pictures, and those in the south requesting society dramas.[3] Local tastes, combined with quixotic censorship restrictions, diplomatic sensitivities, and quota and tax regulations, made supplying the foreign market an extremely complex and often baffling exercise. Sam Morris commented to Jack Warner that catering to the foreign market was a "game of chess."[4]

The producing and distributing companies collated their own data based on box office results to help them formulate rational foreign policies. In 1923 United Artists asked its foreign managers to compile detailed reports on all conditions affecting foreign sales, including "what pictures you release each week and how they are received," and "any suggestions or recommendations you have concerning our product."[5] In 1937 the company was still analyzing the daily receipts of pictures showing in foreign "Key Spots," including pictures distributed by other companies.[6] Douglas Gomery states that Paramount chief Barney Balaban conducted a daily review of reports from "all Paramount theaters throughout the world" from 1936.[7] No absolutely reliable formula could predict foreign reactions, however, and the selection of material for markets abroad sometimes seemed so haphazard that Frederick Herron wondered whether the companies' foreign managers had any say at all about what was sent abroad.[8]

One truism of foreign distribution was that, especially after the introduction of sound, movies based on dialogue—"walk and talk" pictures—fared less well in non-English-speaking territories than did action pictures. This was most obvious when sound technology was new. At that time the Commerce Department reports contained a succession of complaints that early talkies were devoid of action and that they depended entirely on dialogue to explain the plot and develop the story. For example, commenting on the Gloria Swanson comedy-drama *Tonight or Never* (Feature Productions/United Artists, 1931), a United Artists agent in China reported, "This picture is unsuitable for China because it has no action whatsoever and entirely depends upon dialogue. The Chinese public cannot understand this type of picture."[9] After the introduction of dubbing, some companies chose to dub only action pictures, implicitly deeming dialogue-oriented productions unsuitable for foreign distribution outside the English-speaking territories.[10]

Language problems may not have been the only reason that action pictures were more popular abroad. The American consul in Tientsin, China, observed that local audiences were so mystified by movies requiring an understanding of the cultural mores of the Western world that their preference for comedy and "action such as adventure, war and 'western' pictures" was quite understandable.[11] Ironically, although the low-budget western did not need to recoup its costs with foreign revenues, it enjoyed immense popularity in many overseas markets, especially among "laboring and rural classes." In fact, in 1936 United Artists purchased a series of six Rex Bell movies specifically to release in India, the Straits Settlements, and the Netherlands East Indies.[12] In 1937, well after the technical aspects of dubbing and subtitling had been brought to an acceptable standard, Sam Morris was able to produce evidence to show that dialogue-centered dramas still produced consistently poor results in the foreign-language markets. He compared the revenues of four action-based pictures with revenues from six that depended on dialogue (see table 4). Morris' figures show that in this sample the action pictures displayed more total earning potential than the "walk and talk" pictures as a direct result of their comparative attractiveness in foreign-language territories. His figures suggest that a strong economic rationale underpinned the regular production of action-oriented pictures as a major sector of industry output, even if only because of their success abroad. Like action melodramas and westerns, physical comedy proved very popular in non-English-speaking markets: Robert Vogel, head of the International Department at MGM, claimed that Laurel and Hardy made more money abroad for MGM than any other stars.[13]

In addition to providing sufficient action-oriented material for export, every major company made further accommodations to the requirements of leading foreign markets during production.[14] Occasionally projects deliberately incorporated special items of foreign interest,

Table 4
Performance of Action versus Dialogue Pictures in Foreign-Language Markets

Production	Total Gross	Percentage of Income	
		English Version	Superimposed and Dubbed Version
Action Pictures			
I Am a Fugitive from a Chain Gang	$ 870,087	30%	70%
Tiger Shark	417,504	40	60
20,000 Years in Sing Sing	420,257	45	55
Captain Blood	1,049,141	55	45
Dialogue Pictures			
Oil for the Lamps of China	309,261	68	32
Broadway Gondolier	302,424	76	24
The Petrified Forest	212,898	75	25
Page Miss Glory	214,302	84	16
I Married a Doctor	109,518	85	15
Three Men on a Horse	99,315	94	6

Source: Sam Morris, letter to Jack Warner, 12 November 1937, JLW correspondence, box 59, folder 8, Warner Bros. Archive.

and more commonly, movies mooted for export featured stars with international drawing power. *Cavalcade* (Fox, 1933) is an example of a movie that was produced with the foreign sphere in mind, in this case the British Empire. Based on a Noël Coward play, the movie traced modern British history through the fortunes of one family. Fox considered revising the script to make it more relevant to American audiences—specifically by changing the locale to the United States and making the family American—but the studio eventually decided to retain the "pro-English" version. Jason Joy explained the company's reasoning: "It can be made interesting to American audiences, and will be thoroughly appreciated by the audiences of the British Empire, not only for itself but especially because of our willingness to give them back the story in their own fashion."[15] Fox's seriousness about this aspect of the production was evident in a letter from head of production Winfield Sheehan to Joy, requesting that both Joy and Hays comment on the extent to which the production would be "an asset in British countries—England, Canada, Australia, etc."[16] Sheehan also consulted the BBFC before putting the movie into production. Both the studio and the SRC were anxious that the picture should not strike any false notes with foreign audiences, for apart from drawing profits overseas, they hoped that it would act as a piece of international promotional advertising, both for Fox and for the industry as a whole. By the time the movie was released, it had undergone unusually close scrutiny. Joy pronounced it to be "perfect from the standpoint of the Code and of official censorship" and hoped that it would do the industry, "and indeed America," no end of good.[17]

The practice of using individual films for institutional promotion persisted throughout the 1930s. Overseas, especially, the maintenance of "prestige" through the production of films with outstanding technical and/or artistic credentials was held to be vital to Hollywood's dominance.[18] Extravagant and ambitious undertakings like *A Midsummer Night's Dream* (Warner Bros., 1935) constituted a countervailing tendency to the rough-and-tumble of the action pictures. As with all superproductions of this kind, Warner Bros. gambled that success abroad would take the movie into profit. Jack Warner wrote to Sam Morris: "I have received many letters from Hummel [Joe Hummel of Warner Bros.' Foreign Department] about DREAM openings in foreign countries and have written to him to please tell me just how much money we are getting net. I am waiting with open ears the news on just what we are doing financially throughout Europe and the rest of the foreign territory on DREAM. Will appreciate hearing from you as fast as you can get any information of this kind."[19]

The most obvious concession to foreign tastes lay in the selection and promotion of stars with international drawing power. The industry's experience at the beginning of the sound era, when international audiences had rejected movies custom-made in their own languages in favor of those featuring established favorites, had demonstrated the global dimensions of stardom. At the same time, foreign audiences often responded particularly warmly to their own compatriots when they appeared in the international context of the Hollywood industry. When Hollywood producers poached acting talent from other national industries, they not only weakened their competitors but also recruited the affections and loyalties of foreign populations. Gabriel Hess, attorney for the MPPDA, spelled this out in a statement he made before the Immigration and Naturalization Committee of the U.S. House of Representatives:

Some of the world-wide character and appeal of American motion pictures must be credited to the employment of foreign actors in American studios . . . .

It is reasonable to assume that to a certain extent foreign markets have been created and held by the pride and interest of the people of a country in actors of their nationality who in pictures made in America become outstanding international screen personalities.[20]

Hess cited the examples of Greta Garbo, Charles Laughton, and Maurice Chevalier; one could immediately add Marlene Dietrich, Charles Boyer, David Niven, Ramon Novarro, and many others. Australia persisted in taking a proprietorial interest in Tasmanian Errol Flynn, even when it suited Hollywood's promotional strategies better to claim that he was Irish.

Greta Garbo constitutes the most conspicuous example of the influence of foreign tastes. Although she is remembered today as the quintessential screen goddess of the late 1920s and the 1930s, she was never overwhelmingly popular in the United States. Her reputation depended on her immense following abroad, and her films consistently depended on the foreign market to take them into profit.[21] The extent of her standing overseas is indicated by records in United Artists' foreign "Black Books" for 1936, in which she is listed as the most popular actress in twenty-six out of thirty countries surveyed.[22] While MGM could not have predicted Garbo's phenomenal appeal abroad, and particularly in Europe, it seems unlikely that the studio's initial recruitment of a Swede came about by chance. As the American commercial attaché in Stockholm observed in 1927, Sweden had one of the highest per capita expenditures on motion pictures in Europe and an exceptionally large number of cinemas for a country its size. He reminded American producers that they needed to use every effort to adapt their pictures to local tastes if they were to maintain their predominant position in the market.[23]

Of course, not only actors were recruited from foreign industries but also technical workers of all kinds, notably directors and cameramen. The industry could afford to buy up the best staff in the world, and its recruitment policies constituted a logical business move. As a capitalist tactic, this had a kind of elegance. Only the strongest national industries in the world could offer the kind of training and experience that would make a technician attractive to Hollywood; therefore, once the acquisition had been made, not only was the American industry inherently strengthened, but its most immediate competitors were also proportionately weakened. Hollywood justified this policy by claiming that it allowed producing companies to make movies best fitted for international consumption. For example, Hays talked about "drawing into the American art industry the talent of other nations in order to make it more truly universal."[24]

This explanation is not wholly fatuous. Whatever the original intention behind Hollywood's voracious program of acquisition, the fact that the studios contained many émigrés (predominantly from Europe) probably allowed a more international sensibility to inform the production process. Luigi Luraschi, who was a PCA liaison at Paramount in the 1930s, commented that his job was made easier by this international dimension, especially when it came to avoiding offense to foreign nations: the European directors were instinctively alert to areas of sensitivity and treated them cautiously in production.[25] In general, however, this area of influence has been overestimated.[26] In fact, Hollywood production operated within an internally consistent set of aesthetic and representational conventions on which individual directors could work only minor variations. When highly regarded German director G. W. Pabst was preparing to make *A Modern Hero* (Warner Bros., 1934), he received the following memo from production supervisor Hal Wallis:

I want to caution you at this time against changing any dialogue or action or sequences in "THE MODERN HERO" from what has already been agreed upon between us. . . . I am just editing the last Barthelmess picture [*Massacre*] and because of changes that were made on the set, I am going to have to make some re-takes to put the script back into its original version and I don't want to go through this on "THE MODERN HERO." I don't want the thought or the action of any scenes changed nor do I want any dialogue changes so let us all understand this before the picture starts.[27]

If Hollywood movies had global appeal, it was because they were products deliberately designed for global consumption; it was not a serendipitous effect of recruiting an international labor force.

Concessions to foreign tastes could occur not only at the level of a movie's conception but could also be included as an addition to, or inflection of, the production. At the same time as Jack Warner was banking that Shakespeare would pull crowds in Europe, he was hoping that some hard-hitting scenes in *Road Gang* (Warner Bros., 1936), a prison movie, would be a particular hit in France, "where they love this type of brutality."[28] On the other hand, the preeminence of the domestic American market made Universal unusual in its decision to proceed with its 1934 version of *Imitation of Life*, a melodrama with racial overtones, on the basis that "while the company realizes that they may have some difficulty with this kind of picture in this country, they feel that it is the kind of picture which will clean up in Europe."[29]

From the mid- to late 1930s the problems incurred in incorporating foreign influences ranged from the fundamental to the peripheral, as shown in the movies discussed in the sections below. These cases also illustrate different levels of competence in accommodating overseas requirements: some studios were better organized and better informed than others. No aspect of content regulation was completely foolproof, however, and a technical error could always deny a movie part of its potential audience.

The Last Days of Pompeii (RKO, 1935)

The Last Days of Pompeii tells the story of a Roman artisan-turned-gladiator called Marcus, who finds Christ. At the beginning of the movie he enjoys an idyllic though pagan existence in Pompeii with his beautiful wife and baby until both are killed in a freak accident. He turns his energies to amassing money and power ruthlessly until he adopts the orphaned son of a man whom he has killed in gladiatorial combat. With the boy, he goes in search of "the greatest man in Judea" (whom he assumes to be Herod), pursuing the prophecy of a fortune-teller. On the way the boy falls ill and is cured by Christ. Marcus embarks hesitantly on the road to conversion. Later he happens to be in Jerusalem at the time of the Crucifixion, and then in Pompeii at the time of the eruption of Vesuvius. He acquits himself nobly in the movie's last few apocalyptic scenes, and Christ appears in spectral form in time to bless him as he dies.

When Joseph Breen received the script from RKO in April 1935, he worried about the possible reaction to such a subject in Britain. The project of building a story around Jesus Christ, when the British barred his representation, was fraught with difficulty. Breen would have had in mind *The King of Kings* (De Mille Pictures/Producers Distributing Corp., 1927), a feature about the life of Christ by Cecil B. De Mille which had gained only limited distribution in Britain despite its being a prestige production. It had never even been presented to the BBFC because of the certainty that it would be rejected. *Outward Bound* (Warner Bros., 1930) had encountered censorship problems even though it was an allegorical story that only suggested a parallel between God and a character called the Examiner. Breen sought Frederick Herron's advice:

> I hate like blazes to impose upon your goodness to ask you to read the script, but I think it will be necessary that you do so, in order that you understand specifically the worries we have. You will note that the figure of Christ is frequently suggested throughout the story. It is their purpose never, at any time, actually to show the figure of Christ, but as you will note from reading the script, there are some lines which will be spoken by a voice definitely to be suggested as those of the voice of Christ.
>
> Also, they purpose to show, in a long shot, three crucifixes on a dark hill.

The figures on these crucifixes will not be distinguishable, and it is planned briefly to use a copy of the famous painting, which I think you know, and which is the painting with the three crucifixes silhouetted against the reflection of the sky of the setting sun.[30]

This approach was necessary for one good reason:

Radio are planning to spend something like a million dollars on this production, and it goes without saying, they have their eyes fixed quite definitely on the British market . . . .

Maybe your man in England could cable you the substance of what reaction he gets from the Censor Board and from the Lord Chancellor.[31]

James M. Beck, Herron's contact at the BBFC, reported that the voice-over could be used if the text was derived from the Scriptures and if the whole thing was treated with due reverence. The BBFC thought the crosses on the hill ought to be eliminated, and Beck therefore suggested that the movie be constructed in a form sufficiently flexible to allow those shots to be excised for British distribution. He further suggested that "cruelty and horror" sequences be treated very carefully, since they had been deleted in similar productions in the past.

Herron passed all this back to Breen, elaborating the point about cruelty: "In checking over the religious films that have gone to England heretofore, I found that they have cut out shots of cruelty such as gladiators hacking one another to pieces, horror shots such as lions tearing their victims to pieces, wild animals fighting each other, etc. This applies to both *The King of Kings* and *The Sign of the Cross* [Paramount, 1933]."[32] Merian Cooper of RKO welcomed the BBFC's comments, having declared himself fully prepared to "cut his cloth" to suit the requirements of the British.[33] He only balked at the suggestion that the action set in Jerusalem should "not have as a background any sign of the cross going past." He felt he could not dispense with the walk to Calvary and proposed to compromise by showing the top of a cross in the background.

The problems presented by the project were sufficiently delicate for Herron to send the full script of the movie to the BBFC for further reaction. J. B. Wilkinson, secretary of the BBFC, advised:

As you state in your foreword, the story follows, to some extent, the famous novel by Lord Lytton, and from our point of view, is quite permissible.

Attention, however, must be paid to the scenes of fighting in the arena, particularly *scenes 124, 135, 143 and 1083* to avoid brutality and gruesome closeups.

Scene 922 showing Augur sacrificing lamb sounds very unpleasant, and should be modified.

Scene 1084 and subsequent scenes of the eruption of Vesuvius and the destruction of Pompeii must be carefully handled so as not to exhibit too many horrors.

Scene 1122. The visionary figure must, according to our usual standards, be omitted.[34]

The implication of this last, of course, was the sticking point. Christ was a central character in the story, and great ingenuity would be required to keep him off the screen altogether.

RKO almost managed it. When Marcus stops at an inn during his journey to find the greatest man in Judea, some fellow travelers inform him that the man he wants is next door in a stable, only the doorway of which is visible. Christ does not actually appear, and Marcus eventually continues on his way. Nevertheless, the two do soon meet. Marcus is encouraged to present his ailing son to the holy man to be healed. He discovers an open-air congregation, shown in the middle distance, with Jesus concealed by the throng. As Marcus approaches with his son in his arms, the crowd parts, but just as the speaker is about to be revealed, the perspective changes to Christ's point of view, showing Marcus making his way forward. Marcus kneels and says, "Master, Lord, have mercy on my son." A chorus of angels is heard, and the perspective switches back to its original position behind the crowd. As the congregation moves off, still with Christ at its center, Marcus is revealed with the boy, now restored, standing at his side.

The film's next close encounter with Christ occurs at the Crucifixion. The jeering crowds witnessing the walk to Calvary are shown in the distance, with the events in Marcus's story stolidly occupying the foreground. As promised by Cooper, only the tops of crosses can be seen making progress along the road behind the crowd. Later, in a single shot, a collection of crosses can be seen silhouetted on a hill in the extreme distance, but they are so far away that no human figures can be discerned. Finally, at the end of the action, Christ appears to the dying Marcus in a vision. It is the closest the movie comes to putting Jesus on the screen, but technically the shot avoids constituting a *material* vision of Christ: he is a ghostly superimposition, shimmering insubstantially over the ruins of Pompeii.

The scripting and direction of *The Last Days of Pompeii* show how streamlined the accommodation of the foreign market had become in prestige productions by 1935. By inviting the involvement of the BBFC in a consultative role, RKO demonstrated the extent of its willingness to be flexible about treatment wherever necessary to guarantee unimpeded distribution in foreign territories. Breen and Herron's roles as

In order to meet the requirements of the British Board of Film Censors, Christ is kept
offscreen in *The Last Days of Pompeii* (RKO, 1935). The characters, however, can see him
even if the audience cannot. Here they are bathed in a heavenly light emanating from
behind the camera.

middlemen in the negotiations between the studio and a reactive section of its market illustrate an aspect of their work which was always
dominant, but which is often overlooked in comparison with the more
controversial "censorious" functions of the PCA in upholding the
Code. The nature of their advice illustrates their "casebook" approach,
which in this instance involved drawing on their experience of similar
projects by other companies to anticipate the likely pitfalls facing a spectacular religious picture in 1935. Their efforts were certainly successful
in forestalling censorship on the picture's British release: the only action eliminated was a shot of Pontius Pilate washing his hands. The
treatment of Christ in this movie was such a success with the BBFC that
in the following year it suggested that Queen Victoria's presence
should be established in much the same way— by implication rather
than explicit representation—in the Warner Bros. film *White Angel*.

D. E. Griffiths of Warners' London office told Hal Wallis that according to the BBFC, "if it is possible for you to establish the Queen's presence by dialogue, and have Florence Nightingale curtsey to the throne, without showing any actual figure of the Queen, this will be allowed."[35]

In the event, *The Last Days of Pompeii* was one of only two RKO movies produced in the 1930s that earned more in the foreign field than they did domestically (the other being *The Hunchback of Notre Dame*, 1939). Made at a cost of $818,000, *Pompeii* brought in $489,000 from the United States and $491,000 from foreign territories.[36]

The fact that the movie's production was informed at every stage by specific foreign sensitivities significantly affected its form and content. Its central element of deniability—the fact that no one could claim that Christ actually "appeared" in the film—arose entirely from the BBFC's stipulation that such a representation would be inadmissible. At times this treatment gives rise to the odd sense that the principal action in the film is confined to a subplot, with momentous events possibly transpiring just out of view, as in Tom Stoppard's *Rosencrantz and Guildenstern Are Dead*. Yet while on this level the board's influence may have been restrictive, at the same time it provided an incentive to imaginative response, both on the part of the filmmakers and on the part of the audience. To some degree necessity became a virtue as, leaving aside the narrative contortions required to place Christ consistently in the background, the implication of a divine presence may have had the potential to act on the minds of the audience more powerfully and mysteriously than a literal embodiment.

Woman Trap (Paramount, 1936)

As we have seen, Hollywood's relationship with Mexico got off to a bad start. The Mexican resolution of 1922, while offering a precedent for the negotiation of trade agreements through concessions in content, failed to make any immediate impression on the prejudices of Hollywood producers, and by 1923 the products of First National were again banned in Mexico because *Girl of the Golden West* (Associated First National, 1923) had "hurt the sentiments of the Mexican public."[37] Insults were followed by bannings, or threatened bannings, on a fairly regular basis.[38] *The Dove* (Norma Talmadge Productions/United Artists, 1927), which was set in Tijuana, had to be withdrawn from distribution after it occasioned the banning of all United Artists' products in the Mexican market. M. C. Levee, then general manager of United Artists, later recalled, "After consultation with the Mexican Embassy, there seemed nothing that we could do except to change the locale of the story. We shifted it to the coast of Costa Rica and used fictitious names that people never even heard of and consequently the picture suffered."[39]

With the establishment of the Production Code in 1930, some improvement was discernible. First National's adaptation of Porter Browne's play *The Bad Man* (1930) was heavily revised to avoid causing offense in Mexico *before* it went into production. By 1931 the threat to ban had become something of a formality on Mexico's part. In the case of MGM's *Strangers May Kiss* (1931), the Mexican Foreign Office took the position that scenes set in Mexico were insulting, declaring that "unless the picture were withdrawn immediately or the objectionable scenes deleted the Mexican government would be forced to impose an embargo on the producing company."[40] However, when John V. Wilson of the PCA looked at the picture with the Mexican consul, it transpired that the movie could be corrected to everyone's satisfaction with the excision of three simple shots. By 1934 sufficient precedent had been established for the country's sensibilities to be taken into account as a matter of course. In relation to the preparation of Paramount's *The Trumpet Blows* (1934), Maurice McKenzie reported: "As to Mexico. Botsford tells me that before they went into production they sent the script to the Mexican government, some changes were suggested, these changes were made, and they do not anticipate any trouble on that score."[41] In 1935, when the PCA pronounced the Warner Bros. property *The Where to Go Man* to be inherently insulting to Mexico, the studio dropped plans for its production.[42]

Yet however much Hollywood wanted to avoid offending its southern neighbors, the stereotypes adhering to Mexican locations proved irresistible to producers. As Levee maintained, "There is a difference between using the name Tia Juana and some other name that is not known, because it has certain connotations—it has a meaning to the audience and brings a reaction in them that an unknown name cannot."[43] Filmmakers loved the easy exoticism of Spanish names, dusty streets, donkeys, haciendas, sombreros, and erotic Spanish women. Most of all they loved the Mexican Bad Man—a large, raucous, mustachioed bandit who spoke semicomic pidgin English and exhibited varying degrees of barbarous behavior. Understandably, he was anathema to the Mexican government. The conflicting impulses of the producers—to avoid condemnation while retaining a place on the screen for the Bad Man—are embodied in Paramount's 1936 release *Woman Trap*.

Woman Trap has a routine plot involving a spoiled young heiress and a city reporter who get mixed up with a gang of jewel thieves and go through a series of dangerous exploits before being rescued together.

The variation on the theme in this case is that most of the action takes place in Mexico, where the jewel thieves go to hide out. The criminals are sheltered by Ramirez (Akim Tamiroff), described in the movie's advertising as a "self-styled Mexican bad man." They need the local knowledge of this amiable but apparently unscrupulous character to be able to survive in the desert, but they plan to dispose of him before they go. Ramirez becomes involved in the kidnapping of the hero and heroine, Keat and Buff, and he and his servant, Pancho, lead them on a hot and thirsty march across the desert. It finally transpires that Ramirez is not the dangerous oaf that he appears to be but is actually a crafty Mexican G-man who has been working undercover on the case of the missing jewels.

This sleight of hand was hardly original: *Woman Trap* was contemporary with the spate of G-man movies that offered American gangsters a way back onto the screen disguised as detectives, by means of plots involving detectives disguised as American gangsters. Its adaptation to the Mexican problem was unusual, however, and constituted a case of lateral thinking on the part of the studio. As with many of the conventional G-man movies, the fact that the audience is not let into the secret of Ramirez' identity until the end is an important factor in allowing the performative elements of the movie to tell a different story to that claimed by the stated narrative. Paramount's advertising agents had no doubt about how they wanted the audience to experience the movie, and they warned exhibitors not to give the game away in their own advertising: "Wherever the 'bad man' angle is stressed, we should suggest that the true character of this 'bad man' (the fact that he is a Mexican G-man) be kept hidden as it is in the picture. The mystery angle should be retained."[44]

Inasmuch as the value of the G-man device lay in the fact that it enabled Ramirez to be a classic Bad Man up to the last minute while still managing to reflect well on the Mexican government, *Woman Trap* provides another case in which foreign market considerations influenced form and content. Mexican relations also influenced some small-scale details of characterization. For example, John Hammell, Paramount's PCA contact, was concerned about the depiction of Ramirez' servant, Pancho. He contacted Jack Cunningham, who was supervising the movie: "D-9: At the top of this page Pancho, in a bright tone, says: 'Somebody have got to be killed?' The idea here is that the average Mexican glories in killing. This characteristic should not by any means be too strongly stressed."[45] Cunningham took the objection seriously and contacted producer Harold Hurley with appropriate revisions:

Akim Tamiroff plays an undercover member of the Mexican secret police in *Woman Trap* (Paramount, 1936). For most of the movie, however, audiences perceive him as an unreconstructed Mexican Bad Man.

I feel that if there is any virtue at all in the criticism it should be eliminated entirely and the dialogue in this scene . . . has been changed to the following:
Ferguson: You want to make some money? Mucho dinero?—
Pancho: (Shrewdly looking at Ferguson) Mucho dinero?
Ferguson: Yes, a lot of it—you know the country around here pretty well, don't you?
Pancho: Si, Señor—like the inside of my mind—[46]

Two extra scenes were also written, showing Ramirez secretly collecting water from a spring in the desert and supplying it to Keat and Buff. Cunningham explained their purpose to Hurley: "I'd like to state that aside from the story value and interest this might arouse on the part of the audience they were also put in for the sake of the Latin-American character of Ramirez who would by this device not be criticized for torturing Buff and Keat to bring about the capture of Ferguson and his gang. This little situation definitely indicates that he has not caused them unduly to thirst on the desert."[47] These last scenes, however, were never shot. Compared with RKO's careful attention to foreign matters in the shooting of *The Last Days of Pompeii*, Paramount's efforts to eliminate offense in *Woman Trap* were halfhearted. Despite the movie's technical renunciation of the Bad Man persona, *Woman Trap* managed to encourage the most stereotypical American attitudes toward Mexico.

The tone of the depiction can be gauged from the Paramount Publicity Department's suggestions for lobby exploitation:

Sombrero Still Display: A huge sombrero can be cut out of compo board and covered with stills from the picture. This can be either a flat outline of the hat or a real three-dimensional affair, several feet in height.

Hacienda in Lobby: An attractive lobby display can be built easily by erecting the front end porch of a typical Spanish hacienda. Only the front of the building, painted to resemble adobe, is necessary, plus the tilted lean-to roof and a few posts and railings. The doorway leads to a small room—made from the junction of the hacienda with the lobby corner. The interior can be covered with stills from the picture, appropriately lighted. The outside of the hut should be hung with serapes, sombreros on pegs, blankets and other Mexican knick-knacks . . . gourds, lariats, a saddle, etc. Cactus, sand and a hitching post will add to the display. It can be completed by dressing an usher in typical Mexican caballero costume, standing him at the entrance to the hacienda, giving out programs.[48]

Although Ramirez turns out to be Señor del Valle of the Mexican Secret Police, he has lines such as "Here ees a pretty tough hombre, myself, you know!" and "Oh, yes—I am the biggest G's man in Mejico." The evolution of the Mexican male from a sadistic bandit to a genial but cunning clown represented no great improvement. Hays remarked in his memoirs that the Mexicans "preferred that we use American locales in our films, feeling that we were liable to make mistakes in using theirs, even with the best of intentions."[49] While the industry could accommodate complaints about specific aspects of representation, it could offer little response to general objections to its power to fictionalize and stereotype.

Woman Trap resembles *The Last Days of Pompeii* insofar as its producers saw the problems associated with the foreign market as a technical challenge. In *Woman Trap*, however, the solution is located on the level of plot; on the level of performance, the offending characterization is essentially unreconstructed. The element of deniability—the G-man ploy—technically prevents the Bad Man's return, but from the audience's perspective he is present for most of the movie. The movie probably did nothing to improve the industry's relations with Mexico in 1935, nor was it designed to do so. Although as an action movie *Woman*

Trap would have been eligible for fairly general distribution abroad, it would not have depended on the Latin American market to make a profit and might not have been sent there.[50] The movie was primarily designed to appeal to the average patronage of split-week B theaters in the United States and would not have needed wide distribution overseas to recoup its costs.

West of Shanghai (Warner Bros., 1937)

West of Shanghai, which began its production history as *Cornered,* was originally supposed to be a third remake of Porter Browne's *The Bad Man,* but once the studio had decided that the best way to deal with the Mexican location was to move the story to China, any connection with the movie's source became even more tenuous than was usual with Hollywood adaptations. The movie tells the story of a party of Westerners who fall into the clutches of a renegade Chinese warlord, Wu Yin Fang, played by Boris Karloff, anticipating his *Mr. Wong* series at Monogram Studios later in the decade. Like his Bad Man antecedents, Fang's characterization is semicomic. He turns out to be essentially honorable and dispatches the real villain of the piece before facing a firing squad at the end of the movie.

Breen did not want to see a Chinese problem created in lieu of the Mexican one. He contacted Mr. Chang, the Chinese consul in Los Angeles, for his advice on the production, telling Herron, "I have set about, quite frankly, to cultivate the Chinese Consul, and I can see no reason why he cannot be very helpful to us. I have endeavored to arrange to consult him before pictures, which would be likely to come to his attention, go into production: This, I think, is a way to avoid much trouble later on."[51] After having made several recommendations, which were duly adopted, the Chinese consul declared himself to be satisfied with the result, including Fang's characterization, with but one minor exception. The problem was that the uniforms worn by Fang and his bandit army too closely resembled those of the National Army of China. Chang could not approve the movie unless the uniforms were changed. Unfortunately, however, the uniforms appeared throughout the movie. Jack Warner wrote to Sam Morris in New York:

Had we for one moment thought there would be any controversy over the uniforms we would naturally have made them more nondescript. As it is they really are nondescript but in photographing them they do to an extent resemble the regular uniforms of the National Chinese Army.

We have come to an impasse with Mr. Chang, who has been very fair and square in his recommendations, but the last reply he received from the Nan-

In *West of Shanghai* (Warner Bros., 1937) Boris Karloff plays Wu Yin Fang, a Mexican Bad Man transposed to China. The Chinese consulate found nothing to complain about in the movie except the uniforms worn by Fang and his bandit followers—which were in virtually every scene in the picture.

king Government was that they haven't any objections to the picture other than the uniforms. Inasmuch as it is a physical impossibility to change the uniforms of Karloff and his cohorts, which by the way we have shown with several narrative titles that they definitely are bandits and meet their just deserts of death and law and order triumphs, it comes to this, Mr. Chang suggests that we show the picture to the Chinese Ambassador in Washington or someone he may designate as he has gone as far as he can go officially.[52]

Jack Warner was prepared to make several propitiatory gestures to try to ameliorate the situation. He suggested that Warners employee Albert Howson should make appropriate apologies and explanations to the ambassador, assuring him of the studio's good will toward the Chinese; he guaranteed that the company would not send the movie to Hawaii, the Philippines, China, Japan, or any other country in the Far East "where it would cause any comment or dissatisfaction"; and he offered to put a revised explanatory preface on the picture, either of the studio's creation or in "any other wording the Chinese Ambassador can suggest." Warner was prepared to make any changes to the picture that the ambassador suggested, as long as the official understood that it was a practical impossibility to change the uniforms. Warner was even willing to misrepresent the movie in its own advertising campaign to avoid compounding any offense: "In making up any lithographs or ads, inform Einfeld to keep away from any *uniforms*," he wrote to Sam Morris. "Keep Karloff in civilian clothes even if you have to fake it. We are going to camouflage it as having nothing to do with any Chinese soldiery and internal strife."[53]

Morris took up the problem at the New York end, but Herron discouraged him from approaching the ambassador. On the basis of recent experience (presumably of Paramount's *The General Died at Dawn*, 1936), Herron assured Morris that such a course would only cause more headaches, and that in any case the ambassador did not have the authority to approve the picture.[54] Between them Morris and Herron came to the conclusion that in this case no diplomatic way out of the impasse could be found. After all, nothing could be done about the uniforms, and as Morris told Warner, "inasmuch as we have the picture and the opportunity of making some money with it, let's go to it the best way we know how."[55] Far from steering clear of the subject of Chinese internal strife, they decided that "since we are going to be in bad anyway we might as well change the title to *West of Shanghai* as this title will undoubtedly mean extra dollars in countries where the picture can be released."[56]

The result for the movie itself was that as well as gaining a new title it acquired the following carefully worded preface:

China is a vast country with far-flung borders. To the north, beyond the reach of steel rails, is a region sparsely inhabited but rich in oil and mineral deposits—an area very difficult to police. In every country, such a frontier has its adventurers, and China is no exception. With their followers, in uniforms made to look as much as possible like those of regular troops, men with illusions of grandeur assume false military titles, and ape the mannerisms of high-ranking officers. The career of such a bandit is a short one, for the efficient Chinese government soon runs him to earth. This is the story of Wu Yin Fang, who marched from nowhere with a marauding band at his heels, and was soon swept into oblivion.

Compared with the complex accommodations of the foreign market that were made in *The Last Days of Pompeii* and *Woman Trap*, this addition was relatively inconsequential. It had no impact on the movie's narrative construction or characterization, and little effect on the experience of the audience, except perhaps to make them wonder why their attention was being drawn to the bandits' uniforms. On the other hand, the interventions in all three movies employed strategies of denial to circumvent elements potentially offensive to sections of the foreign market.

Prefaces had been used since the early silent film days to establish ideological frameworks for movie narratives. This one followed the same principle by attempting to define a context within which the audience's narrative elaborations would be contained. Whether or not parameters for imaginative experience could be set in this way under any circumstances, it seems unlikely that prefaces would have had the desired effect within the context of exhibition in the United States, where showings were continuous and audiences regularly drifted in after the film had started. In practice, prefaces spoke more to institutions than to audiences, particularly to censors, to reformers, and in this case to the Chinese consulate. The existence of the preface reflects the studio's recognition of the Chinese government's influence within the industry.

Indeed, the studio had maintained cordial relations with the consulate in the early stages of production, and Jack Warner's correspondence demonstrates his willingness to keep the Chinese legation happy. The eventual abandonment of this cooperation in favor of recovering money already invested illustrates the point at which diplomacy ceased to make economic sense. As Warner himself insisted, the movie was unlikely to achieve a high enough profile to be of any diplomatic consequence: "[E]xplain very clearly to the Chinese Ambassador that this picture is not an important one," he wrote to Sam Morris. "It is a class B production and will not be shown in any of the class A theaters of any consequence in the world. . . . It really will be distributed and

forgotten as it is not an important picture."[57] The more important consequence of the movie's low-budget status was that, to an even greater
extent than *Woman Trap*, it did not need to bring in revenues from
throughout the foreign field. Sam Morris upheld Warner's decision not
to send the movie to the Far East and suggested that some South American markets ought to be excluded as well. Any losses incurred would
not be too sorely missed, since, as he remarked, "between America,
England and Scandinavia, and a few other places, we should get our
money back with a good profit."[58]

Breen himself viewed the whole experience as contributing to the
pressure on producers to circumscribe their field of representation. He
told Herron that the various consuls seemed to be quite unreasonable
in their demands and added that "if we are to pay serious attention to
all of them, I am afraid we shall have to very materially confine our
story development within a rather restricted orb."[59] He continued:

> The companies are not insensible to the danger in the situation. The studio
> folks, of course, seek everlastingly to secure and to hold the widest possible
> field within which to set their drama. They resent anything suggestive of restric-
> tion in this field—what they call "free flow" of story development. Against
> this, of course, is the practical problem as to where we are going to show these
> "free flow" pictures, if they give offense to various foreign nationalities.
>
> As I view it—we can be "free, sovereign and independent," and tell every-
> body to go to hell, and make all the pictures we want, with Chinese, German,
> French (or anybody else) characterized in every way possible. On the other
> hand, if we want to continue to maintain our very lucrative foreign fields, we
> shall have to be, possibly, less "free and sovereign—and less independent."[60]

This comment neatly sums up the attitude that the wider industry had
to adopt in relation to its international customers. Like it or not, the
foreign market was a basic factor in the economic life of Hollywood,
and its appeasement was an essential part of the business. Every level
of production was under a certain amount of pressure to conform to
international requirements, even though products near the bottom of
the range were more likely to slip through the MPPDA's net, as is demonstrated by both *West of Shanghai* and another Karloff vehicle, *Devil's
Island*.

Devil's Island (Warner Bros., 1939)

France objected to the filming of stories about the French Foreign Legion, mainly because filmmakers tended to identify it with cruelty and
suffering. The same problem adhered to stories set in the penal settlement of Devil's Island in French Guiana: the location provided an op-

portunity to subject the hero to terrible trials imposed by a brutalizing regime, none of which reflected very well on the French. Despite their potential for creating trouble in France, however, both Foreign Legion and Devil's Island stories proved irresistibly fascinating to American producers in the 1920s and 1930s. Twenty-six movies involving the Foreign Legion were filmed during this period (including three comedies), and six pictures were substantially set on Devil's Island.[61]

In 1938 Columbia made the Foreign Legion picture *Adventure in Sahara*, and Warner Bros. made *Devil's Island*. Paramount's high-budget remake of *Beau Geste* followed in 1939. All three pictures encountered difficulty with the French consulate. In order to avoid a boycott of its products in France, Columbia had to withhold *Adventure in Sahara* from any distribution outside the United States and had to limit the movie's domestic release to two months. Paramount, which certainly needed a foreign release with *Beau Geste*, was much more careful with the movie's preparation: the studio employed a former Legionnaire as a technical adviser from the start. Nevertheless, Paramount was obliged to recall the picture more than a month after its release, so that modifications could be made according to instructions from French diplomatic officials.[62] *Devil's Island* only made it to the world's screens after a protracted wrangle involving Warner Bros., the PCA, and the French government.

The history of *Devil's Island* demonstrates the operations of industry regulation in their least effective form. Some studios made every effort to anticipate Breen's requirements in both themes and details, but Warner Bros. was not one of them.[63] Like every other company, the studio had a censorship department to maintain contact with the PCA and to scrutinize scripts to see that nothing was shot that could not be distributed, but at Warners the department's advisory power seems to have been very limited. For example, in January 1937 the in-house "censors" suggested some cuts in the dialogue of *Ever since Eve:* "I couldn't work on a full stomach—no matter whose," and "Men seldom make passes at girls who wear glasses." Their advice was immediately overridden by Walter MacEwen, assistant to Hal Wallis, who sent a memo to producer Earl Baldwin saying, "You need not make any dialogue changes in these spots unless the Breen office says so, and only then provided Mr. Wallis approves the Breen change. I have told the censorship department to discontinue overlapping with the Breen office's duties and to stick to mechanical items such as names, telephone numbers, etc."[64]

In the context of Warners' overall production output, *Devil's Island* was probably particularly untroubled by the censorship department.

Like *West of Shanghai*, it was made under the supervision of Bryan Foy, head of the studio's B production unit. He operated with a comparatively free hand because the movies he produced were invariably low-budget, with correspondingly low profit margins. The income they could expect to draw from the foreign market was proportionately insubstantial. In fact, the evidence suggests that Foy neither knew nor cared much about what happened to his movies overseas and that, beyond technically satisfying the dictates of the Production Code, he was less than anxious to make his products conform to Breen's advice. This attitude sometimes put him at loggerheads not just with the PCA but also with executives in his own company.

In the case of *Devil's Island*, the choice of the subject itself demonstrated a disregard for the more sensitive areas of the industry's foreign relations. In Foreign Legion stories the Legion could, with careful handling, be used as a colorful background to romance and adventure, but in Devil's Island stories it was very difficult to escape the central situation of oppression and violence. For example, advertisements for Goldwyn's 1929 production *Condemned to Devil's Island* promised that the hero would be "Condemned to an Island of Lost Souls, Tormented by Power-mad Guards . . . See Fever-infested Swamps . . . Sordid Horrors of Prison Ships . . . Desperate Criminals!"[65]

Upon receiving the first parts of the script of *Devil's Island* in late June 1938, Breen invoked the Production Code, reminding Warner Bros. of its obligation to treat the history, institutions, prominent people, and citizenry of other nations fairly. Valentin Mandelstamm had ceased working in Hollywood in the early 1930s, but Breen warned that French consular officials remained alert to anything in the movies that affected their national image. He suggested that the producers should consult their Foreign Department "for an opinion as to the likely reception of the picture abroad."[66]

Sure enough, the French consulate had lodged its first complaint before the end of July. Acting consul G. Raoul-Duval had heard a rumor that the picture was to be based on a recent autobiographical book called *Dry Guillotine* by escaped convict René Belbenoit, and he informed both Breen and Warner: "These misrepresentations, even if the picture is not shown in France, would, by giving to the American public an erroneous idea of our penitentiary colony, cause a great ill feeling in my country . . . not only against the picture itself but also against all American productions."[67] In fact, Warners never cited Belbenoit's book as a source for the story, but the movie was undeniably similar in theme, and the notoriety of the book and its author certainly would have given the picture a more topical—and more controversial—flavor. In practice Breen could do little beyond hoping that the studio would proceed with care. Herron promised to try to "quiet the French Embassy down," but he observed fatalistically: "Of course, they have always objected to any picture made with Devil's Island surroundings."[68]

The movie tells the story of a brain surgeon, Dr. Charles Gaudet (Boris Karloff), who is unjustly convicted of treason in a French court and sent to jail in French Guiana, where he endures horrible privations at the hands of the sadistic commandant, Colonel Armand Lucien. When Gaudet performs an operation that saves the life of Lucien's young daughter, he earns the gratitude of Madame Lucien, who tries to help him escape and later asks the minister for penal colonies to intervene to save his life. Finally Gaudet is pardoned, Lucien is arrested for misconduct, and the minister promises to institute reforms.

Breen saw the picture in early September 1938. He wrote to Herron:

My personal judgment is that it is certain to prove highly offensive to the French government and the people, on three major counts:

   a. The questionable sequence showing a French court passing a sentence of punishment *unjustly* upon a distinguished doctor;

   b. The characterization of the French military officer, who is in charge of the penal colony, as a dishonest, crafty and brutal person; and

   c. The general suggestion that the prisoners on Devil's Island are treated brutally and inhumanely.

The picture comes within the strict provisions of the Production Code, and is carefully handled from that angle. However, because of the danger from the standpoint of the French, I discussed the whole problem with Jack Warner and Bryan Foy last Friday morning. At their suggestion, I showed the picture on Friday afternoon to the local French Vice-Consul.

This gentleman, after he recovered his composure, promised to let me have in writing his impression of this picture, and its likely reception at the hands of his people and government in France.

This morning he telephoned to make an appointment to come here this afternoon at four o'clock, which appointment was made. At about half past three, however, he telephoned that he would not come, and that he had decided not to write me the letter he promised last Friday afternoon to write.

He told me over the phone that he had made a detailed report setting forth his impressions of the picture, and sent this, both to his foreign office in Paris, and to the Ambassador in Washington. He further expressed great apprehension about it, and while he did not commit himself *definitely,* or *officially,* he did say that he felt that the repercussion in France, because of this picture, would be very, very bad. . . .

I shall see Jack Warner tomorrow and recommend to him that he send a print of the picture to his man in Paris, and get to work on it from that point.

Dr. Charles Gaudet (Boris Karloff) has a hard time in *Devil's Island* (Warner Bros., 1939). It was a reasonable bet that the French would object to this characterization of their penal colony, but to some degree the B unit that produced the picture seems to have operated outside the control of company chiefs.

When I asked Bryan Foy why he did not heed to the several recommendations made to him in our letters, that he consult his foreign department about this release before proceeding with this picture, he answered that inasmuch as the picture was not to be released in France (or in England), he felt that this was not necessary. He also stated that our letters were passed on to their legal department here, and that this department evidently saw no danger in the situation because they had given him an OK to go ahead with the picture.[69]

The last sentence shows the extent to which Foy either disregarded or misunderstood the basis on which Breen's advice was offered, since legal infractions had never been a major concern of the PCA. As for Foy's claim that he thought withholding the film from circulation in France and England would obviate its foreign relations problems, perhaps he was just being disingenuous. Limiting overseas distribution had not proved a satisfactory response to French demands in the past. On the other hand, it is possible that Foy knew very little about the problems faced by the marketing and distribution branches of his company.

The "factory" system of studio production depended on motion pictures being passed from specialist to specialist, and the scale of the operation meant that different sections of a studio's operation were strongly compartmentalized. Just as writers often failed to recognize the commercial and industrial pressures that confronted a script in production, so production personnel were often strangely isolated from the exigencies facing their products during the phases of distribution and exhibition. At the most general level, this condition was manifested in the different priorities that characterized East Coast and West Coast operations. As Robert Vogel has commented,

Basically, of course, at the top in all of the companies there was a pull between New York and Hollywood in the respect that the New York people felt that the Hollywood people made fine pictures, but spent so much money doing it that the company couldn't make a profit. And the folks in Hollywood said, "These fellows in New York are bankers and know nothing about making movies." And they were both right. But the pull between the two worked to the advantage of everybody. The pendulum would swing a little one way or the other and then find the middle.[70]

The physical separation of the personnel in New York and Hollywood mirrored the distance between the opposing forces that determined the characteristics of the industry's products. Breen's job was to mediate between the two sides, and the authority granted him to enforce the Production Code ensured that in this he was relatively successful. But beyond the technical requirements of the Code, he had to depend on economic arguments to make his case. In the case of *Devil's Island*, he had to deal with an executive supervisor who was responsible for overseeing the release of twenty-seven movies in 1939, none of which represented a great risk in terms of money invested. Pictures of this kind were produced too quickly to warrant extensive research and preparation, notwithstanding the damage that a single controversial product could cause to the industry's long-term prospects in overseas markets. In any case, *Devil's Island*'s last scenes already constituted a gesture toward the appeasement of the French government, by claiming that a more humane system of administration had been introduced after the final credits. Beyond this, it is likely that, to Foy, "marketing" and "sales" were simply someone else's problem. Herron complained to Breen, "It is a great pity because this whole thing will be dumped in my lap here. It will go to the Embassy, from the Embassy to the Commercial Attaché in New York, and from him to me." He added, "I hope you have brought this to the attention of Mr. Hays because it would probably be brought to his attention if a formal protest is made by the French Embassy to the State Department."[71]

Breen decided temporarily to withhold the movie's Production Code seal, delaying its distribution while everyone decided how best to proceed. It was one of four Warner Bros. movies that caused the PCA concern in 1938. The others were *Angels with Dirty Faces* (1938), *The Sisters* (1938), and another Bryan Foy production, *King of the Underworld* (1939). These faced Code problems, respectively involving crime and kidnapping, representation of a brothel, and gangsters "in armed and violent conflict with the police." All of these difficulties were eventually resolved through script and editing modifications. Breen considered using the Code to force changes in *Devil's Island* as well but decided that it would be difficult to justify such a position when much of the film's material was based on "pretty well authenticated books. . . . The picture tells no new story, and it would be difficult to establish the fact that the French government, or people, were not fairly represented in this story."[72] Under these circumstances he had to grant the movie a seal, but he still hoped that the studio would introduce extensive modifications before releasing it.

Evidently some argument ensued within Warner Bros. itself about the way the French problems should be handled, reflecting the tension that existed between long-term security and short-term profits. At first Jack Warner assured Breen that "anything which definitely ties it in with the French" would be removed from the picture. The title was to be changed, and several scenes deleted, "with a view to putting the locale of the picture in some unidentified country, and definitely and affirmatively to establish it that the penal colony, where most of the action takes place, is *not* a French colony."[73] Foy declared himself ready to go along with this timeworn strategy of denial, and Breen told Hays that the changes would be made. When Warner and Foy looked more carefully at the economics of the situation, however, they decided that the "considerable expense" involved could not be justified and announced their intention to release the movie, unchanged, within the United States.

Meanwhile, Warner Bros.' Foreign Department, which operated out of New York, was doing its best to have the movie modified or scrapped. Sam Morris, head of the department, had never wanted *Devil's Island* to be made in the first place. Now he apparently tried to convince the West Coast that if changing the picture was uneconomic, then it was even more uneconomic to jeopardize the company's chances in France with what was, after all, only a B movie. Unexpectedly, Breen received word from Herron that Joe Hummel of Warners Brothers' Foreign Department had "called up Friday and said that they'd thrown *Devil's Island* in the ashcan. It was a long bitter fight before they were able to do this but the foreign department finally won out."[74] Hummel and Herron were both wrong: Warner Bros. went ahead and put the picture into domestic release on 7 January 1939. Such was the indignation of the French government, however, that the studio was forced to withdraw it from circulation shortly afterward, and it was not shown in most of the eastern states, including New York. The company also suffered a two-month punitive suspension of its license to operate in France. Herron thought this treatment to be very lenient under the circumstances, commenting, "I have no doubt that their Paris man can get around the two months suspension proposition without any great harm to his company."[75]

The final twist in the movie's history was yet to come. By 1940 World War II had rendered the French market unviable. At a stroke, the matter of France's national feelings disappeared from Hollywood's agenda, and *Devil's Island* was rereleased, this time to both the domestic and the foreign fields. Its only modification was the addition of the following preface:

Devil's Island . . . Scene of martyrdom for Dreyfus, until Zola's fiery crusade won his freedom. An island of dread . . . ruled of necessity by an iron regime . . . for here the most dangerous enemies of France were herded into exile. . . . Of purely fictional material, this story pictures that time, now past. A modern understanding of penal administration has brought a change.

Today humanity makes easier the burden of correction. For modern France is committed to the task of remaking men . . . not breaking them.

Variety commented, "In view of the fact that it goes out more than a year later than when first available, the picture most likely will gain some boxoffice benefit from the publicity attendant to its withdrawal, but intrinsically it is just another meller [melodrama] of the dreaded isle down in the Caribbean." The review also noted that "Globe, first date for the film in New York, is ballyhooing the famous Devil's Isle as being 1,000 times tougher than Alcatraz, which should be good showmanship."[76]

Idiot's Delight (MGM, 1939)

Robert E. Sherwood's play *Idiot's Delight* was a Broadway hit in 1936 and as such would normally have found its way to the screen within a year or so. But the play was full of political elements that made the studios wary about attempting an adaptation. It featured the interactions of a group of travelers stranded in a mountain resort in Italy at the beginning of a new world war, a war attributed to Fascist aggression. Geoffrey Shurlock, who had joined the PCA from Paramount in 1932, read the play for the PCA in March 1936. He recorded the following opinion:

The main question raised by this play is one of industry policy. It seems extremely likely that a picture based on this play would be banned widely abroad, and might even cause reprisals against the American company distributing it. The play is fundamentally anti-war propaganda, and contains numerous diatribes against militarism, fascism, the munitions ring, etc. The action centers around the starting of a new European war, in which Italy is specifically shown to be the aggressor against France, with the indication that the other nations are about to ally themselves on one side or the other.[77]

Breen told Herron in April that four companies, including Warner Bros. and Pioneer, had had informal discussions with the PCA about acquiring the property, but all had considered it "too dangerous an undertaking." With a reputed price tag of $125,000 on the motion picture rights, acquiring the play was also an expensive proposition.[78] In August RKO flirted with the idea of purchasing it but wanted to clarify the movie's chances in the foreign field first. At the studio's request, Breen wrote to James Beck at the BBFC, enclosing the script:

One of our companies would like to purchase this play to be adapted for screen presentation. I am fearful that the British Board in London will not be disposed to look with favor on a story of this kind, and I should like to get their reaction to it.

The offensive sex angle in this story can be easily changed. The point I worry about is the definite suggestion of a war between two great European nations. Will you be kind enough to ask Mr. Wilkinson to read this play and let us have his reaction to it. We would like, particularly, to know if it would materially help the story, in his judgment, if, instead of indicating the outbreak of hostilities between two great European powers, the countries involved would be two of the smaller European countries—say, two of the Balkan countries.[79]

The British board suggested that the conflict should be between two "unidentifiable" countries instead.[80] Whether for this or some other reason, RKO lost interest in the property, and by December Breen was discussing it "unofficially and off the record" with MGM.[81]

MGM maintained a particularly cooperative relationship with the PCA. One reason was that the economic structure of its parent organization, Loew's, Inc., differed somewhat from that of the other major companies. Whereas 20th Century–Fox and Warner Bros. each owned several hundred theaters across the United States, Loew's had taken a more cautious approach to cinema acquisition and had limited its holdings to about 150 theaters, principally in New York City.[82] Consequently, Loew's earned a comparatively large proportion of its total revenues from film rentals, as opposed to ticket sales.[83] It needed to produce movies that could be successfully marketed to cinemas that were not under its direct control, and MGM's products therefore needed to be attractive and low-risk. Even its lower-budget, routine productions displayed a quality in casting and art direction that set them apart from the more modest B movies produced at other studios. The comparative care devoted to the preparation of MGM's products was reflected in its willingness to work with the PCA to find solutions to problematic themes and treatments that may have jeopardized its products' chances in the marketplace.

This careful attitude extended to the accommodation of pressures arising from the foreign market. Higher levels of capitalization meant that MGM depended particularly heavily on foreign sales, and as far as possible potential causes of foreign offense were eliminated during the course of production. Robert Vogel, who supervised the preparation of international versions in the 1930s, advised producers of possible foreign problems from the earliest stages of script revision, and major problems were usually eliminated by the time the PCA reviewed the finished picture. If difficulties affecting international distribution were thought to be insurmountable, the picture would not be made.[84] It is notable, for example, that MGM was the only major studio not to attempt a Foreign Legion or Devil's Island picture in the 1920s or 1930s. In making *The Good Earth* in 1937, MGM maintained extensive contact with the Chinese consulate and managed to avoid any trouble from that quarter.[85]

Herron was relieved when he learned that MGM had purchased *Idiot's Delight* since, as he remarked to Breen, "if Metro are going to make it they will clean it up from an international standpoint."[86] On the other hand, relations with the Italian market were deteriorating as political tensions heightened. There had been a crisis in the market in 1936, when the Italian government had tried to impose a stricture that would have kept approximately three-quarters of all box office revenues in Italy. The situation was only resolved to the satisfaction of the American companies after a temporary boycott of the Italian territories and a personal visit by Hays to Italy, where he discussed the situation with Mussolini.[87] The Italian censors rejected twenty Hollywood pictures outright between 1935 and May 1937.[88] This resulted in part from the increasing tendency of the censors to clamp down on Italian characterizations, but to Herron this stance was barely more than a pretext. He commented that "it is quite evident to me that the Italians are out to give us all the trouble they can. . . . it is just one trouble after another in that territory." He hoped that under the circumstances the studio officials would approach *Idiot's Delight* "with their eyes wide open."[89]

When the Italian consulate approached the PCA about the movie in June 1937, some of its demands were, as expected, problematic. Vice Consul Robert Caracciolo informed Breen that the film would be allowed to enter distribution in Italy only under the following conditions:

First. The Metro-Goldwyn-Mayer studio is willing to change the script completely so that it will have no connection with the original story and that it will contain nothing that could offend or hurt my Country in any way;

Second. The script will be sent to me for examination in order that we will both agree on its final production;

Third. The name of Mr. Sherwood will be eliminated in all the editions that are to be distributed in Italy.[90]

MGM producer Hunt Stromberg replied diplomatically, "I am certain the Vice-Consul will understand, when it is explained to him, that it would not be within any policy to buy a story and then discard it in its entirety."[91] Nevertheless, he was sure that the changes the studio would introduce to the script would leave the Italians no cause for complaint. Rather than abandoning the original story, MGM planned to change its emphasis, so that the love story—involving a couple who had had a brief affair many years previously, and who met again by chance in the hotel—would become the center of dramatic interest, and the impending war would constitute only "incidental background." Events in the earlier lives of the two principals, which were only spoken about in the play, would be fully dramatized to emphasize the development of the romance. Stromberg promised to delete any "speeches or ideas" that would tend to indict any nation. "[W]e are trying to make these countries nondescript, but if this is impossible for story clarity and interest, we will identify the nations, but without any attempt to render judgment as the play itself suggested to some. . . . There is no doubt that an argument against war will prevail in this underlying treatment of theme, but that argument will be expressed by private individuals with no governmental connections whatsoever and by characters of American and English nationality, definitely not Italian."[92]

Stromberg offered to arrange a private screening for representatives of the Italian government when the picture was finished, and both he and Breen made strenuous efforts to keep the consulate informed of the progress of the picture, while discussing between themselves the best tactics for maintaining its geographic and political neutrality. For example, Stromberg cabled Breen in late June 1938: "Planning in casting to use personalities like Conrad Veidt for Weber and Edward Raquello for Italian officer. Raquello played this part in New York stage production. These actors speak with accents which from our point of dramatic view adds to character of the story and since we do not identify them by name or dialogue as being of any specific nationality do you think we are safe on accents? Please wire immediately stating your opinion."[93] In order to avoid using the Italian language, MGM decided to use Esperanto for the foreign dialogue in the picture.

MGM dealt extensively with Vice Consul Caracciolo on the strength of his assurance that he had been authorized to represent the official view of the Italian government in negotiations with the studio. Stromberg sent Caracciolo a copy of the script, and through Breen, the vice consul was consulted about the casting of some minor characters in the film. At one point Caracciolo expressed his concern that, although Italy was not specifically mentioned (characters continually talked about trying to cross "the border" without specifying which border it was), audiences might suspect that the location was Italy from various geographic clues in the film. He recommended that the movie contain a specific denial of this implication: "I personally believe that to avoid all misunderstanding, besides eliminating these geographical references, it would be advisable to put in the picture a new character of definite Italian nationality, and make him participate in the discussions that

Clark Gable finds himself traveling in the company of a generically European extra in *Idiot's Delight* (MGM, 1935). Although the original play placed the drama in Italy, MGM went to great pains to obscure the movie's geography. The travelers become stranded at "the border." We never find out which border it is.

take place in the hotel, together with the Americans, the English, the French, and the Germans. Said Italian character should also leave for Italy when all the others go back to their respective countries."[94] Although the scriptwriters did not go so far as to create a major new character, they did introduce a fur-coated traveler who, when ordered off a train near the beginning of the movie, cries, "But I must get back to my country—I must get back to Italy!" After this, the man is occasionally seen in the background at the hotel, but he plays no further direct part in the action.

Everything seemed to be going well until, on 30 July 1938, studio general manager Eddie Mannix received a telegram from his Rome office saying that the Italian government was fundamentally opposed to the production of *Idiot's Delight* and would certainly ban the movie. Although the vice consul promised to cable Italy to straighten out the problem, it became clear that he was helpless in the matter. He stopped taking Breen's calls, although Breen complained that "I have tele-phoned to him twenty-five times, at least."[95]

The studio regarded all this very seriously. Louis B. Mayer became involved in the situation personally, which was most unusual; he asked Breen to provide an account of what had gone wrong and to explain how the Italian market had been lost. But in this case, the fault did not lie with either the studio or the PCA. Ironically, the Fascist politics that Stromberg had taken such pains to keep off the screen had resulted in the closing down of the Italian market, even while *Idiot's Delight* was in production. Throughout 1938 a gradual tighten-ing of import restrictions occurred, leading up to the establishment, in early 1939, of Ente Nazionale Industria Cinematografica (ENIC), a gov-ernment office with monopolistic control of distribution. From that point on, films could only be distributed in Italy through agents or subagents of the monopoly. In response, the American industry very publicly withdrew from Italy, with Hays announcing to the press that business conditions there were intolerable.[96]

It is surprising, therefore, to, discover *Idiot's Delight* circulating in Italy in 1939. A letter from Fayette W. Allport, the MPPDA's European manager, dated 23 October, reports that the sound of air-raid sirens was cut out of the picture at the start of the war, at which time the movie was playing widely in the Italian market. Despite the official rhetoric on both sides, small numbers of American films—especially those made before 1938—did continue to play in Italy, especially in rural and second-run theaters. Luigi Freddi, the director general of cinematography in Italy, feared that the total banishment of the Holly-wood product would threaten the economic viability of domestic exhi-bition, which would in turn further weaken the struggling Italian film industry.[97]

A postscript to the case of *Idiot's Delight* involves *The Adventures of Marco Polo* (Samuel Goldwyn/United Artists, 1938), whose script-writer also happened to be Robert E. Sherwood. Such was the Italian government's hostility to the original stage version of *Idiot's Delight* that, according to the consulate, Sherwood's association with *Marco Polo* threatened to cause Goldwyn "considerable difficulty marketing his pictures in Italy."[98] Eventually the Italians dropped their demands that Sherwood's name be removed from the movie's credits, but they remained critical of the fact that, with his record, the writer had presumed to take as his subject one of the great figures from Italian history. The ambassador told Herron that the movie ran the risk of being "hissed in the theatre." To make matters worse, the Italian government had offered Goldwyn technical assistance and the use of "actual" locations in Venice, but he had turned down this offer in favor of shooting in California, which provided him with sites representing "Italy, Persia, the Gobi Desert, the Ural Mountains, North China, Indo-China, and the ancient capital Pekin."[99] In September 1938 it seemed that the only way for United Artists to get the movie approved in Italy would be to pay Freddi about twenty thousand lire.[100]

Whether or not this payment was actually made, the Italian censors rejected the movie on 21 September 1938. Yet six months later it was playing to packed houses, presumably because of some deft negotiations with ENIC as well as some conciliatory modifications that had been made to the content of the movie. In order to counter its particular public relations problems in the Italian market, the movie had been reconstructed to feature a hero that was no longer Italian, but Scottish. The first part, originally set in Italy, had been removed. All references to Venice had been cut out, as had the hero's discovery of macaroni in China. In a shining example of the compromises that could be visited on film content in the name of wider distribution, *The Adventures of Marco Polo* had been transformed into *McVeigh; or, A Scotsman in the Court of the Grand Khan.*[101]

7

The Big Picture

The Politics of "Industry Policy"

In Hollywood's universe, "industry policy" measures included any area subject to regulation that was not included under the purview of the Production Code. Technically, advice issued from the PCA relative to matters of industry policy was merely cautionary, whereas pronouncements concerning the Code were binding. However, the distinction between the two areas of responsibility often proved hazy. For example, a resolution adopted by the MPPDA in 1937 concerning the depiction of drinking and drunkenness effectively fell between the jurisdictions of the Code and industry policy. In the mechanisms of self-regulation, corporate and "professional" matters were routinely negotiated alongside sexual, criminal, and "gruesome" subjects. The Production Code was really only a specialized category within the wider field of industry policy constraints, all of which originated in the actions of censor boards, public relations problems, or market negotiations.

As communicated to producers by the MPPDA, industry policy not only covered the depiction of foreigners and foreign locales but also affected the depiction of the social fabric of the United States. It ensured the general probity of onscreen public officials, as well as the benevolence of cinematic bankers, lawyers, doctors, teachers, social workers, newspapermen, and police. Where villainous professionals were depicted at all, they were shown to be renegades, soon pulled back into line by bosses or colleagues; "compensating" characterizations were designed to counter hostile reactions to the depiction of professional irresponsibility. In general, both public administration and private enterprise were shown to be motivated by altruism, and the benefits of capitalism were not subject to challenge.

While Hollywood's social world may have been significantly colored by the application of "balance" in the depiction of commercialism and professional conduct, at the level of individual narratives the introduction of such compensating elements caused little disruption. Where themes and subjects were not amenable to this type of facile amelioration—the guidelines issued to producers in 1927 contained Don'ts as well as Be Carefuls—these gradually disappeared from Hollywood's realm. Political subjects, including any discussion of the relationship between capital and labor, were generally absent from the Classical cinema, as were revolutionary themes. Explorations of racial conflict were also largely ruled out. It was in these little-publicized areas of the MPPDA's activities that its effects were, in practice, most censorious.

By contrast, despite the fact that most of the industry's public relations problems were caused by sexual subjects, themes with sexual overtones—both "illicit sex" and "pure romance"—remained staples of Hollywood's output. The Production Code's very preoccupation with sexual matters reflects the industry's determination to continue finding ways of putting these themes on the screen. Although the manner of their representation was constantly at issue and their treatment involved an endless series of displacements and obfuscations, the general effect of these evasive tactics was often, paradoxically, to heighten the screen's erotic impact. Similarly, strategies designed to avoid international offense by circumventing explicit foreign representations tended to relegate non-American locales to an amorphous category of the foreign "other," exacerbating rather than ameliorating the implication that the world outside the United States comprised picturesque exotica.

In the charged political atmosphere at the end of the 1930s, Hollywood's centralized system of content regulation came under attack. It is arguable that the MPPDA's regulatory processes were simply too successful, since they had resulted in a body of movies so consistent in outlook and ideology that the industry's critics could claim with some justification that Hollywood allowed no room for "opposing" views. Ironically, despite the ongoing publicity surrounding contentious sexual and criminal representations, it was the prohibition of political debate—a cornerstone of industry policy, designed to protect Holly-wood's status as a medium of harmless entertainment and to free it from political contentiousness—that fueled governmental criticism of the industry and reinforced complaints that Hollywood essentially acted in restraint of trade. Ultimately, these complaints would lead to the disruption of the stable industrial system that underpinned Classi-cal Hollywood's consensual world.

Professions and Commerce

Crime, bloodshed, heartache, and anxiety occupied the foreground of many Hollywood narratives, but everything was played out against a social background that was curiously utopian. It was not just that law and order triumphed in the end and that virtue was rewarded. In a vari-ety of more subtle ways, the social fabric that underpinned the action was benign, especially in movies with contemporary American set-tings. In particular, industry policy protected political, legal, medical, and other professional institutions. In Hollywood's world, doctors, lawyers, and bank managers were motivated by altruism, and the po-lice force pursued wrongdoers largely untroubled by graft and corrup-tion. Exceptions certainly occurred, and when they did they often occu-pied the foreground of the action, before being revealed as temporary aberrations within a fundamentally stable and reliable social system.[1]

In 1938 the PCA took stock of the nineteen thousand letters of advice that it had issued since the organization of its office under Breen in 1934 and recorded some "general statements of policy" concerning the han-dling of issues that were not covered under the Code. "Professions" were treated according to the following rubric:

> All of the professions should be presented fairly in motion pictures.
>
> There should be no dialogue or scenes indicating that all, or a majority of the members of any professional group, are unethical, immoral, given to criminal activities, and the like.
>
> Where a given member of any profession is to be a heavy or unsympathetic character, this should be off-set by showing upright members of the same pro-fession condemning the unethical acts or conduct of the heavy or unsympa-thetic character.
>
> Where a member of any profession is guilty of criminal conduct, there should be proper legal punishment for such criminal conduct—such punish-ment to be shown or indicated clearly.[2]

This policy had evolved from the general need to protect the indus-try from the disapprobation of any professional body that was apt to form itself into a lobby. As the National Billiard Association had demonstrated in 1924, it was possible for quite peripheral groups to receive attention if they were sufficiently well organized. Circus operators, for example, had threatened to take legal action over the inclusion of a circus tent fire in *Rain or Shine* (Columbia, 1930), and when a similar incident was planned for *Auction in Souls* (KBS Productions/World Wide Pictures; Fox, 1933), Maurice McKenzie alerted James Wingate that "the circus people have a most effective organization composed of substantial people who get to work immediately, the minute they think any wrong has been done to them."[3] More centrally, clergymen and missionaries were treated with great caution; the Code specifically prohibited "ridicule of the clergy."

Social workers and charity workers were also handled with kid gloves. They came from the same stable as the "reformers," women's clubs and philanthropic organizations who were apt to lobby against motion pictures and whom the industry was particularly anxious to befriend. Social workers worked with "delinquents" and, if provoked, were in a good position to accuse the motion picture industry of corrupting the nation's youth—a charge which was particularly dangerous to Hollywood's public relations, and one which the industry devoutly wished to avoid. Social workers first forced changes to a finished picture in *It* (Paramount Famous-Lasky, 1927).[4] In 1929, as a result of protests arising from *The Godless Girl* (C. B. De Mille Productions/Pathé), the American Association of Social Workers was invited to advise the SRC on "all stories that directly or indirectly deal with some aspect of social work."[5] Jason Joy expressed concern about the proposed characterization of a heartless social worker in *Street Scene* (Feature Productions/United Artists) in 1931: "[T]he fight will not come from the social workers themselves, but from the bankers, lawyers, businessmen et al.—the very backbone of our country who are not only interested in social work per se, but are responsible in every large city for the development and continuance of the community chest and other philanthropic functions."[6] In this case the SRC's protest was unsuccessful, as Samuel Goldwyn and the writer, Elmer Rice, insisted on sticking to their original script. By the late 1930s, however, when the mechanisms of self-regulation had become more consistent, "meddlesome and tyrannical" social workers had largely vanished from Hollywood's repertoire.

As long as the industry was determined to avoid controversy, it had to accommodate the sensitivities of all manner of powerful institutions, not only those with a moral or professional agenda. The mollification of corporate interests was a major area of industry concern. While the studios all tried to avoid possible causes of protest from industrial and commercial sources, the bases for such action were sometimes difficult to predict. For example, an apparently innocuous short comedy called *Furnace Troubles* caused considerable difficulties for Fox in 1929. The movie's plot revolved around the trouble a householder experienced with his smoky anthracite-burning furnace, which constantly demanded his attention while he was trying to play a game of cards. The operators of the anthracite minefields of northeastern Pennsylvania saw this as "propaganda circulated without disclosure of the interested parties on behalf of oil heating" and organized a boycott of Fox pictures.[7] The situation was only resolved after two officials from the MPPDA personally visited the coalfields to apologize and the movie was withdrawn from circulation.

By the mid-1930s the industry had learned to be extremely vigilant. *Imitation of Life* (Universal, 1934) was controversial because of its theme of race relations, but Maurice McKenzie was also alert to a problem involving a proposed incident of a rail crash at the town of Camden: "Have you considered the fact that Camden is served by only the Pennsylvania railroad and that a reference to a disastrous wreck at Camden might be resented by the Pennsylvania railroad . . . ?"[8] The Warner Bros. property *Oil for the Lamps of China* (1935) was more problematic, since it was based on a book detailing the experiences of a Standard Oil Company employee in China and his exploitation by the company. Although the studio changed the name of the company to American Oil Company and inserted a preface complimenting the oil business, Breen remained uncertain about the advisability of the project. He warned the studio to "take serious counsel before actually putting this picture into production in order to escape any possible serious criticism from some of the oil companies, if not actual litigation."[9] When Warner Bros. proceeded with the production, it did so in consultation with both Standard Oil and the Chinese consulate.[10]

By 1938 it was standard practice for studios to decenter any material reflecting on industry in favor of an overarching love story, in the same way that international politics were consigned to the background of *Idiot's Delight*. Arthur Houghton of the PCA expressed surprise that the British Chamber of Shipping should object to a David Selznick project on the sinking of the *Titanic*. As he commented to Hays, "I am positive that they are unable to see a picture as we see it, probably running for six and a half reels of love story and the incidents in peoples' lives and the last reel and a half being devoted to the tragedy at sea and their reactions to it. Also the possible building up at the finish of the fact that the benefits and improvements resulting from the TITANIC disaster are the very things that stand out as making sea travel on all ships so perfectly safe today."[11] Nevertheless, the movie, which was to have been directed by Alfred Hitchcock, was not made. *Central Airport* (Warner Bros., 1933) was also essentially a love story, but in this case the story included a plane crash. The property did finally reach the screen, but only after extensive consultations between the studio and the Los Angeles Chamber of Commerce Aviation Committee, as well as the scrapping of the crash sequence, which had reportedly cost $50,000 to stage, out of a total budget of $365,000.[12]

The SRC and the PCA encouraged producers to afford particularly careful treatment to opinion-formers such as newspaper publishers and broadcasters. Radio and newspapers posed a potential threat to the motion picture industry not only because they could give bad publicity to individual projects but also because they could turn the tide of public opinion against the industry as a whole. William Randolph Hearst, in particular, was a declared proponent of federal censorship who was inclined to make his opinions known in the editorial pages of his newspapers.[13] The relationship between movies and the press was strained enough without producers throwing aspersions at press "barons" and reporters on the screen. Joy was so concerned about repercussions from the characterization of a "despicable" newspaper editor in *The Street of Chance* (Paramount Famous-Lasky, 1930) that he convinced the studio to remove the character from the script entirely.[14] In *The Front Page* (Caddo/United Artists, 1931) he was again confronted with a "rough, uncouth and unscrupulous characterization of newspapermen." On this occasion, at the suggestion of the SRC, the film's director, Lewis Milestone, held discussions with Hearst as part of the process of determining a treatment that would not bring about reprisals from the press.[15]

As part of the same cycle, Warner Bros. decided to film the newspaper story *Five Star Final* (Warner Bros., 1931), despite the fact that an MPPDA reviewer thought the property to be "exceedingly dangerous." The story concerned the salacious muckraking tactics of the *Evening Gazette*, a fictional New York tabloid. The SRC advised the studio to deflect media criticism by drawing a strong distinction between the tabloids and the respectable press: "We believe that you should make every effort to make it unmistakably clear that a tabloid is a paper quite separate and distinct from the usual paper. To do this we believe that it should be shown that the real newspapers of the city are unanimous in condemning the Gazette for its tactics. . . . This could be done by showing inserts of articles in the other papers."[16] Unfortunately for the studio, newspaper proprietors largely failed to notice this distinction, and the film was severely criticized. The *Free Press* in Ventura, California, accused the movie of painting "a viciously false and untrue picture of American journalism," and the *Press* in Binghamton, New York, echoed many other publications in claiming that "self-respecting American newspapers have been targets for what amounts to a campaign of inferential misrepresentation and vilification by the motion picture industry." In Boston, the mayor banned the showing of the film "upon the urgent insistence of the editors of the local Hearst papers."[17]

Joy tried to explain the need for tactful handling to Darryl Zanuck, producer of *The Strange Love of Molly Louvain* (Warner Bros., 1932): "As you know, the industry has been severely criticized of late by important newspaper editors and publishers for what they believe to be unfair descriptions of newspapermen. It will take very little more to tip over the cart and have some of the strongest newspapers in the country on our necks, calling for further regulation."[18] Advice to studios to revise drunken, corrupt, and/or generally derogatory characterizations of newspapermen appeared throughout the 1930s, most conspicuously in 1937, which saw a flurry of newspaper subjects.[19] Breen might have preferred that the studios drop the subject altogether, but because of the immediate profitability of newspaper properties, the PCA's influence was felt in the amelioration of negative stereotypes of editors and reporters rather than in their abandonment. In *His Girl Friday* (Columbia, 1939), a remake of *The Front Page*, the introduction of a comic love triangle decentered the theme of unscrupulous journalism that had been perceived as dangerous in the original. *Mr. Smith Goes to Washington* (Columbia, 1939), although the subject of intense negotiation, still managed to cause offense, both to the press and to the U.S. Congress.[20]

Two against the World, also known as *One Fatal Hour* (Warner Bros., 1936), illustrates the PCA's practice of inserting "compensating" elements to balance negative characterizations, in this case in the context of radio broadcasting. The story is essentially a remake of *Five Star Final* and involves a broadcaster who attracts the prurient interest of his listeners by hounding a woman who had been exonerated in a murder case twenty years previously. The investigation disrupts her life, causes her husband to lose his job, and ruins her daughter's wedding plans. Eventually she poisons herself, and her husband shoots himself. Breen told Jack Warner that he was "gravely concerned, as a matter of policy," about the movie's commentary on the ethics of the broadcasting industry.[21] Hays himself took an interest in the project and asked Breen to make sure that the treatment of the broadcasting chains was "absolutely corrected": "From what I gather of the story, it is one which will invite reprisals from the radio people—and properly so—if we present them in such a sordid and unfair light. It must be shown that there is no attack or inferential criticism of the major broadcasting chains. . . . The name of the Broadcasting chain should not be anything like United Broadcasting System (UBS) or Universal Broadcasting System, or some similar name which will carry the impression that it is a nationwide broadcasting service."[22]

Breen conferred with Bryan Foy, the movie's production supervisor, "with the object of discussing the objections and finding some means of avoiding or eliminating them."[23] As in *Five Star Final*, they adopted the strategy of differentiating between responsible and irresponsible elements in the industry, but this time they proceeded with less subtlety. Between them they devised a new sequence to be inserted into the script:

A scene will be played in the offices of an association of broadcasting chains and broadcasting stations. In the group will be a number of men, presumably representing the big broadcasting chains, and Dr. McGuire [a priest], whom we will meet earlier in the picture.

The chain representing the broadcasting stations will thank Dr. McGuire for bringing to their attention the reprehensible practices indulged in by the UBC and will put themselves on record, representing the legitimate radio stations and the national broadcasting chains, as not only opposed to such reprehensible tactics and wanting no part in them, but stating that they, themselves, will endeavor to bring the whole nasty business to the attention of the Federal Communications Commission in an attempt to have the license for the UBC stations revoked.

The point involved here is to separate the sheep from the goats—definitely to indicate that the better type, the more legitimate, broadcasting stations do not sanction any such reprehensible practices as we know the UBC to have indulged in; to condemn these practices and to lend every possible aid to prevent such practices recurring.[24]

The sequence was scripted as follows:

(A full shot in a council room. On the door are carved letters Association of Broadcasters. Five men, comprising the board of directors of the Broadcasters' Association, are seated in tall-backed leather chairs about an oval council table. Elderly businessmen who have about them that air of dignity and erudition becoming to a group of Supreme Court judges, they are listening with sympathetic attention to Dr. McGuire, who is standing. Jim Carstairs is seated alongside the doctor.)
Dr. McGuire (with righteous anger): Of all the deliberately vicious things for one man to do to another, I tell you gentlemen there has never been anything to parallel it. This man Reynolds has not the slightest shred of common decency.
(Cut to close shot, board chairman, kindly and grey. Near him sits a board

member. Both are listening to the almost impassioned doctor, expressions of wholehearted interest on their faces.)

Dr. McGuire's voice, continuing: He is using his broadcasting station for nothing more than personal gain, denying Mr. Carstairs and his wife their inalienable right to live in peace and happiness.

(At this point, the chairman and the board member look at one another. They are deeply impressed. Cut to full shot, council room, favoring Dr. McGuire and Jim Carstairs.)

Dr. McGuire, continuing: Mrs. Carstairs paid her debt to society long ago for the murder of the man who had been her husband when a jury exonerated her. Reynolds and UBC must not be allowed to persecute her any longer. It's—it's inhuman! (then quietly) That, gentlemen is my own personal appeal to you who represent all the big national broadcasting companies.

(As he sits down there is a pause—then the board chairman rises.)

Board chairman: Dr. McGuire, we have been watching Reynolds for some time. He and his kind constitute a real threat to honest broadcasting. They are known as bootleg broadcasters and operate just inside the law. We now have sufficient evidence to lay the case before the Federal Communications Commission. There can be no doubt as to the outcome—Reynolds' license will be revoked and he will be driven out of the business. As chairman of this board, I want you to know you have done us an invaluable service.

(All rise and we hear ad libs of "We've been waiting for this chance!" and "Now we've got him." The board chairman exits from the scene toward Dr. McGuire and Jim Carstairs.)[25]

A faithful version of this scene was included in the finished film. Breen was certainly the author of its outline, if not of the final text. The influence of the PCA was not, of course, acknowledged in script credits, although Breen's stamp regularly appeared on the products of the late 1930s, even when he made no direct contribution to screenplays. The influence of such characters as Hearst and Hays in the wings is less distinct but is nevertheless discernible.

Politics

Under Breen anything that could be construed as "subversive of the best interests of society" would not earn a seal.[26] In 1935 Warner Bros. succeeded in making *Black Fury,* about a strike in the coal-mining industry, but only after the studio had inserted some lines indicating that "conditions of the coal industry have vastly improved and are getting better all the time." As Breen explained, "The point here is to get in a line or two that may establish the fact that the miners have little to complain against and that Croner [a character hostile to company policy] is unjust in his criticism of the employing company."[27] Warner Bros.

In *Two against the World* (Warner Bros., 1936), radio network UBC is guilty of gutter journalism. Joseph Breen was instrumental in inserting this new scene into the movie, in which responsible broadcasters decide to report UBC to the Federal Communications Commission: "The point involved here is to separate the sheep from the goats—definitely to indicate that the better type, the more legitimate, broadcasting stations do not sanction any such reprehensible practices as we know the UBC to have indulged in."

executive Robert Lord remarked that the PCA seemed to be "extremely touchy" about the subject of capital and labor.[28] Columbia's *Mills of the Gods* (1934), which depicted industrial unrest, lost much of its virulence on the way to the screen, evolving into a "turgid family melodrama."[29] *Together We Live* (Foy Productions/Columbia, 1935) exposed some young men's involvement in a Communist-inspired strike as a "youthful mistake." The movie was only approved by the PCA after the removal of "any direct attacks on organized labor, capitalism, or constituted forces of law and order," and after it was made clear that the strike was caused by Russian agitators.[30]

The SRC and the PCA were nervous about passing such material for fear of stirring up trouble with censors, not only at home but also abroad. Revolutionary themes were judged objectionable in Spain, Sweden, and parts of China in the late 1920s, and in Japan, Italy, Iran, and Poland in the late 1930s. Greece banned any subject suggestive of revolution, including the French Revolution, throughout both decades. Turkey maintained a ban on all subjects depicting political tendencies of any kind except the broadly democratic, and in Yugoslavia the slightest hint of communism was vigorously suppressed. Warner Bros. realized that it was taking a risk in treating the subject matter of *Juárez* (1939) because of the growing tendency to ban themes of a revolutionary nature abroad.[31] Production supervisor Henry Blanke stressed to Robert Taplinger, the director of studio publicity, that the story would be built up around the central heroic figure of Juárez. Blanke may or may not have helped the situation abroad by suggesting that Juárez should be portrayed as the "Mexican Lincoln."[32] Within the United States several state censor boards, especially the New York Censor Board, deleted direct references to revolution. Hays worried about the inclusion of riot scenes in *Manhattan Melodrama* (MGM, 1934), and at Breen's insistence a scene of a socialist rally was amended to eliminate speeches about world revolution, even though the speakers were offscreen and wholly marginal to the plot. In discussions on *Oil for the Lamps of China* Breen suggested that Warner Bros. avoid mentioning the Communist revolution; then, on second thought, he decided that "it might be well not to make any reference to communism at all."[33]

Breen was concerned about the "flavor suggestive of propaganda or radicalism" in RKO's *Winterset* (1936), and he made several suggestions, including the following:

Page 63—If you can do it, we suggest that you eliminate entirely the speech of the Radical as set forth in scene 151, et seq. Of course, if this is to be played for comedy, it will be acceptable, but it is dangerous in any event.

If you use this speech, you should eliminate the expression from speech 285: "members of the proletariat" and "capitalist oppression," as well as the word "rich" in the fifth line.

Page 67—speech 297—We suggest that you eliminate the expression "tread down the poor." Possibly you could substitute: "tread down a helpless old man."

Page 68—speech 302—We suggest that you substitute the word "lunatic," or some other word, for the word "capitalist."[34]

In general it became difficult for the industry to treat political or industrial subjects in anything other than conventional terms of praise for American democracy and corporate capitalism, even when more controversial discourses were present in American culture. Jason Joy had established a precedent during the Depression whereby even outright poverty had to be treated with an eye to its political implications, as he had explained to Irving Thalberg in relation to *Tin Foil*, released as *Faithless* (MGM, 1932):

It seems to us that the moral issues involved are complicated by the current economic situation. If it is to be suggested that the depression not only has stripped the nation of its wealth but has reduced its women to going on the streets as prostitutes to obtain the bare necessities of life, then our whole national life is depicted at a low point. There would be justifiable resentment of this insinuation, particularly in view of the rather heroic efforts being made by the relief organizations, individuals, and the government itself to take care of the needy.[35]

By the mid-1930s it was clear that pointed political themes had little or no chance of reaching the screen. Sinclair Lewis' novel *It Can't Happen Here*, describing a Fascist takeover of the United States, was never filmed, even though MGM had purchased the rights for a reported sum of two hundred thousand dollars. Olga Martin commented on the fate of the property: "Representing as it did a caricature of the European conflict transferred to American soil, the story was a potential tinder-box. When the studio, which bought first and thought afterward, realized what it was juggling, and what the total destruction and loss in goodwill and other more tangible assets would amount to, if it were created, the story was shelved."[36] The pressure to circumscribe the terms of Hollywood's political discourse, arising from worldwide institutions of censorship and mediated by the MPPDA, helped to reinforce the perceived status of Hollywood movies as objects of entertainment devoid of political significance. According to Martin Quigley, editor of the *Motion Picture Herald*, movies which adopted a political stance had "nothing whatever to do with the amusement industry."[37]

The caution that adhered to the treatment of contemporary issues also helped to maintain the industry's central interest in the safely conservative subjects of love and marriage. As Thomas Elsaesser has pointed out, popular culture has characteristically "refused to understand social change in other than private contexts and emotional terms."[38] The displacement of the site of political discourse into the realm of the personal, however, was certainly reinforced in Hollywood's case by the operation of industry regulation. The only difficulty for the MPPDA in pursuing this course was that such a fine line separated romance from sex. The point at which conventional limits of sexual representation were transgressed was the point at which the personal became controversial and reentered the realm of politics. While "romance" constituted a sanctioned theme for motion picture subjects, the problem facing the industry was not so much how to remove sex from the screen as how to render it invisible.

Eroticism

The movies' discourse on sexual matters became increasingly oblique as a result of the industry's search for "vagueness and delicacy of treatment."[39] In the early 1930s the sexual consummation of a relationship could be suggested inexplicitly but unmistakably, often by the use of a discarded item of clothing combined with the suggestion of a passage of time. For example, in *The Devil Is Driving* (Paramount, 1932) the hero's hat blows out of the window of his lover's apartment when the two get into a clinch, and a dissolve reveals it kicked and battered beneath the feet of early morning pedestrians. In *Ann Vickers* (RKO, 1933) the camera follows the slide of Ann's coat to the floor as she is embraced, and then pans to the window, where the scene dissolves from evening to early morning. Such suggestions had a way of hardening into clichés with repeated use, committing producers to a quest for ever more subtle avenues of representation. In August 1933 James Wingate advised Jack Warner to modify a scene in *Bureau of Missing Persons* (Warner Bros., 1933) that was almost identical to the one in *Ann Vickers*, requesting that he introduce the fade earlier in the sequence: "This will eliminate the shot of the feet where the girl rises on her toes and where the man's hat drops into the scene."[40]

By 1934 the fade itself had become questionable. Karl Lischka of the PCA, when reporting on the script of *Evelyn Prentice* (MGM, 1934), told Breen that "[t]he affair between Evelyn and Kennard is so written that it does not necessarily imply intimacy—at least it would not if their 'fade out' on their kiss (p. 62) were omitted, and this could be omitted without harm to the story structure."[41] By the mid-1930s many obvious and not-so-obvious codes for implying sexual suggestiveness had been ruled out of bounds: in 1935 the PCA objected to a scene of rain falling on a closed door in the script of *The Devil Is a Woman* (Paramount, 1935) on the grounds that such shots "are established over many years as the set up in motion pictures for an illicit relationship."[42]

If the suggestive nature of sexual representation meant that the producers renounced responsibility for the inferences that could be drawn from the lacunae in their movies, this representational style, by granting the audience imaginative license, was also essentially erotic. The "repressed" of the movie was available to return as expression in the minds of the viewers. The implications of this process were not entirely lost on the production personnel who had to work within the constraints of the system. When self-regulation first began to be exercised through the medium of the SRC, some elements within the industry were violently opposed to it on the grounds that it would place their work in an imaginative straitjacket.[43] Others, like screenwriter Paul Bern, however, considered that the disciplines involved in self-regulation could have powerfully erotic implications:

The restraints are not necessarily harmful. The fade out is often much more effective and naughtier in suggestion that the full scene would be if played through. Ernst Lubitsch . . . in his "Marriage Circle" and "Forbidden Paradise" through the fade out and by suggestion and innuendo, titillates the audience by making them think they see things in a way that gives them much more pleasure than if they actually saw them. What I mean is the innuendo of a scene in which you see two characters kissing, the door closing and the picture fading out slowly—and you all begin to think about what is happening behind the closed door.[44]

Under Breen, the erotic collusion between audience and text became less overt. In sexual comedies the knowing wink of Maurice Chevalier or Mae West was supplanted by the apparent innocence of the world of screwball comedy, or perhaps even displaced into the precocious performances of Shirley Temple.[45] The audience was left to take full responsibility for its own sophisticated response. Carole Lombard in *My Man Godfrey* (Universal, 1936) and Katharine Hepburn and Cary Grant in *Bringing Up Baby* (RKO, 1938) were innocent inhabitants of a movie universe in which sexuality was so thoroughly identified with naïveté that one hardly ever occurred without the other.[46] The stars' glamorous personae were essential ingredients of this world: glamour, in both its onscreen and offscreen manifestations, represented the sublimation of public sexuality into a "pure," safely delimited, and consumable form.[47]

The part the PCA played in promoting the complex innocence of Hollywood's cinematic universe is exemplified by its contact with RKO during the preparation of its 1939 comedy *Bachelor Mother.* The movie is built around an absurd misunderstanding that leads everyone to imagine that a young single woman, Polly Parrish (Ginger Rogers), is the mother of a baby whom she has actually found abandoned on the doorstep of an orphanage. She is unable to convince anyone that the baby is not hers, and when her boss's son, David Merlin (David Niven), becomes involved in the case, she is obliged to assume the role of the baby's mother in order to keep her job as a salesgirl in Merlin's Department Store. As the action progresses, the baby proves to be irresistible. Instead of having too few claimants, now it has too many. David's fa ther, J. B. Merlin (Charles Coburn), decides to adopt the baby in the mistaken belief that it is his grandson, and Polly decides she cannot part with it. While a romance develops between Polly and David, the plot moves through a compounding series of misunderstandings about the baby's paternity. The absurdity of the whole situation, and of the movie's consistent failure to recognize the usual mechanics of parenthood, culminates in a pronouncement by J. B. Merlin that "I don't care *who* the father is—I'm the grandfather!" When in the end David and Polly decide to get married, David still believes that the virginal Polly is the baby's natural mother.

Much of the movie's humor stems from its several layers of sexual suggestiveness, but none of these implications dawn upon the characters themselves. Polly's main concern is how she will continue to earn a living, not her sudden acquisition of the status of an unmarried mother. David earnestly tries to sort out the situation on a practical basis, even when it becomes clear that he is widely assumed to be the baby's father (which, given his supposedly libertine background, might be a possibility, although the movie does not pursue it).

The file of correspondence between the PCA and the studio demonstrates that Breen and his staff played an active role in defining the appealing naïveté of the central characterizations. For example, in relation to a scene in which a social worker informs David of Polly's abandonment of the baby, Breen warned RKO that "there should be no comedy suggesting that David's apprehension is based on the fear that he is the father of an illegitimate child." At the point when the social worker stresses that Polly is Miss and not Mrs. Parrish, Breen insisted that there should be no indication "*through David's reaction*" (his emphasis) that this was "a comedy play upon a suggestive situation." He applied the same stricture to a sequence in which David's father engineers a meeting with David and Polly in a park in order to see the baby, whom, unbeknownst to them, he assumes to be his grandson. The central comedy of the situation is never made overt, and Polly and David remain innocent of J.B.'s subtextual motives until the final moments of the scene. Even then nothing is directly articulated: as J.B. leaves, the two look at each other in sudden apprehension, Polly laughs, and David runs after his father. In relation to a similar scene in which David chats with a colleague of Polly's, unaware that the man believes him to be the father of Polly's baby, Breen expressly advised RKO that "we recommend that this material be read perfectly straight."[48] The *New York Times* reviewer greatly enjoyed the resulting performance style, characteristically choosing to attribute its formulation entirely to the director, Garson Kanin: "Mr. Kanin has wisely kept his cast in check and, having a wise cast, has seen that the audience enjoys the joke alone. The spectacle of Miss Rogers and David Niven struggling forlornly to prove their innocence of parenthood and winning no credence at all is made triply hilarious by the sobriety of their performance, and by the diabolic plausibility of the circumstantial web enmeshing them."[49]

The change undergone by the movie's tag line is typical of the influence of the PCA on the production. Originally the final exchange between Polly and David, in which they discuss their marriage, ended with the line "And have I got a surprise for you!" When Breen saw this in the script, he pointed out that it was "open to objectionable interpretation" and requested that it be deleted or changed. However, the line was still in the movie when it was shown to a preview audience in June 1939. The audience found the joke to be very funny—perhaps too funny. *Variety* claimed that it was "one of the greatest film tag lines ever heard for adults."[50] Breen held fast to his opinion that the line was offensively suggestive and refused to issue a seal to the picture until something was done about it. The studio considered appealing to the MPPDA Board of Directors but eventually decided to substitute a new ending. The version that received general release contains the original build-up—"So you still think I'm the mother of that baby?" "Of course!"—but the tag line is replaced with a little ironic laugh by Polly. She has used the same laugh earlier in the movie in response to David's naive confidence that his father's shop would issue a refund for a broken toy. By escaping articulation, the joke becomes unassailable. The tone of the laugh is also important: it indicates a private joke, as opposed to the public invitation to interpretation contained in the original line. Like the movie as a whole, it refuses public acknowledgment of its own implications.

The self-contained "innocence" of the world of *Bachelor Mother* represents a logical outcome of Classical Hollywood's ambition to satisfy audiences which varied widely in age and experience. In the late 1920s Joy's principle of deniability was applied to individual incidents and episodes, but in this case the entire movie works on two levels at once, with the virginal unmarried mother and the moralistic libertine enmeshed in a set of sexually suggestive situations which they consistently fail to recognize. The distance maintained between their misrecognitions and our own "sophisticated" knowledge of their situation permeates the whole movie with a light sense of dramatic irony.

A governing ironic principle can be seen as a more general characteristic of Hollywood movies produced in the late 1930s. As was especially noticeable in contemporary settings, cinematic reality differed

from the everyday in predictable and consistent ways, from the inevi-
tability of moral resolution to the reliable absence of toilets and pregnant women. Because under the PCA this system of codes and ab-
sences was applied not to individual texts but to the whole body of
the industry's output, the Hollywood universe was established as a
conventionalized arena with its own internal set of logical processes
and outcomes. The palpable mismatch between this set of realities
and the reality inhabited by audiences outside the cinema underlined
the status of the movies as constructed objects of entertainment. By
maintaining a conventionalized aesthetic distance between viewer
and text, this system of representation always left the door ajar to
sophisticated readings arising from the ironic recognition of the contract between movie and audience.

Exoticism

Irony also permeated Hollywood's representation of exotic locations.
By the mid-1930s the movies themselves often made elaborate denials
that they bore any relationship to the geopolitical sphere whatsoever,
largely as a result of repeated foreign protests. Yet such denials did not
merit much credence, especially to a mode of interpretation dependent
on reading beyond the evidence presented on the screen. Spurious
disclaimers were part of the language of the movies, as exemplified by
the preface that preceded *British Agent,* which was based on a "true"
book by Bruce Lockhart, detailing his experiences as a British diplomat
in Moscow: "This picture was made purely as entertainment and in no
wise does it purport to be a political or historical document. It is not
intended as a true picture of the times and the persons and characters
portrayed are entirely fictitious." Hays claimed that the reason for the
frequent choice of foreign locations—although they were usually
filmed on studio back lots—was that "producers felt that an occasional
character from a 'foreign' nation added contrast and color to a story
filled with Americans."[51] In other words, producers had no interest in
portraying foreign locations or societies authentically. The question of
"realism" was never at issue, and the industry was merely engaged in a
quest for the picturesque.

The geographic and/or temporal removal of plots from contemporary American contexts was also encouraged by the fact that certain
aspects of domestic censorship were sometimes relaxed when the action took place in fantastic settings. The National Board of Censorship
set a precedent for this in the early silent era when it exempted frontier pictures from conforming to its usual standards: "[The] board will

Ethnic and cultural stereotypes help to establish an air of the exotic in *Morocco* (Paramount, 1932).

not tolerate the rough handling of women and children except where
the life depicted is undoubtedly pioneer. . . . Under normal conditions, it will not pass pictures which show the successful balking of
the law. Some latitude should be shown perhaps to pictures of the
'wild and woolly' variety where next to impossible deeds are pictured. The conditions are such that the motion-picture patron would
find it impossible to duplicate them, and the whole action takes place
in an atmosphere of rough romance."[52] To escape censorship, producers had an interest in investing their foreign and historical locations
with "rough romance," regardless of the sociological reality. The practice of social displacement most obviously encouraged the production
of westerns but was also expressed in the adoption of foreign locations: *Her Man* (Pathé, 1930), for example, was moved "Cubawards"
to avoid U.S. censorship difficulties.[53]

The problem with overtly equating Hollywood's idea of the foreign
with any actual political or historical entity surfaced early in the history
of the SRC. Joy predicted trouble with the United Artists production of
The Bad One in 1930: "In considering the French attitude: We believe

Never mind the romance: the thing that was likely to offend Spain in this scene from *Call of the Flesh* (MGM, 1930) was the open drain.

there will be serious objection to the manner in which the modern port city of Marseillaise [*sic*] is pictured. The impression given is that it is an unkempt city, full of narrow and dirty streets, architecture of the middle ages, and populated mostly by smocked peasants."[54] This was exactly the kind of characterization which caused most offense in Europe, Mexico, and South America, partly because of its outright inaccuracy and presumably also because of the negative message it conveyed to potential investors and trading partners. Unfortunately, it also represented one of the notions of the "foreign" that appealed most strongly to American filmmakers.

The adoption of fictional foreign locales seemed to offer a painless way out of the impasse. Olga Martin proposed this as an unproblematic solution in her guide for scriptwriters: "Unless the political story pays tribute to a foreign nation in some way, Hollywood does not attempt to use an existent political entity. A mythical kingdom is used instead."[55] The ploy of the mythical kingdom operated much like the industry's treatment of sex, however, in the sense that it rendered the object of foreign sensitivity invulnerable to objection without necessarily making it go away. As noted in chapter 4, mythical locations were rarely completely unattributable, since they were usually built on recognizable cultural stereotypes, even when these were not openly acknowledged in the movies themselves. It is arguable that such stratagems exaggerated the problem of cultural offense rather than alleviating it, since they licensed filmmakers to exercise their most extreme prejudices with little fear of effective protest.

As early as 1934 director Ernst Lubitsch burlesqued the cliché of the fairy-tale European kingdom in the opulent musical comedy *The Merry Widow* (MGM, 1934). The movie begins with a standard establishing shot of a map of Europe, but a magnifying glass has to be introduced to the shot in order to bring into focus the tiny kingdom of Marshovia, sandwiched between Hungary and Romania. Marshovia itself is a quaint, underdeveloped, self-important nineteenth-century European nation-state in which Lubitsch parodies Hollywood's notion of the European exotic. The standard European stereotypes of a hierarchical aristocracy and a bucolic peasantry are overlaid in absurd combinations in the decor: the royal palace, and even the royal bed, are adorned with elaborate sculptures of sheep and horses, reflecting the agricultural basis of Marshovia's economy. But the action, which revolves around the sexual adventures of libertine Count Danilo (Maurice Chevalier) and his romance with a wealthy Marshovian widow, Sonia (Jeanette Macdonald), is not confined to Marshovia. Danilo is obliged to go to Paris on a mission to seduce Sonia back to the kingdom. Through this maneuver, "real" European culture and history is implicated in the satiric vision of the movie, albeit in lighthearted and usually ridiculous terms.

A French-language version (*La veuve joyeuse*), also starring Chevalier and Macdonald but featuring different minor actors, was shot alongside the English version. Although only the two languages were used, the foreign material was sufficiently sensitive for four different cuts of the film to be prepared, for distribution in the American, French, British, and Belgian markets. According to *Variety*, certain scenes in the film were "emphasized for the English speaking audience and others played down for foreign consumption."[56] The movie's budget of nearly two million dollars certainly justified the extra care, but the need for the different versions reflects the fact that "mythical kingdoms" could not easily be divorced from the sociopolitical sphere.

The Merry Widow's action and dialogue are rife with sexual overtones, to the extent that it tested the bounds of permissible treatment in

In the musical comedy *The Merry Widow* (MGM, 1934), director Ernst Lubitsch (pictured here on the set with Una Merkel) burlesqued the conventional "mythical kingdom" ploy, with his high-camp version of the bucolic European kingdom of Marshovia. He used the same ironic approach to defuse some of the sexual suggestiveness inherent in the dialogue and action by making his protagonists innocents abroad in a fairy-tale world.

1934. Following a spate of protests, the movie had to be recalled from circulation on its original release and modified by the PCA. Breen concluded that the movie should be made more naively frivolous to negate any "offensively suggestive" implications. He assured Will Hays that reducing the wanton, knowing aspects of Danilo's characterization would make him "a more attractive character to mass audiences and less sophisticated perhaps than those which are now viewing the picture on Broadway."[57] Even with the extra cuts, the movie flirted with "rejectionable" material, but it managed to escape further censure partly because some of its import was abstracted in songs, and partly because the sexual situations were handled with the same sense of parodic self-consciousness that characterized the settings. Because the action was framed in the artificially picturesque environment of a child's fairy tale, it was characterized by an absurdly heightened version of the "innocence" that routinely rendered movies safe for general distribution. As in the case of *Bachelor Mother*, Breen's interventions only served to heighten the comic tension between what was stated and what was implied. A recognition of the exigencies of the Production Code and "industry policy" was available to audiences at both textual and subtextual levels.

Only Angels Have Wings (Columbia, 1939) contains a more routine example of the way cinematic mythical kingdoms were deployed, although it takes itself only slightly more seriously. Its nominal location, "Barranca," is a South American diplomat's nightmare. The setting is literally rendered as a banana republic, with Barranca's fullest geographic and political description occurring in a title which declares it to be a "port of call for the South American banana boats." The establishing shots show a night scene of a crowded wharf bustling with peasants, children, dogs, donkeys, ducks, and loads of bananas. Bonnie Lee (Jean Arthur) descends from a boat to experience the local color and discovers the natives, who for some reason are holding an impromptu song and dance in the middle of an operating port, to be charming and musical. Nevertheless, she is outraged when approached by two young men (Allyn Joslyn and Noah Beery, Jr.), until she discovers that they are Americans. She exclaims, "Why, I thought you were a couple of—!" (Perhaps "Barrancans" would have sounded too ridiculous.) "It sure sounds good to hear something that doesn't sound like pig-latin," she tells them. The party is nearly run over by a quaint-looking vehicle mounted on rails, driven by hat-waving locals, blasting its horn, and pursued by cheering children. "What was that?" asks Bonnie. "Fifth Avenue bus line," reply her companions. They take her through more throngs of banana-toting natives to meet Dutchy, the "postmaster and leading banker of Barranca."

There is clearly an element of conscious artifice in all this; the movie proclaims itself to be an adventure yarn and revels in its own fictional status. Barranca is therefore identified as a wholly imaginary location—or is it? When Edgar Dale analyzed the content of motion pictures in 1935, he distinguished those pictures set in "foreign locales" from those set in "imaginary" settings. In the "foreign" category he included a "quite adequate presentation of Orambo, a little, hot, dreary town some place on the coast of South America."[58] To this extent *Only Angels Have Wings* is South American too. In his auteurist study of Howard Hawks, Robin Wood does not hesitate to claim that "the opening shots vividly create Barranca, the South American town in which the film is set."[59] At a certain level the movie's denials fail, and Barranca proclaims the ethnic, cultural, and economic superiority

In the banana republic of Barranca, Bonnie Lee (Jean Arthur) sorts the Americans from the foreigners in *Only Angels Have Wings* (Columbia, 1939).

of the United States. The plot claims to be uninterested in any of these issues, even though the "Maguffin" which motivates much of the action is the securing of South American airline contracts, reflecting the contemporary corporate colonialism of American carriers such as TWA. More generally, cultural offense persists on the level of performance and decor, as it did in *Woman Trap*—in the characterizations of the natives, in the easy sexuality of the local girls, and in the ubiquitous bananas.

Both *The Merry Widow* and *Only Angels Have Wings* insist on the quintessentially picturesque nature of the foreign. As a port, Barranca bears a remarkable similarity to the version of Marseilles contained in *The Bad One*, but with a South American accent: the peasants wear broad-brimmed hats instead of smocks. The mythical kingdom was not an empty signifier; rather, it contained a quaint exoticism of its own which could be equally brought to bear on regional representations as diverse as Europe or South America—a condition encouraged by the fact that most foreign subjects were shot on the same studio lots. As a result, although "foreign" locations were dressed differently, they often shared similar qualities of the picturesque. Since foreigners' national origins were deliberately obscured, the population of Hollywood's universe came to be broadly comprised of "Americans" and "others."

This divide is highlighted by contradictions that characterize movies featuring nominally "foreign" protagonists. In *Blockade* (Walter Wanger Productions/United Artists, 1938), Henry Fonda plays Marco, a Spanish peasant. Unlike General Fang in *West of Shanghai* or Ramirez in *Woman Trap*, Marco is a sympathetic character with whom the audience is intended to identify. Consequently, while his costume is "foreign," his performance, and indeed his character, are not. Unlike his compatriot Luis, who speaks with a heavy accent, Marco expresses himself eloquently in standard American English. There is an odd exchange in the movie when a visiting American woman, Norma (Madeleine Carroll), comments that her father used to sing Spanish peasant songs. Marco protests, "But you're a foreigner!" She and he, who literally speak the same language, are in fact equally "American." The peasant Luis and Norma's father—who also speaks with a strong accent and wears a beard to boot—are the real foreigners on the level of performance.

If a single factor distinguished Hollywood's amorphously drawn cinematic foreigners from each other in the 1930s, it was less nationality or ethnicity than class. As *The Merry Widow* recognized, foreign civilians were typically either peasants or members of an aristocratic elite. While similar distinctions existed between working-class and upper-class American characters, the screen also had room for a confident and prominent middle class that was overwhelmingly an American preserve. Despite the fact that Henry Fonda's character in *Blockade* professes to be enamored of the peasant life, he is no peasant at heart: unlike the indolent Luis, he uses chemical fertilizers on his fields, plans to buy a tractor, and looks forward to a future of material prosperity. In Hollywood's world, middle-class aspirations, especially as defined by consumerist behavior, were the norm even when (or especially when) the action took place in a lower-class or ethnically distinct community. The struggle to achieve affluence against the odds was a particularly heroic cinematic enterprise. The aspiration toward a consumerist utopia was certainly not confined to Americans, but the image-oriented, materially based vision that it implied was associated with American culture wherever it occurred, whether it was celebrated or reviled.[60]

If Hollywood's vision was essentially middle-class, consumerist, and "American," then the aristocracy, the working class, and the "foreign" all constituted aspects of the screen's exotica. They represented alien cultures whose mores and customs were objects of fascination precisely because they were mysterious. In this context the exotic was closely related to the erotic, especially in the 1920s and early 1930s: the drunken, tattooed cinematic sailor and the lower-class "floozy" were both characterized by sexual excess, but so were the sophisticated and moneyed "fast set" and the European aristocrats with whom they were frequently identified. These characters' behavior, particularly their sexual behavior, was presumed to exceed middle-class convention and was therefore perceived to be open to limitless erotic possibilities, for better or worse. Foreigners, whether they were peasantry or aristocracy, were particularly liable to be eroticized through the implication that they operated according to alien and unknowable sociosexual norms.[61] This contributed to the air of dangerously heightened sensuality associated with performers like Marlene Dietrich and Greta Garbo, whose intensity of desire seemed to know no limits on the screen. Their "foreign" personal credentials featured prominently in their publicity and were easily carried over to their onscreen personae.

The erotic potential of these "alien" characterizations was particularly potent when a role was distinguished by *both* class and ethnicity. Many of Garbo and Dietrich's roles were as either prostitutes— Dietrich in *Blonde Venus* (Paramount, 1932) and *The Devil Is a Woman* (Paramount, 1935), Garbo in *Anna Christie* (MGM, 1930) and *Susan Lennox (Her Fall and Rise)* (MGM, 1931)—or royalty—Dietrich in *The Scarlet Empress* (Paramount, 1934), Garbo in *Queen Christina* (MGM, 1934). In *Madame Du Barry* (Warner Bros., 1934) Dolores Del Rio plays both a lower-class courtesan and a lady of the French court in the same role. Similarly, in *As You Desire Me* (MGM, 1931), Garbo is simultaneously the prostitute Zara and the countess Maria Varelli. The most sensational male example of this phenomenon is Rudolph Valentino, who was the quintessential object of desire for millions of women around the world in the silent period. In *The Sheik* (Famous Players–Lasky/ Paramount, 1921) Valentino, himself an Italian immigrant, plays an Arab sheik who threatens to rape his female captive. At the end of the movie he is revealed to be "really" an English aristocrat, and the reconciled pair depart on their honeymoon. Thus in the one performance Valentino manages to combine the various frissons of untamed lower-class/immigrant masculinity, unrestrained (or, in practice, barely restrained) "ethnic" sexual potency, and the aestheticized sensuality of the aristocratic upper class. Miriam Hansen has written of Valentino's "exotic eroticism": for his female audience, he was "the exotic-aristocratic male other" who combined "barbaric masculinity with romantic passion."[62]

The introduction of sound made such overdetermined performances less feasible by forcing actors to commit themselves vocally to one level of characterization or another. It became much more difficult to be credibly both aristocratic and barbaric in the same breath, and the potent mixture of elements that had made movies like *The Sheik* so attractive was lost. The Eastern/European/Latin lover largely disappeared in the 1930s. Ricardo Cortez, who had been groomed by Paramount as a Latin lover in the Valentino mold in the 1920s, continued his career in the sound era but less as an object of erotic fascination than as a journeyman performer in B pictures. Maurice Chevalier was one of the few linguistically distinct romantic male leads in the early 1930s, and his roles were confined to musical comedy. Female leads with foreign accents could make the transition to sound with fewer problems; their class status was less absolute, as cinematic women could "marry up" or fall from grace with relative ease. Given the incoherence inherent in the representations of women that were abroad more generally in Western society, the erotic dichotomy between exalted and debased characterizations in female roles could be maintained with a less evident sense of contradiction. The additional factor of an exotic European background simply added to the characters' allure.

With the exception of English actors such as Leslie Howard and David Niven, both male and female leads of patently foreign origin became more scarce as the 1930s wore on. Charles Boyer was an exception, but far from reprising Valentino's steamy sexuality, he epitomized sophisticated Gallic charm. Ingrid Bergman, who was Garbo's nearest successor, did not play in her first American movie, *Intermezzo, a Love Story* (Selznick International/United Artists), until 1939. Austrian Hedy Lamarr arrived in Hollywood to much publicity in 1938, but the asexual Norwegian ice skater Sonja Henie was the only foreign female star of any note in the late 1930s. In general, in line with the general effacement of ethnic difference on the screen, the exotic became less erotic throughout the decade, and correspondingly less central to Hollywood's obsessions. Bonnie Lee goes to Barranca to find romance in *Only Angels Have Wings*, but the object of her desire turns out to be not a Barrancan but Cary Grant.

The System under Fire

July 1938 saw the institution of a federal antitrust suit against all the major motion picture companies. The Paramount Suit eventually led to a wholesale reorganization of the industry, when in 1948 the producing companies were ordered to divest themselves of their distribution and exhibition branches.[63] This was the result that the organized industry had feared most, since its vertical organization was at the basis of its exclusivity and underpinned all of its business practices. The industry was *built* on a restraint of trade and so was always vulnerable to charges of monopolistic practices.[64] Charges had already been brought against Famous Players–Lasky in 1921 and against Paramount in 1927 by the Federal Trade Commission. In 1938 the charge was widened beyond the industry's industrial and economic practices to include its regulation of motion picture content. Specifically, it complained: "There is no opportunity for new forms of artistic expression which are not approved by those in control of the major companies, even though there exist communities which would support them."[65]

This charge implied a criticism less of "forms" per se than of themes. With war brewing in Europe, there was widespread concern that the political response of the motion picture industry would be determined by the political attitudes of the few key men in the industry. Freedom of political expression was already a matter of debate within American society. *Blockade* had made comparatively discreet reference to the Spanish Civil War, but it still inflamed passions on all sides, with loyalist sympathizers complaining that it was unduly censored, and a Catholic contingent headed by the Knights of Columbus arguing that it should never have been released at all.[66] In 1937 Judge Louis E. Levinthal overturned a decision of the Pennsylvania State Board of Censors to suppress a feature-length film called *Spain in Flames* (Agencies of the Spanish and Russian governments/Amkino, 1937) on the grounds that it could properly be considered a documentary. The film incorporated Spanish and Soviet newsreels and had a commentary by Ernest Hemingway and Archibald MacLeish; the judge found that its content was "timely and of continuing interest, since the Spanish rebellion is still current."[67] On the other hand, if the movie had been classified as a feature, the cuts would presumably have been allowed to stand.

A rather more emphatic ruling against the same Pennsylvania board was delivered by Judge P. J. Bok in December 1937, when he overruled a ban on a Russian docudrama, *Baltic Deputy* (Lenfilm/Amkino, 1937). The movie concerned the life of a Russian scientist named Timiriazev and his conversion to Bolshevism. Judge Bok used the occasion of his ruling to rebuke the board: "[W]e do not regard the present attitude of Pennsylvanians toward Communism as sufficiently enthusiastic to warrant the assertion that a local or national emergency exists which justifies the suppression of the picture. Only such a condition would, in our opinion, permit the Censors to extend the definition of 'immoral' to include a controversial subject unrelated to a matter of public decency. Without it, the power of censorship is unbridled if we allow it to roam at large in the field of 'mores' or custom, whether economic, political, social or philosophic." He responded scathingly to the board's assumption that anything pertaining to the Russian Revolution should automatically be banned from view: "According to the Censors, a revolution by Communists is objectionable whereas a revolution against Communists would not be: a bitter attack against government in Russia is immoral, but one in France is not immoral because France and Russia are different countries. It is difficult to decide a law case on stuff and nonsense like this."[68]

It was possible to argue that if the state censors were susceptible to criticism of this type, then it was hardly supportable for the PCA to recommend deletion of political material on the grounds that it would be vulnerable to subsequent censorship action. Critics of the screen could maintain that conservatism on this level constituted an intolerable restriction of expression when the MPPDA controlled access to almost every regular site of exhibition in the country. Even more susceptible to criticism was the notion that the material on American screens should respond to pressures from foreign "dictators" in line with the MPPDA's usual policy of motion picture appeasement. The whole idea of "industry policy" was drawn into question, since its basis was the accommodation of influences arising from powerful interest groups. Because industry policy did not exist as a charter and therefore was unavailable for public scrutiny, it was open to criticism as a conspiratorial and prejudicial aspect of PCA activity. Hitherto neither Joy nor Breen had seen any difficulty in ideologically scrutinizing movies before issuing them with a seal. Now the problem confronting Hays was that the very mechanisms that had been instituted to avoid adverse public reaction to the industry threatened to provide its critics with the ammunition to attack its most vulnerable flank: its restraint of trade through oligopolist control.

Hays enlisted his chief vice president, Francis S. Harmon, to look into the problem and find out whether the advice emanating from the PCA unnecessarily laid the MPPDA open to criticism. Harmon carried out an audit of the opinions handed down by the PCA between 1 March and 10 March 1938. He found that during that period the PCA wrote 110 advisory letters to the studios. Seventy-two of these contained routine approvals of scripts, lyrics, or completed pictures, while eight letters requested changes to be made under the Production Code. The remaining thirty letters, which involved advice stemming from industry policy or known censorship standards, contained seventy references to censorship, compared with only thirty-eight items that were

questioned under the Code. In the majority of instances where censorship was invoked, it was merely brought to the studio's attention as a
potential risk, but in sixteen cases changes were actually requested "to
avoid political censor cuts."[69] Harmon reported the matters of industry
policy that featured in these opinions as follows:

> Proposed characterization of Thomas E. Dewey (1 letter)
> Rejection of advertising film by PCA (2 letters)
> Association of negroes and whites in same sequence and probability of
> southern objection thereto (1 letter)
> Portrayal of South American Revolution and use of U.S. Marines in connec-
> tion therewith (1 letter)
> Incidental policy questions including one reference to President Roosevelt,
> one reference to former U.S. Senator, one characterization of an existing U.S.
> Senator as being involved in the sale of munitions to foreign countries, one
> reference to the Appropriations Committee of the House of Representatives in
> 1914, one reference to Boy Scouts, one to lodge uniforms, and one to Pan-
> American Airways, one to Los Angeles, one to New York, and three to the
> cooperation extended by the United States Navy in connection with certain
> scripts in pictures.[70]

This analysis confirmed that the PCA was monitoring a much wider
range of issues than those strictly governed by the Code. Breen argued
that the PCA had the responsibility to advise producers "that a proposed course of action, while it may prove financially profitable, may
bring in its train results which are not felt to be for the best interests of
the organized industry."[71] However, Harmon recognized that the statistics could support the accusation that the MPPDA was exceeding its
jurisdiction and unreasonably restricting the freedom of the screen. He
recommended that henceforth a clear distinction should be maintained
between the administrative and advisory functions of the PCA. Hays
passed on Harmon's conclusions to Breen in a memo titled "Advisory
Function of the PCA": "If something is objectionable under the Code it
should be omitted on that basis, without invoking political censorship.
Where no Code violation is involved but deletion is possible or certain
the producer should be so advised without recommending or requesting that the change be made. Policy matters should also be raised without the PCA making specific requests. Policy and Code matters should
be dealt with in separate letters."[72]

Breen's strength in the early 1930s had been his propensity to lay
down the law to the producers. His definite notions about the bounds
of representation and his blunt personal style had contrasted favorably,
in the eyes of the concerned public, with Joy's attitude of compromise
and negotiation. Company executives in the East had been relieved to

have a West Coast agency to take issue with producers over major causes of offense that would otherwise jeopardize the smooth distribution of their products. Now that circumstances had changed, some aspects of Breen's approach began to be represented as liabilities. He told Hays, "You may want to consider further this phase of the problem, before setting down any definite regulations regarding it. The studio executives, I am certain, will want no change whatever in the present procedure. They will want us to urge upon their producers, *as vigorously as possible,* the elimination of material, which is likely to be deleted pretty generally by censor boards, irrespective of how the *letters,* carrying those recommendations, may read to people not concerned with the problem of making motion pictures."[73] In fact, the plan to deliver Code and advisory opinions in separate letters seems not to have been consistently adopted, since letters were certainly sent in 1939 that combined the two functions. Nevertheless, with Breen's position comparatively weakened, Harmon seems to have gained the upper hand in the internal politics of the MPPDA.[74]

At a meeting with Carl Milliken and Ray Norr in June 1938, Harmon drafted a statement of "General Policy" which declared in part: "If the film deals with a controversial subject, but is free from that which offends decency or is listed in the Code as morally objectionable, then the sole remaining question to be decided by the PCA should not be whether the film is 'desirable' but whether the presentation deals fairly and honestly, and without deliberate deception, with the subject matter."[75] Breen, who was away at the time of the meeting, later approved the draft, with the removal of the phrase "fairly and honestly," which he felt was so vague as to be meaningless. His personal feelings about the situation come through clearly in his response to a complaint from Samuel Goldwyn about *Boy Meets Girl* (Warner Bros., 1938):

> In accordance with your request, I have seen the Warner picture, *Boy Meets Girl,* and I am sending this to let you have my reaction to it.
>
> It is my considered judgment that this screenplay is in conformity with the provisions of the Production Code. Because of this, our certificate of approval was issued.
>
> You understand, I think, that we, of the Production Code Administration, have no authority in passing judgment on motion pictures submitted for our approval, to go beyond the provisions set forth in the Code. This means that we have no authority to venture any judgment as to whether or not a picture acceptable under the Code is acceptable, or unacceptable, on *other grounds*—the grounds, for instance, of general industry good and welfare. We have no authority to refuse approval of a picture—acceptable under the Code—on the theory that it might do injury to this, or any other, industry.

Consequently, in our judgment of *Boy Meets Girl*, we confined ourselves solely to our responsibility under the Production Code. We agree that the picture is in accordance with the provisions of the Production Code, and thus, having no further responsibility in the matter, issued the certificate of approval.

I have my personal viewpoint regarding the general advisability of producing a picture dealing with the general subject of *Boy Meets Girl*, but inasmuch as my personal opinion in such matters is of little importance, I withhold giving expression to it to you.[76]

Breen left the PCA, disaffected, in 1941, only to return to the job the following year.[77] But before the new regime could have much influence at the level of production, Hollywood was overtaken by external events. The onset of war in Europe in 1939 had thrown the foreign market into disarray. The U.S. Department of Commerce remained optimistic that the industry would retain its global dimension through the application of "sound business principles, with a shrewd, judicious appraisal of world psychology and world-outlook," as indeed it had through the Depression and the introduction of sound, but the studios prepared to reorganize their business practices in the face of expected foreign losses.[78] In the event, the war transformed the foreign situation in ways that no one could have foretold in 1939. The industry forged conspicuous new links with the State Department, and as revenues from Latin America increased, offsetting losses in Europe, Hollywood cooperated closely with the Office of Inter-American Affairs, adopting a new, high-profile role in ideological promotion.[79]

War-related developments brought powerful new factors into play in the industry's balancing act of social, diplomatic, and economic factors, and postwar conditions eventually rendered the system unworkable. The evolution of motion picture self-regulation into the complex forms of the late 1930s had depended on the relatively stable framework provided by the cooperative operation of large, vertically integrated companies. When Hollywood entered peacetime in 1945, in the "soundest financial condition in its history," its industrial disruption by the Supreme Court's ruling on the Paramount Suit lay only three years away.[80]

Conclusion

Since Hollywood was the most visible, and arguably the most influential, cultural institution on earth between the world wars, an understanding of its particular vision of the world constitutes a vital part of the cultural history of the twentieth century. In this book I have sought to contribute to that understanding, less by offering an interpretation of Hollywood's world than by trying to account for it, exploring the specific historical and industrial factors that informed the Classical Hollywood system of production. This account suggests that at several levels distribution strategies determined production policies.

Axiomatic to Hollywood's phenomenal international success was the close interdependence that existed between its production, distribution, and exhibition wings after its period of consolidation in the late 1910s and early 1920s. Clearly, vertical integration gave the largest companies a huge economic advantage, and a barely legal one at that, but the consequences for the American cinema were more far-reaching than the exclusion of market competition. Where production and distribution were combined under one management, the activities of the West Coast studios could be constantly informed by the exigencies of distribution, both global and domestic, as orchestrated from New York. With the MPPDA acting as a mediating agency, pressures arising from the marketplace could be assimilated swiftly into the production process. Hollywood's themes, its treatments, its casting choices, and, indeed, its filmic style were all shaped by the demands of unclassified exhibition and wide-scale distribution. The movies were uniquely designed for "vertical" consumption across barriers of age, experience, and predilection in a single site of exhibition, and "horizontal" consumption across widely diverse geographic and cultural territories.

The regulation of the motion picture industry has often been understood in relation to the sexual and criminal taboos that chiefly constitute the Production Code. This study demonstrates that, while these subjects were always prominent among the industry's public relations concerns, the range of subjects that came under regular scrutiny was much broader. The SRC and the PCA tried to limit offense wherever it could rebound on the industry, and producers were cautioned about political and industrial matters as well as strictures arising from the international arena, all under the rubric of "industry policy." The demands of official censor boards strongly informed the operations of industry regulation, but they were part of a wider pattern of institutional influence that included pressure from professional and business organizations, as well as from government administrations.

A notable consequence of distribution and exhibition pressures was the formulation of "open" texts which were amenable to a variety of different readings—a consequence in marked contrast to the reputedly censorious functions of the PCA. Ambiguous treatments offering a choice of interpretations helped to compensate for the movies' loss of flexibility after the introduction of sound and also facilitated their continued consumption by widely heterogeneous audiences. Subjects vulnerable to objection, while occasionally abandoned, were more often rendered sufficiently cryptic to defray hostile analysis, or displaced into forms that roundly declared their own fictional status, such as screwball comedies or "fantasies" set in mythical kingdoms.

Although it was a cornerstone of the industry's public relations policy that all its products should be rendered "fit" for general consumption at home and free from international offense, individual pictures were not necessarily exhibited everywhere. Most overseas markets were selective in their choice of films, and the American market was itself fragmentary.[1] Movies did not receive uniform distribution within the United States any more than they did abroad. A film's expected field of distribution had a significant effect on the way in which it was handled during production, with expensive movies needing to be more scrupulously prepared to meet the needs of the whole market. On the other hand, it cannot be assumed that a decrease in capital investment necessarily implied the restriction of a movie's release to the domestic field: the very cheapest pictures, the action westerns and adventure serials, were consistently popular with the nonliterate and non-English-speaking sections of the foreign market, as well as with nonmetropolitan audiences in the United States.[2]

To avoid the threat of governmental regulation, censorship, or public protests, the industry tried to ensure that its products were free from political and social contentiousness. This encouraged the construction of Hollywood's world as a realm apart, a self-contained universe, melodramatic but fundamentally benign, with little direct relevance to the experience of its audiences outside the cinema. The studios drew upon an eclectic range of material as the basis for motion picture adaptation, but every movie was subjected to similar standardizing treatments that guaranteed Hollywood's products a uniform ideological outlook. It therefore makes little sense to evaluate specific adaptations based on their "accuracy" or "faithfulness" to the original novels or plays. Source material was only the most basic grist for Hollywood's mill.

Similarly, Hollywood was not concerned with "realism" in its depiction of the historical or geopolitical spheres, as its treatment of foreigners and foreign locations amply demonstrates. While the studios were prepared to modify details of representation in an effort to secure unimpeded distribution for their products, their depictions of the foreign remain rife with colorful stereotypes. This came about not through ignorance, carelessness, or prejudice on the part of particular production personnel, but through the deliberate packaging of salable elements. The picturesque, the exotic, and the quaint were all staple ingredients of Hollywood production; like spectacle, romance, and heroism, they formed part of the admixture of motion picture ingredients that the industry delivered for the price of a cinema ticket.

The division of Hollywood's demographic world into "Americans" and "others" is surely one of the most ironic effects of industry regulation, for it was precisely the international expansion of Hollywood's range of distribution that led it to develop a deliberate policy of effacing ethnic and cultural difference on the screen. The result was the creation of a strangely skewed, homogenized picture of the social and racial characteristics of both urban America and the world beyond. Many studies have concentrated on Hollywood's depiction of individual ethnic and cultural groups, but the fact is that these groups were imperfectly differentiated from each other, just as they were imperfectly differentiated from the denizens of Hollywood's "mythical kingdoms." All were subsumed under the amorphous and fantastic category of the foreign. As the production history of *West of Shanghai* illustrates, the difference between Mexico and China was only a matter of costuming. In either case, foreign characters in a strange land provided the requisite exotic foil to the normative vision of bourgeois American characters. Whether the action of a movie was ostensibly set in China, New York, Indiana, or Mars, Hollywood offered audiences the chance to become "American" tourists in a fictionalized and romanticized world. European, African, and even American audiences became practiced at the subjective realignment necessary for the consumption of movie narratives ostensibly set in their own backyards.

Indeed, Hollywood *constituted* its audiences as "American" in a remarkably literal fashion. By involving audiences in its particular vision, which was characterized by bourgeois and consumerist behavior, it in fluenced attitudes and behavior both inside the United States and abroad. At the same time, as a result of the "openness" of its texts, Hollywood invited individual audience members to complete or interpret the action on the screen according to their own imaginative desires. Perversely, by devising a standardized formula for playing to endlessly diverse audiences, the American industry arrived at a filmic style which allowed it to play a peculiarly personal role in the lives of its audiences. The identification of audiences with the world of the movies—reflected in and encouraged by the industry's historical links with consumer culture, and regardless of national or cultural context—was fundamental to Hollywood's impact on the life of the twentieth century.

In this book I have described some of the cases that tested the bounds of permissible representation in the 1920s and 1930s, but these were necessarily unusual. Especially in the mid- to late 1930s, only a handful of cases presented any real problems at any given time, and the great majority of properties reached the screen in conformity with industry requirements with little or no trouble. The result of centralized regulation was the creation of a self-consistent, if oddly delimited, cinematic realm. Stars could change movies, but the peculiar collection of moral and political assumptions governing their existence remained broadly the same, as did many of their world's formal characteristics: its conventional fade-outs and ellipses, its fondness for erotic suggestion, and its almost surreal, yet strangely familiar, exotic backdrops. To this extent Hollywood's cinematic universe itself achieved a kind of coherence as a fantastic kingdom, both strange and familiar to its diverse audiences. Because the particular set of constraints that determined the parameters of its world evolved as an integral part of the American studio system, its claim on this realm is unique. Hollywood's idiom has always been incongruous when employed by other film industries with other histories. However paradoxically, Hollywood has been able to establish an international reputation as the only home of "authentic" cinematic fantasy.

Notes

Works Cited

Index

Notes

Introduction

1. "Suggested Code to Govern the Production of Motion Pictures," in Richard Maltby, "Documents on the Genesis of the Production Code," *Quarterly Review of Film and Video* 15, no. 4 (1995): 41.

2. For a historical approach to this subject, see Barry Salt, *Film Style and Technology: History and Analysis* (London: Starword, 1983). A more lighthearted discussion is contained in Penny Stallings, *Flesh and Fantasy* (New York: Harper and Row, 1978).

3. See Charles Eckert, "The Carole Lombard in Macy's Window," *Quarterly Review of Film Studies* 3, no. 1 (1978): 1–21.

4. The definitive features of "Classical" Hollywood—usually identified with the "studio" system of production—are discussed in David Bordwell, Janet Staiger, and Kristin Thompson, *The Classical Hollywood Cinema: Film Style and Mode of Production to 1960* (London: Routledge, 1985).

5. See Joan Shelley Rubin, *The Making of Middlebrow Culture* (Chapel Hill: University of North Carolina Press, 1992).

6. Leonard J Loff and Jerold L. Simmons, *The Dame in the Kimono: Hollywood, Censorship, and the Production Code from the 1920s to the 1960s* (New York: Grove Weidenfeld, 1990); Lea Jacobs, *The Wages of Sin: Censorship and the Fallen Woman Film, 1928–1942* (Madison: University of Wisconsin Press, 1991); Gregory D. Black, *Hollywood Censored: Morality Codes, Catholics and the Movies* (Cambridge: Cambridge University Press, 1994). See also Richard Maltby, "The Production Code and the Hays Office," in *Grand Design: Hollywood as a Modern Business Enterprise, 1930–1939*, by Tino Balio (New York: Charles Scribner's Sons, 1993), 37–72. Gerald Gardner utilized the PCA archives to produce *The Censorship Papers: Movie Censorship Letters from the Hays Office, 1934 to 1968* (New York: Dodd, Mead and Co., 1987). His characterization of the PCA's operations as a "dark and dirty business" (xi), however, hardly constitutes a useful contribution to our understanding of the mechanisms of industry regulation.

7. Estimations of the gross revenue returned by the foreign market between the wars vary from 25 to 50 percent, with most analysts, including the U.S. Department of Commerce, settling on an average of 35 percent. In 1927 Sidney R. Kent, general manager of Paramount Famous-Lasky, offered the figure of 25 percent when addressing a group of Harvard University students.

His estimate seems surprisingly low considering the fact that his company
had a particularly wide-ranging foreign network. In the same speech he referred to 115 foreign exchanges in 73 countries. See Sidney R. Kent, "Distributing the Product," in *The Story of the Films,* edited by Joseph P. Kennedy (Chicago: A. W. Shaw Co., 1927), 203–32. Douglas Gomery gives a figure of 50
percent, but without supporting documentation; see Gomery, *The Hollywood
Studio System* (London: BFI, 1986), 12. C. J. North and Nathan D. Golden, of
the Motion Picture Division of the Bureau of Foreign and Domestic Commerce in the U.S. Department of Commerce, estimated in 1932 that the Depression had caused a fall in foreign revenues from 30–40 percent of the gross
to 25 percent; see North and Golden, "The European Film Market—Then and
Now," *Society of Motion Picture Engineers Journal* 18 (1932): 442. By 1936
Golden's estimate was back to 30–40 percent; see Golden, "Brief History and
Statistics of the American Motion Picture Industry," *Motion Pictures Abroad,* 14
August 1936, 2. In 1937 and 1938 he quoted a figure of 40 percent: see Golden,
"Brief History and Statistics of the American Motion Picture Industry," *Motion
Pictures Abroad,* 1 August 1937, 2; and idem, "American Movies Still Conquer-
ing Obstacles Abroad, Says Nathan D. Golden," *World Wide Motion Picture
Developments,* 28 October 1938, 1.

Recent research has confirmed an average figure of 34 percent for MGM
between 1924 and 1948, and at least 30 percent for RKO between 1932 and 1946.
See Mark Glancy, "MGM Film Grosses, 1924–1948: The Eddie Mannix Ledger,"
Historical Journal of Film, Radio and Television 12, no. 2 (1992): 129; and Richard B.
Jewell, "RKO Film Grosses, 1929–1951: The C. J. Tevlin Ledger," *Historical Jour-
nal of Film, Radio and Television* 14, no. 1 (1994): 42.

8.   Julius Klein, quoted in *Hearing before Subcommittee of House Committee on
Appropriations,* 69th Cong., 1st sess. (Washington, D.C.: GPO, 1926), 302.

9.   See, for example, Rick Altman, *The American Film Musical* (London:
BFI, 1989), 328ff. For convenience I have used the term "Hollywood" synony-
mously with the American film industry after World War I, while recognizing
that the industry's business operations were always based in New York. The
wider concept represented by Hollywood is discussed in later chapters. More
problematic in the context of this project is the adoption of the term "American" to refer to the products of the United States, in contradistinction to those
of its continental neighbors. However, this terminology is so entrenched in the
sources I have utilized, both primary and secondary (cf. Altman), that with a
certain reluctance I have decided to conform to common usage.

10.   Some recent studies have, however, pointed up a more subtle interac-
tion between Hollywood and its consumers. See, for example, David Ellwood
and Rob Kroes, eds., *Hollywood in Europe: Experiences of a Cultural Hegemony*
(Amsterdam: VU University Press, 1994).

11.   Kristin Thompson, *Exporting Entertainment: America in the World Film
Market, 1907–1934* (London: BFI, 1985).

12.   See, for example, Sarah Street, "The Hays Office and the Defence of
the British Market in the 1930s," *Historical Journal of Film, Radio and Television* 5,
no. 1 (1985): 37–55.

13.   Ian Jarvie, *Hollywood's Overseas Campaign: The North Atlantic Movie Trade, 1920–1950* (Cambridge: Cambridge University Press, 1992). Canada makes a strange case study in this context, since the major American producers all treated it as part of the domestic market.

14.   See Thompson, *Exporting Entertainment*, 1–60.

15.   Paul Kerr, ed., *The Hollywood Film Industry* (London: BFI, 1986), 1.

Chapter 1. Image Making

1.   Joel W. Finler, *The Hollywood Story: Everything You Always Wanted to Know about the American Movie Business But Didn't Know Where to Look* (London: Octopus Books, 1988), 36.

2.   For a detailed account of the American industry's early foreign trade, see Thompson, *Exporting Entertainment*.

3.   See H.F.H., "Lack of American Enterprise in Foreign Countries," *Moving Picture World*, 11 February 1911, 310, 312.

4.   Thompson, *Exporting Entertainment*, 63–71. Thompson argues that this shift was initially occasioned by a British ban on the export of unlicensed motion pictures.

5.   David P. Howells, described as the man "who handles the First National and United Pictures for the entire world outside of the United States and controls Metro and Selznick for the Orient," quoted in "The Foreign Outlook," *Wid's Year Book, 1919–20*, n.p.

6.   Thompson, *Exporting Entertainment*, 71–74.

7.   C. B. Stephenson, "The Development of the Industry Abroad," *Commerce Reports*, 2 January 1922, 34.

8.   Gomery, *Hollywood Studio System*, 14, 5.

9.   See Thompson, *Exporting Entertainment*, 103.

10.   Will H. Hays, *The Memoirs of Will H. Hays* (New York: Doubleday and Co., 1955), 507.

11.   See Louis Galambos, *The Public Image of Big Business in America, 1880–1940: A Quantitative Study in Social Change* (Baltimore: Johns Hopkins University Press, 1975), 7ff.

12.   See John Izod, *Hollywood and the Box Office, 1895–1986* (London: Macmillan, 1988), 120–31; and Simon N. Whitney, "Antitrust Policies and the Motion Picture Industry," in *The American Movie Industry: The Business of the Motion Pictures*, edited by Gorham Kindem (Carbondale: Southern Illinois University Press, 1982), 161–204.

13.   For a discussion of the fate of the Motion Picture Patents Company, see Jeanne Thomas Allen, "The Decay of the Motion Picture Patents Company," in *The American Film Industry*, edited by Tino Balio (Madison: University of Wisconsin Press, 1976), 119–34; and Robert Anderson, "The Motion Picture Patents Company: A Reevaluation," in *The American Film Industry*, edited by Tino Balio, rev. ed. (Madison: University of Wisconsin Press, 1985), 133–52.

14.   J. Dannenberg, "Outlook and Résumé," *Wid's Year Book, 1920–21*, 64d.

15. Whitney, "Antitrust Policies," in *American Movie Industry*, ed. Kindem, 163.

16. "Censorship," *Wid's Year Book, 1919–20*, n.p.

17. *Wid's Year Book* (entitled *The Film Year Book* from 1922, and *The Film Daily Year Book* from 1928) consistently attributes 14 percent of domestic income to New York State.

18. "The Foreign Outlook," *Wid's Year Book, 1919–20*, n.p.

19. Data concerning motion pictures were included in the "Miscellaneous" and "Specialties" sections of the *Daily Consular and Trade Reports* (*Commerce Reports* from 1914) published by the U.S. Department of Commerce.

20. William L. Sherrill, quoted in "Opinions on Foreign Outlook," *Wid's Year Book, 1920–21*, 261.

21. See Thompson, *Exporting Entertainment*, 93–99; and Leslie Midkiff Debauche, "Practical Patriotism: NAMPI Enlists in World War I," *Velvet Light Trap*, no. 23 (1989): 16–38.

22. W. A. Robbins (Cooperative Film Exchange), quoted in "Opinions on Foreign Outlook," *Wid's Year Book, 1920–21*, 259.

23. See Arthur G. Pettit, *Images of the Mexican American in Fiction and Film* (College Station: Texas A&M University Press, 1980); and Allen Woll, *The Latin Image in American Film*, rev. ed. (Los Angeles: UCLA Latin American Center Publicat.ons, University of California, 1980).

24. Peter Stanfield, "The Western, 1909–14: A Cast of Villains," *Film History* 1 (1987): 97–112.

25. Thompson, *Exporting Entertainment*, 140.

26. See Ellis W. Hawley, Murray N. Rothbard, Robert F. Himmelberg, and Gerald D. Nash, *Herbert Hoover and the Crisis of American Capitalism* (Cambridge, Mass: Schenkman Publishing Co., 1973), 3–33, 59–85. See also Galambos, *Public Image of Big Business*.

27. See, for example, Lamar Trotti, "Regulation and Self-Restraint in the Motion Picture Industry," 1926, Trotti file, reel 2, Motion Picture Producers and Distributors of America Archive, Motion Picture Association of America, New York (hereinafter cited as MPPDA Archive).

28. Hays, *Memoirs*, 333.

29. Thomas G. Patten, letter to Will Hays, 12 May 1923, Will H. Hays Collection, Indiana State Library, Indianapolis (hereinafter cited as Hays Collection). See also Helen Delpar, " 'Goodbye to the Greaser': Mexico, the MPPDA, and Derogatory Films, 1922–1926," *Journal of Popular Film and Television* 12, no. 1 (1984): 34–41.

30. See Lary May, *Screening Out the Past: The Birth of Mass Culture and the Motion Picture Industry* (New York: Oxford University Press, 1980); and Stanley Coben, *Rebellion against Victorianism: The Impetus for Cultural Change in 1920s America* (Oxford: Oxford University Press, 1991).

31. See Judith Mayne, "Immigrants and Spectators," *Wide Angle* 5, no. 2 (1982): 33–40.

32. Hays, *Memoirs*, 506.

33. Galambos, *Public Image of Big Business*, 18, 127.

34. This perception persisted throughout the 1910s and into the 1920s. See, for example, the evidence of Mrs. Rufus M. Gibbs, a member of the Citizens' League for Better Motion Pictures, in *Federal Motion Picture Commission*, 69th Cong., 1st sess., H.R. 4094 and H.R. 6233 (Washington, D.C.: GPO, 1926), 172.

35. Charles M. Feldman, *The National Board of Censorship (Review) of Motion Pictures, 1909–1922* (New York: Arno, 1977), 20–24.

36. Evidence of Walter W. Erwin (general manager, VLSE), in *Federal Motion Picture Commission*, Committee on Education, 64th Cong., 1st sess., H.R. 456 (Washington, D.C.: GPO, 1916), 57.

37. Thompson, *Exporting Entertainment*, 1–27.

38. May, *Screening Out the Past*, 46.

39. *Federal Motion Picture Commission*, Committee on Education, 63d Cong., 2d sess., H.R. 14895 and S. 4941 (Washington, D.C.: GPO, 1914); *Federal Motion Picture Commission* (1916).

40. Testimony of William Sheafe Chase, in *Federal Motion Picture Commission* (1916), 154.

41. J. Hinman, "Pathé Exchange vs. the Motion Picture Commission of the State of New York," Supreme Court Appellate Division, 7 July 1922, p. 7, Censor-Newsreel file, reel 1, MPPDA Archive.

42. Ibid., p. 6.

43. Testimony of Mrs. Eleanor Freeland (chairman, Moving Picture Committee of United Women of America, 2d division), in *Federal Motion Picture Commission* (1916), 93.

44. Evidence of Mrs. Everett Hamilton (representative, General Federation of Women's Clubs), stenographer's record, New York State Legislature, Senate Committee of Finance and Assembly and Committee on Ways and Means, *Minutes of Proceedings*, New York State Bill 694, Assembly Bill 877, and Assembly Bill 75, 6 March 1923, Repeal of New York Censor file, reel 1, MPPDA Archive.

45. At a hearing on an act to abolish the New York Censor Board, Chase complained that the motion picture business was in the hands of four or five men, who "have control not only in New York State, but in the United States and all the world." Legislature of the State of New York, *Minutes of Proceedings*, Senate Bill Introductory no. 694, Assembly Bill Introductory no. 877, Assembly Bill Introductory no. 75, 6 March 1923, p. 15, State Sittings—Repeal of Censor file, reel 1, MPPDA Archive. See also William Harrison Short, *A Generation of Motion Pictures: A Review of Social Values in Recreational Films* (New York: National Committee for the Study of Social Values in Motion Pictures, 1928), 153ff.

46. For a late example of these attitudes, see William Marston Seabury, *Motion Picture Problems: The Cinema and the League of Nations* (New York: Avondale Press, 1929). Seabury, for instance, complains of movies that "seriously impair American prestige abroad and stimulate world animosity and unfriendliness against America and everything American" (14).

47. Ellen O'Grady, quoted in Legislature of the State of New York, *Minutes of Proceedings*, Senate Bill Introductory no. 694, 6 March 1923, p. 28, State Sittings—Repeal of Censor file, reel 1, MPPDA Archive.

48. *Federal Motion Picture Commission* (1926), 135.

49. *Federal Motion Picture Commission* (1916), 263–64.

50. Ibid., 15.

51. Feldman, *National Board of Censorship*, 149–53.

52. May, *Screening Out the Past*, 203–314.

53. Filmmaking started in the Los Angeles area in 1907 and in Hollywood proper in 1911. By 1915 "Hollywood" was being used colloquially to encompass all filmmaking in southern California. See Christopher Finch and Linda Rosenkrantz, *Gone Hollywood: The Movie Colony in the Golden Age* (London: Weidenfeld and Nicolson, 1979), 1–14. In 1921 two-thirds of the world's pictures were made in California, according to "The Days of '49 in California Moving Picture History," *Wid's Year Book, 1921–22*, 69. The use of the term "Hollywood" to represent the glamour and fantasy attached to the American movie business was probably reflected and encouraged by the 1923 Paramount Famous-Lasky production *Hollywood*, directed by James Cruze. The film was a star-studded feature about life in the movie colony.

54. See Richard deCordova, *Picture Personalities: The Emergence of the Star System in America* (Urbana: University of Illinois Press, 1990), 117–51; and David A. Yallop, *The Day the Laughter Stopped: The True Story of Fatty Arbuckle* (London: Hodder and Stoughton, 1976).

55. Signatories to the MPPDA's certificate of incorporation were Albert T. Banzhaf, Philip G. Bartlett, Rufus S. Cole, Benjamin P. DeWitt, William Fox, Frank J. Godsol, David Wark Griffith, Siegfried F. Hartman, Will H. Hays, Karl Kirchwey, Harry G. Kosch, Carl Laemmle, Marcus Loew, Saul E. Rogers, J. Robert Rubin, Lewis J. Selznick, George A. Skinner, and Adolph Zukor. See Raymond Moley, *The Hays Office* (Indianapolis: Bobbs-Merrill, 1945), 36.

56. See "What Hays Can Do for the Movies," *Literary Digest*, 28 January 1922, 12–13.

57. *That Marvel—the Movie: A Glance at Its Reckless Past, Its Promising Present, and Its Significant Future* (New York: G. P. Putnam's Sons, 1923), n.p.

58. "Policy of the Department of Public Relations," Meeting—Committee on Public Relations file, reel 2, MPPDA Archive.

Chapter 2. The Open Door

1. Articles of Incorporation, quoted in Moley, *Hays Office*, 226. Moley's book is the standard account of the MPPDA. He was highly sympathetic to the association and its progressive business methods. Because he was given access to the organization's records during the book's preparation, *The Hays Office* is a useful source of information, but it is nevertheless a frankly partial account.

2. *New York Times*, 7 March 1921, 7, quoted in Feldman, *National Board of Censorship*, 192–93. The resolution was passed on 6 March 1921.

3.   Hays, quoted in stenographic report, "Minutes of the Meeting of January Fourth of the Committee on Public Relations," 4 January 1923, p. 2, and Will Hays, letter to Albert Warner, 5 September 1922, both in Civic Committee file, reel 1, MPPDA Archive.

4.   The committee comprised representatives from the following groups (organizations with two representatives are noted): Academy of Political Science, Actor's Equity Association, American City Bureau, American Civic Association, American Federation of Labor, American Home Economics Association, American Legion (2), American Library Association, American Museum of Natural History, American Sunday School Union, Associated Advertising Clubs of the World, Boy Scouts, Boys Club Federation, Camp Fire Girls, Chamber of Commerce of the United States (2), Chautauqua Institution, Child Health Organization of America, Child Welfare League of America, Colonial Dames of America, Commonwealth Club of California, Community Service, Cooper Union for the Advancement of Science and Art, Council for Jewish Women (2), Dairymen's League Co-operative Association, Daughters of the American Revolution, Federal Council of Churches of Christ in America, General Federation of Women's Clubs, Girl Scouts (2), Girls' Friendly Society in America, International Federation of Catholic Alumnae, Jewish Welfare Board, National Association of Civic Secretaries, National Catholic Welfare Conference, National Child Labor Committee, National Civic Federation, National Community Center Association, National Congress of Parents and Teachers (2), National Council of Catholic Men, National Council of Catholic Women, National Education Association, National Health Council, National Safety Council, National Security League, National Society for Prevention of Blindness, National Tuberculosis Association (2), New York Child Welfare Committee (2), New York City Federation of Women's Clubs, Russell Sage Foundation, Safety Institute of America, Salvation Army, Sons of the American Revolution, United Society of Christian Endeavor, War Department, Woodcraft League of America, Women's Trade Union League, YMCA (2), Young Men's Hebrew Association, YWCA (2), Young Women's Hebrew Association. Mrs. Frank H. Percells, Mrs. Charles S. Whitman, and Mrs. Charles Bull were on the committee without institutional affiliation. Memo, "Committee on Public Relations," June 1922, Civic Committee file, reel 1, MPPDA Archive.

5.   The organizations represented on the Committee of Twenty were the American Federation of Labor, the American Legion, the Boy Scouts, the Camp Fire Girls, Community Service, the Daughters of the American Revolution, the Federal Council of Churches of Christ in America, the General Federation of Women's Clubs, the Girl Scouts, the National Catholic Welfare Conference, the National Congress of Parents and Teachers, the Russell Sage Foundation, the Women's Trade Union League, the YMCA, and the YWCA. Memo, "Committee on Public Relations," June 1922, Civic Committee file, reel 1, MPPDA Archive.

Subcommittees were the Business Committee, the Committee on Motion Pictures Dealing with Industry, the Committee on Motion Pictures Using Book

Titles, the Committee on Historical and Patriotic Information, the Committee on Local Better Films Committees, the Committee on Religious Pictures, the Committee on Pedagogic Pictures, the Committee on Music in Motion Picture Theatres, the Committee on Community Needs, the Committee on Classification and Listing of Motion Pictures by National Organizations, and the Committee on Children's Matinees. Jason Joy, "Minutes of the Luncheon Meeting of the Executive Committee," 10 March 1923, Civic Committee file, reel 1, MPPDA Archive.

6. Charles McMahon, quoted in stenographic report, "Addresses Delivered at the Get-Together Meeting of the MPPDA," 22 June 1922, Civic Committee file, reel 1, MPPDA Archive.

7. James West, quoted in "Minutes of the Meeting of January Fourth of the Committee on Public Relations," 4 January 1923, Civic Committee file, reel 1, MPPDA Archive.

8. Ibid., quoting Hays.

9. "Minutes of Meeting of the Committee of Twenty," 18 October 1922, reel 1, MPPDA Archive.

10. See Federal Council of the Churches of Christ in America, *The Public Relations of the Motion Picture Industry* (N.p.: Department of Research and Education, Federal Council of the Churches of Christ in America, 1931), 67.

11. *Federal Motion Picture Commission* (1926), 33. For example, Jason Joy sent the novel *The Garden of Allah* (produced by MGM and released in 1927) to Mrs. McGoldrick for evaluation and comment. She consulted a number of prominent Catholic clergy and laity in preparing her response and found the finished product to be "a fine example of the good faith the producers kept with those of us whose advice was asked in the beginning." Rita McGoldrick, letter to Carl Milliken (secretary, MPPDA), 2 October 1927, *The Garden of Allah* file, Production Code Administration Archive, Margaret Herrick Library, Academy of Motion Picture Arts and Sciences, Beverly Hills, Calif. (hereinafter cited as PCA Archive).

12. A. E. Smith (Vitagraph), letter to Charles McMahon, 25 September 1924, *Between Friends* file, reel 1, MPPDA Archive.

13. At a committee meeting in May 1924, Joy remarked, "I don't suppose I should be discouraged because more people don't come. I wonder if I am failing because they are not attractive meetings." Joy, quoted in "Committee Meeting Summary," 13 May 1924, Committee on Public Relations file, reel 1, MPPDA Archive.

14. Information in parentheses following film titles gives the producing company followed by the distributing company (where they are not the same), and the year in which the movie was released in the United States.

15. Jason Joy, "Committee Meeting Summaries: Second Annual Meeting," 6 March 1924, Committee on Public Relations file, reel 1, MPPDA Archive.

16. Miss Leighton, quoted in stenographic report, "Meeting of Committee on Public Relations," 8 July 1924, p. 11, Committee on Public Relations file, reel 1, MPPDA Archive.

17. Ibid., p. 4, quoting Hays.

18. "Meeting of Committee on Public Relations," 8 July 1924, pp. 7–8, MPPDA Archive.

19. See Margaretta Reeve (president of the National Congress of Parents and Teachers), letter to Lee Hanmer, 18 November 1924, National Congress of Parents and Teachers file, reel 1, MPPDA Archive. Reeve's resignation came nearly a year after the controversy over *West of the Water Tower*. The General Federation of Women's Clubs' representative, Mrs. John D. Sherman, withdrew for similar reasons in January 1925, and the Girl Scouts' representative also resigned.

20. Courtland Smith, telegram to Fred Beetson, 26 February 1924, AMPP file, reel 1, MPPDA Archive.

21. J. J. O'Neill, memo to Courtland Smith, 14 January 1925, Protests file, November 1924, reel 1, MPPDA Archive. O'Neill suggested specific cuts and alterations and added, "At the same time, however, it might be well to let our directors know that there have been a couple of kicks about Pool Room pictures and to suggest that the directors lay off them."

22. Motion Picture Producers and Distributors of America, *The "Open Door"* (New York: Motion Picture Producers and Distributors of America, 1924).

23. "Minutes of the Luncheon Meeting of the Executive Committee," 10 March 1923, Civic Committee file, reel 1, MPPDA Archive.

24. MPPDA, press release, "An 'Open Door' Policy in the Moving Picture Industry," 28 March 1925, Open Door file, reel 2, MPPDA Archive.

25. Herron asserted in a court deposition in February 1939 that he had held the job of foreign manager for fifteen years; see "Deposition of Frederick L. Herron," February 1939, reel 12, MPPDA Archive. He was certainly part of the organization in September 1923, when he accompanied Hays to England, although Moley claims that his first three years on the job were spent building up contacts and acquaintances. See Moley, *Hays Office*, 171.

26. Frederick Herron, letter to E. C. Raftery, 29 October 1926, O'Brien legal file, box 7, folder 9, United Artists Collection, Wisconsin Center for Film and Theater Research, Madison (hereinafter cited as United Artists Collection).

27. James C. Robertson, *The British Board of Film Censors: Film Censorship in Britain, 1896–1950* (London: Croom Helm, 1985), 148.

28. For a discussion of the British situation, see Rachael Low, *The History of the British Film, 1918–1929* (London: Allen and Unwin, 1971), 87ff.

29. For a detailed analysis of Hollywood's relationship with Germany, see Thomas J. Saunders, *Hollywood in Berlin: American Cinema and Weimar Germany* (Berkeley: University of California Press, 1994).

30. For an analysis of Hollywood's relationship with the German market in the 1920s, see Jan-Christopher Horak, "Rin-Tin-Tin in Berlin; or, American Cinema in Weimar," *Film History* 5, no. 1 (1993): 49–62.

31. The most substantial of these was a contract between Paramount, MGM, Universal, and the German studio Ufa for the distribution of films in Germany through a joint company, Parufamet. See Horak, "Rin-Tin-Tin in Berlin," 54–60.

32. "Report of the Sub-Committee as Appointed by Mr. Hays," 15 January 1925, Meeting—Foreign Managers file, reel 2, MPPDA Archive. Those attending were Shauer (Famous Players–Lasky), Brock (First National), Mannheim (Universal), Abel (Fox), Frederick Herron, and Courtland Smith. Other items on the meeting's agenda concerned new French legislation about nonflammable stock and the protection of American prints from pirating.

33. Hays, speech transcript (context unrecorded), "Foreign Relations and Anti-Censorship Activity of the MPPDA," 21 April 1927, MPPDA file, reel 3, MPPDA Archive.

34. MPPDA internal memo, "Certain Factors and Conditions Affecting the European Market," 20 November 1928, p. 21, Foreign Relations file, reel 5, MPPDA Archive.

35. Ibid., p. 19.

36. Ibid., p. 39.

37. Ibid., pp. 2–3, quoted.

38. U.S. Department of Commerce, Bureau of Foreign and Domestic Commerce, "The Chinese Motion Picture Market" (1927), compiled by C. J. North, *Trade Information Bulletin*, no. 467, p. 7.

39. Ibid., p. 8.

40. "Trade Follows the Motion Pictures," *Commerce Reports*, 24 April 1922, p. 191; Lamar Trotti, "The Motion Picture as a Business" (speech to be delivered by Carl Milliken in Boston), 3 April 1928, Trotti file, reel 5, MPPDA Archive.

41. *Hearing before Subcommittee of House Committee on Appropriations*, 69th Cong., 1st sess., 302–4.

42. "Bureau of Foreign and Domestic Commerce Reports," *Film Year Book* (1926), 854.

43. Lamar Trotti, "The Motion Picture as a Business," 3 April 1928, p. 9, Trotti file, reel 5, MPPDA Archive.

44. "Certain Factors and Conditions Affecting the European Market," 20 November 1928, pp. 1–2, Foreign Relations file, reel 5, MPPDA Archive.

45. Ibid., p. 1.

46. Hays, *Memoirs*, 509.

47. Lamar Trotti, "International Unity," 3 December 1928, Trotti file, reel 5, MPPDA Archive.

48. See Richard Maltby, *Harmless Entertainment: Hollywood and the Ideology of Consensus* (Metuchen, N.J.: Scarecrow, 1983), 10–17.

49. Lamar Trotti, "International Unity," 3 December 1928, Trotti file, reel 5, MPPDA Archive.

50. Mr. Serruys, report of remarks of 7 July 1928, enclosed in Edward G. Lowry, letter to Hays, 24 July 1928, Foreign Relations file, reel 5, MPPDA Archive. The rhetoric used on this occasion strongly prefigured the debates surrounding the treatment of cultural properties during the General Agreement on Tariffs and Trade (GATT) talks of 1993. In the 1990s, too, the French argued that cinema and television warranted special exemption from free trade arrangements because of their cultural and ideological significance.

51.   For a discussion of the French attitude toward American films at this time, see David Strauss, "The Rise of Anti-Americanism in France: French Intellectuals and the American Film Industry, 1927–1932," *Journal of Popular Culture* 10, no. 4 (1977): 752–59.

52.   Paul Koretz, letter to Hays, 19 July 1928, Foreign Relations file, reel 5, MPPDA Archive.

53.   "Speech made by the Hon. Hugh Wilson, U.S. Minister to Switzerland, to the Geneva Conference on July 7, 1928," Foreign Relations file, reel 5, MPPDA Archive.

54.   Hays stated that "whatever the alleged grounds for foreign objection or opposition, our negotiations usually discovered a perfectly natural economic rivalry at the bottom of them" (*Memoirs*, 507). He also suggested that Mexico's objection to the use of Mexican locales by American producers in the early 1940s stemmed from the fact that "Mexico, leading the Spanish-speaking lands in production, was soon producing upward of a hundred films a year" (556).

55.   Herron, memo to Hays, 13 March 1929, Hays Collection.

56.   Strictly speaking, both the Studio Relations Committee and the Production Code Administration came under the jurisdiction of the AMPP rather than the MPPDA. The AMPP, however, mainly rubber-stamped decisions that were taken in New York, the real center of administrative power.

57.   See Motion Picture Producers and Distributors of America, "The Don'ts and Be Carefuls (1927)," in *The Movies in Our Midst: Documents in the Cultural History of Film in America,* edited by Gerald Mast (Chicago: University of Chicago Press, 1982), 213–14.

58.   Moley, *Hays Office,* 64.

59.   Charles McMahon, quoted in "Addresses Delivered at the Get-Together Meeting of the MPPDA," 22 June 1922, Civic Committee file, reel 1, MPPDA Archive.

60.   Moley, *Hays Office,* 63.

61.   Joy, memo to Hays, 18 January 1928, Department of Public and Industry Relations file, reel 4, MPPDA Archive.

62.   See Diane Collins, *Hollywood Down Under: Australians at the Movies, 1896 to the Present Day* (Sydney: Angus and Robertson, 1987), 64–65. According to Collins, Woodle discovered that Australians objected to American nationalism and historical inaccuracies (especially in relation to Britain and Europe) and were bored by films about American institutions, especially American football. The Australians with whom Woodle spoke also expressed irritation with "the bad spelling and American slang in many titles and synopses."

63.   Hays, speech transcript, "Foreign Relations and Anti-Censorship Activity of the MPPDA," 21 April 1927, MPPDA file, reel 3, MPPDA Archive.

64.   Alvin H. Marill, *Samuel Goldwyn Presents* (New York: A. S. Barnes, 1976), 35, 37.

65.   "Heirlooms of Napoleon for 'Madame Sans-Gene,' " *Morning Telegraph,* 5 October 1924.

66. Jerome Beatty, "Daily Report," 2 October 1926, Titles file, reel 5, MPPDA Archive.

67. Ibid. For documents relating to anti-German propaganda films of World War I, see Richard Wood, ed., *Film and Propaganda in America: A Documentary History*, vol. 1 (New York: Greenwood, 1990).

68. Dr. G. Heuser (acting German consul general), letter to Hays, 20 December 1926; Hays, letter to Joe Schenck, 21 December 1926; and Joe Schenck, letter to Hays, 29 December 1926, all in Titles file, reel 5, MPPDA Archive.

69. See Vance Kepley Jr. and Betty Kepley, "Foreign Films on Soviet Screens, 1922–1931," *Quarterly Review of Film Studies* 4 (1979): 429–42.

70. "The Outlook Abroad for 1928," *Film Daily Year Book* (1928), 977.

71. Sam Morris of Warner Bros. suspected that unlicensed duplicates were being made of American films that entered Russia in the 1930s. He advised Jack Warner not to send any films there for preview. See Sam Morris, letter to Jack Warner, 12 May 1936, JLW correspondence, box 59, folder 8, Warner Bros. Archive, Department of Special Collections, Doheney Library, University of Southern California, Los Angeles (hereinafter cited as Warner Bros. Archive).

72. Thompson, *Exporting Entertainment*, 133.

73. Kepley and Kepley, "Foreign Films on Soviet Screens," 439.

74. The consistent characterization of Russians as villains did not concern the industry because it did not affect profits; it was disregarded by the U.S. State Department because the United States did not recognize the government of the Soviet Union. It is difficult to estimate the extent to which this stereotyping may have informed later political and diplomatic developments, but it is reasonable to assume that its legacy was felt during the Cold War, and it may help to account for Ronald Reagan's extraordinarily melodramatic condemnation of the Soviet Union as the "Evil Empire." See Michael Paul Rogin, *Ronald Reagan, the Movie: And Other Episodes in Political Demonology* (Berkeley: University of California Press, 1987).

75. Hays, letter to Joe Schenck, 21 December 1926, MPPDA Archive.

76. Possibly its inclusion was influenced by the appearance of a similar clause in the recommendations of an International Film Congress that was hosted by the League of Nations in 1926. The MPPDA decided not to attend the congress, although it was widely supported by the European industry. See Thompson, *Exporting Entertainment*, 114–15.

77. Hays, *Memoirs*, 431–32. See also Charles R. Metzger, "Pressure Groups and the Motion Picture Industry," in *The Annals of the American Academy of Political and Social Science*, edited by Thorsten Sellin (Philadelphia: American Academy of Political and Social Science, 1947), 110–15.

78. See Hays, letter to Charles Smith (president, American Association for the Advancement of Atheism), 2 November 1927, Protests file, reel 3, MPPDA Archive.

79. Thompson, *Exporting Entertainment*, 119–20.

80. Herron, review, 14 September 1928, *Plastered in Paris* file, PCA Archive.

81. Herron, letter to N. L. Mannheim, March 1928, Censor—Foreign file, reel 4, MPPDA Archive.

82.   Robert Cochrane, letter to Hays, 29 March 1928, Censor—Foreign file, reel 4, MPPDA Archive.

83.   Herron, letter to Joy, 16 May 1928, Censor—Foreign file, reel 4, MPPDA Archive.

84.   The brutal sergeant in Paramount's 1939 version of *Beau Geste* is called Markhoff.

85.   Herron, memo, 1928 (no other date), Censor—Foreign file, reel 4, MPPDA Archive.

86.   E. J. Montagne, letter to Fred Beetson, 21 June 1928; Joy, letter to Hays, 22 June 1928; and Hays, telegram to Joy, 26 June 1928, all in *I Take This Woman* file, PCA Archive.

87.   Charles McMahon, press release through National Catholic Welfare Conference News Service, 25 July 1927, *The Callahans and the Murphys* file, PCA Archive. See Francis R. Walsh, " 'The Callahans and the Murphys' (MGM, 1927): A Case Study of Irish Catholic and Catholic Church Censorship," *Historical Journal of Film, Radio and Television* 10, no. 1 (1990): 33–45; and Francis G. Couvares, "Hollywood, Main Street, and the Church: Trying to Censor the Movies before the Production Code," *American Quarterly* 44, no. 4 (December 1992): 599–607.

88.   Joy, memo to Hays, 18 January 1928, Department of Public and Industry Relations file, reel 4, MPPDA Archive.

Chapter 3. Sound Effects

1.   See Rudolf Arnheim, *Film as Art* (Berkeley: University of California Press, 1957), 226–28.

2.   Quoted in Annette Kuhn, *Cinema, Censorship and Sexuality, 1909–1925* (London: Routledge, 1988), 35.

3.   Kevin Brownlow and David Gill, "Thames Silents Become Channel Four Silents," program notes for *The Four Horsemen of the Apocalypse*, London Film Festival, 1993. The extent to which this practice was commonplace is a matter of debate among historians, and the subject is in need of further research.

4.   For a discussion of classification and ratings, see Stephen Farber, *The Movie Rating Game* (Washington, D.C.: Public Affairs Press, 1972).

5.   "Résumé of Dinner-Meeting of the Studio Relations Committee Held in the Offices of the Association," 19 October 1927, p. 13, Department of Public and Industry Relations file, reel 3, MPPDA Archive.

6.   The information about censoring charges in this paragraph comes from a pamphlet by Edwin W. Hullinger, *Free Speech for the Talkies?* rpt. from *North American Review* (N.p., June 1929).

7.   Orrin Cocks, "Paternalism in Morals," quoted in *Federal Motion Picture Commission* (1914), 231.

8.   Aaron Brylawski, in *Federal Motion Picture Commission* (1914), 171.

9.   Donald Ramsey Young, *Motion Pictures: A Study in Social Legislation* (Philadelphia: Westbrook, 1922), 15.

10.   Joy, letter to Alvin McElvaine, 16 January 1929, *King of Kings* file, PCA Archive.

11.   Stenographic report, "Trade Practice Conference of the Motion Picture Industry on Fair Methods of Competition in the Motion Picture Industry, October 10–15, 1927," pp. 154 and 343, Fair Trade Practices Conference file, reel 3, MPPDA Archive.

12.   See Guy Croswell Smith, letter to Arthur Kelly, 16 May 1930, O'Brien legal file, box 6, folder 1, United Artists Collection; and U.S. Department of Commerce, Bureau of Foreign and Domestic Commerce, "European Motion-Picture Industry in 1929" (1930), *Trade Information Bulletin*, no. 694, p. 26.

13.   Lamar Trotti, "The Motion Picture as a Business," 3 April 1928, p. 17, Trotti file, reel 5, MPPDA Archive. Article 6 of the French Film Decree required that films be submitted "in the identical form in which they have been exhibited in the country of their origin with reproduction of original titles and subtitles of which the French translation will be provided."

14.   Irish Censor Board report, *Resurrection* file, PCA Archive.

15.   *Trade Information Bulletin*, no. 694, p. 54.

16.   U.S. Department of Commerce, Bureau of Foreign and Domestic Commerce, "Motion Pictures in Argentina and Brazil" (1929), *Trade Information Bulletin*, no. 630, p. 4.

17.   Joseph I. Anderson and Donald Richie, *The Japanese Film: Art and Industry* (Tokyo: Charles E. Tuttle, 1959), 24.

18.   Kent, "Distributing the Product," in *Story of the Films*, ed. Kennedy, 207–8.

19.   For example, the first *Trade Information Bulletin* on the Chinese motion picture market, issued by the U.S. Department of Commerce in 1927, listed five fan magazines by Chinese publishers that combined articles on foreign and native productions and performers. Fan magazines printed in the United States and Europe were also available. See *Trade Information Bulletin*, no. 467, pp. 33–35.

20.   Jostein Gripsrud analyzed the Norwegian response to Fairbanks and Pickford in "Mary and Doug and Modernity: Hollywood Stars in Norway, 1924," paper presented to the Society for Cinema Studies Conference, New York, 2–5 March 1995.

21.   Kepley and Kepley, "Foreign Films on Soviet Screens," 437.

22.   David Bordwell, *Ozu and the Poetics of the Cinema* (London: BFI, 1988), 19. Bordwell cites two instances from the sound period, one in which the protagonists of a movie go to see a Betty Boop cartoon (*Tonari no Yae-Chan/Our Neighbor Miss Yae*, 1934), and one in which "two marching students compare their situation to Gary Cooper's in *Morocco*" (*Hanagata senshu/Star Athlete*, 1937).

23.   Rufus Steele, *7 News Stories about the Movies*, rpt. from the *Christian Science Monitor*, 30 July 1926 (New York: Motion Picture Producers and Distributors of America, n.d.), 10. Nothing has changed. According to a Disney publicity agent, the reason that the actors playing the Disney cartoon characters at Disneyland never speak is that "people from every part of the globe visit the

Magic Kingdom, all of them believing that Mickey speaks only their language."
"Michael Takes the Mickey," *TV Times*, 13–19 October 1990, 27.

24.   Central American censor distribution agent's report on *The Rough Riders*, enclosed in J. H. Seidelman (assistant manager, Foreign Department, Paramount), letter to Herron, 2 July 1929, Censor—Elim—Foreign file, reel 6, MPPDA Archive.

25.   Arthur Kelly, "Following Are Censorship Cuts in United Artists Pictures in Australia," memo to other foreign managers, 20 September 1929, Censor—Elim—Foreign file, reel 6, MPPDA Archive.

26.   "Report of the Royal Commission on the Moving Picture Industry in Australia," quoted in U.S. Department of Commerce, Bureau of Foreign and Domestic Commerce, "Motion Pictures in Australia and New Zealand" (1929), *Trade Information Bulletin*, no. 608, p. 30.

27.   Memo from Foreign Department of MPPDA, n.d., re Australian censorship action on *Love Me and the World Is Mine*, O'Brien legal file, box 97, folder 11, United Artists Collection.

28.   Ibid. Between 1925 and 1927, 7.5 percent of the 2,133 films viewed by the Australian censors were absolutely rejected, while a further 3.5 percent were initially rejected but later passed after reconstruction. Forty-two percent were passed after routine eliminations had been made. See *Trade Information Bulletin*, no. 608, p. 12.

29.   T. P. Mulrooney, letter to Dennis F. O'Brien, 27 March 1928, O'Brien legal file, box 56, folder 1, United Artists Collection.

30.   Report of censorship eliminations in First National pictures, contained in "Résumé of Dinner-Meeting of the Studio Relations Committee," 19 April 1928, Department of Public and Industry Relations file, reel 4, MPPDA Archive.

31.   U.S. Department of Commerce, Bureau of Foreign and Domestic Commerce, "Motion Pictures in Mexico, Central America, and the Greater Antilles" (1931), *Trade Information Bulletin*, no. 754, p. 19.

32.   For example, *The Cat and the Canary* (Universal, 1927) was banned in Czechoslovakia for containing "awe-inspiring and mysterious scenes which might influence persons of weak nervous systems so as to threaten public order and safety." See report on rejected films contained in "Résumé of Dinner-Meeting of the Studio Relations Committee," 26 January 1928, Department of Public and Industry Relations file, reel 4, MPPDA Archive.

33.   *Trade Information Bulletin*, no. 467, p. 27.

34.   Remarks of Douglas Miller, reported in "Résumé of Dinner-Meeting of the Studio Relations Committee," 25 November 1927, Department of Public and Industry Relations file, reel 3, MPPDA Archive. When studios later produced multiple-language versions of movies at the beginning of the sound era, at least one studio (MGM) found that the German cut tended to be longer than the other language versions. See Barbara Hall, "Robert M. W. Vogel Oral History," 1991, p. 40, Margaret Herrick Library, Academy of Motion Picture Arts and Sciences, Beverly Hills, Calif.; and Joseph Garncarz, "Hollywood in Ger-

many: The Role of American Films in Germany," in *Hollywood in Europe*, ed. Ellwood and Kroes, 94–135.

35.   Rowland V. Lee, quoted in stenographic report, "Production Economy Meeting between Producers and Directors," Conference of Academy of Motion Picture Arts and Sciences, 14 July 1927, pp. 40–41, AMPAS file, reel 3, MPPDA Archive.

36.   John V. Wilson, memo to Carl Milliken, 23 November 1928, California Office file, reel 4, MPPDA Archive.

37.   Joy told Hays, "I find the mass of detailed office work connected with this phase of our activities to be considerably greater than any of us anticipated, but I am determined to carry it through, successfully, without permanent additions to the payroll." Joy, letter to Hays, 15 June 1928, Department of Public and Industry Relations file, reel 4, MPPDA Archive.

38.   See, for example, "Résumé of Dinner-Meeting of the Studio Relations Committee," 25 November 1928, pp. 11–23, MPPDA Archive.

39.   Joy, letter to Hays, 26 May 1928, Department of Public and Industry Relations file, reel 4, MPPDA Archive.

40.   Joy, letter to Hays, 15 June 1928, Department of Public and Industry Relations file, reel 4, MPPDA Archive.

41.   Lamar Trotti, "The Future of Motion Pictures," 7 November 1928, Trotti file, reel 5, MPPDA Archive.

42.   Hays, quoted in "Résumé of Dinner-Meeting of the Studio Relations Committee," 24 July 1928, p. 4, Department of Public and Industry Relations file, reel 4, MPPDA Archive.

43.   See Douglas Gomery, "The Coming of Sound to the American Cinema: A History of the Transformation of an Industry" (Ph.D. diss., University of Wisconsin–Madison, 1975), 110–84.

44.   Hays, quoted in "Résumé of Dinner-Meeting of the Studio Relations Committee," 24 July 1928, Department of Public and Industry Relations file, reel 4, MPPDA Archive.

45.   M. S. Kusell (manager, Paramount's New York exchange), letter to George Schaefer, 18 June 1928, California Office file, reel 4, MPPDA Archive.

46.   Joy, "Résumé of Dinner-Meeting of the Studio Relations Committee," 24 October 1928, Department of Public and Industry Relations file, reel 4, MPPDA Archive.

47.   E. C. Grainger (Fox), letter to Gabriel L. Hess (general attorney, MPPDA), 20 August 1928, Censor—Sound file, reel 5, MPPDA Archive.

48.   Abel Carey Thomas (Warner Bros.), letter to Hays, 30 August 1928, Censor—Sound file, reel 5, MPPDA Archive.

49.   Hays, letter to Jack Warner, 25 June 1928, Don'ts and Be Carefuls file, reel 4, MPPDA Archive.

50.   William C. de Mille, "The Future of the Photoplay," in *Introduction to the Photoplay*, edited by John C. Tibbetts (1929; Shawnee Mission, Kans.: National Film Society, 1977), 330.

51.   Rita McGoldrick, "Endorsed Motion Pictures," broadcast 9 May 1929, IFCA file, reel 7, MPPDA Archive.

52.   Early musical synchronizations of Hollywood-produced films were carried out on the East Coast, and for a while it seemed that New York would become the sound movie capital of the United States. "Paramount's Long Island studio, on which a million dollars had been spent for sound, was expected to start its first production in July [1928]; MGM was talking of starting sound shooting at its Cosmopolitan Studios, New York; First National announced it would use the old Biograph stages; Warners . . . had their Vitaphone studios there still." Alexander Walker, *The Shattered Silents: How the Movies Came to Stay* (London: Harrap, 1978), 90.

The establishment of the Eastern Studio Relations Committee is documented in a memo from Maurice McKenzie, 23 May 1929, and in a letter from McKenzie to H. W. Fitelson (Tiffany-Stahl Productions), 20 September 1929, both in Eastern Studio Committee file, reel 7, MPPDA Archive. See also Vincent Hart, letter to A. W. Doidge (Educational Films Corp. of America), 18 January 1934, Educational Films file, reel 10, MPPDA Archive; and Vincent Hart, letter to Frederick Herron, 28 July 1934, Production Code file, reel 10, MPPDA Archive.

53.   The Eastern SRC also reviewed foreign films which required a seal for distribution in the United States.

54.   For example, official rejection followed extensive contact with the German consul on *All Quiet on the Western Front* (Universal, 1930), the Mexican consul on *The Gay Caballero* (Fox, 1932), and the Italian consul on *Idiot's Delight* (MGM, 1939). In each case the problem was eventually resolved. On *Idiot's Delight*, see chapter 6.

55.   Joy, "Résumé of Dinner-Meeting of the Studio Relations Committee," 13 September 1928, p. 1, Department of Public and Industry Relations file, reel 4, MPPDA Archive.

56.   Evidence of Joy, in *Federal Motion Picture Commission* (1926), 363.

57.   See Mrs. Benjamin O. Holbrook (chairman of Indian Welfare for the Los Angeles District Federation of Women's Clubs, Glendale), letter to Hays, 22 March 1932, and B. D. Weeks (president of Bacone College), letter to Hays, 19 April 1932, both in *Laughing Boy* file, PCA Archive.

58.   See, for example, Joy, letter to Joe Schenck, 27 March 1930, *The Bad One* file, PCA Archive: "Mr. Mandelstamm's authority to represent the point of view of the French Foreign Office is clearly established and we feel certain that the first inquiry raised from that direction will be as to whether the French government's official representative in Hollywood has been consulted in the production of this picture."

59.   Herron, letter to Joy, 9 August 1928, *Condemned* file, PCA Archive.

60.   Mandelstamm, letter to Arthur Hornblow, enclosed in letter from Mandelstamm to Joy, 15 May 1929, *Condemned* file, PCA Archive.

61.   Samuel Goldwyn, letter to Hays, 21 June 1929, *Condemned* file, PCA Archive.

62.   Mandelstamm's demands for payment were still a subject of intense irritation in the MPPDA in December 1931, when John V. Wilson wrote to Herron asking if France could possibly accredit a different individual. Neverthe-

less, Howard Hughes agreed to pay Mandelstamm a fee in that month for his work on *Cock of the Air*. See Wilson, letter to Herron, 3 December 1931, *Cock of the Air* file, PCA Archive.

63.   Mandelstamm, letter to John V. Wilson, 21 March 1930; Joe Schenck, letter to Joy, 28 March 1930; and Herron, letter to Joy, 29 March 1930, all in *Du Barry, Woman of Passion* file, PCA Archive.

64.   John V. Wilson, letter to B. P. Schulberg, 8 October 1930, *Morocco* file, PCA Archive.

65.   Zanuck, letter to Joy, 21 February 1931; Herron, letter to Joy, 24 March 1931; and Harold Smith, letter to Herron, 23 July 1931, all in *Fifty Million Frenchmen* file, PCA Archive.

66.   Mandelstamm, letter to William Koenig, 22 July 1931, *Fifty Million Frenchmen* file, PCA Archive.

67.   Ibid. The SRC did not have much confidence in Mandelstamm's good will. John V. Wilson told Herron that *The Painted Woman* (Fox, 1932), for example, was "handled very nicely and unobjectionably from the standpoint of the French. I do not believe that the slightest question can be raised from that point." He noted, however, that "Mandelstamm is aware that the picture has been in production. He knows nothing about the story and has not seen the picture, but because of Fox's attitude toward him since he got back from France he is likely to send out bad reports ahead of the picture." Wilson, letter to Herron, 27 July 1932, *The Painted Woman* file, PCA Archive.

68.   See, for example, Colonel John A. Cooper, letter to Carl Milliken, 20 April 1927, Canadian Office file, reel 3, MPPDA Archive; Will Hays, letter to Louis A. Tascherou, 14 June 1929, Canadian Office file, reel 6, MPPDA Archive; and Will Hays, letter to William A. Orr, 20 July 1929, Censor—Canada file, reel 6, MPPDA Archive. Production Code Administration files regularly cite comparatively severe instances of Canadian censorship.

69.   *Trade Information Bulletin*, no. 694, p. 36.

70.   See, for example, U.S. Department of Commerce, Bureau of Foreign and Domestic Commerce, "The European Motion-Picture Industry in 1927" (1928), by George R. Canty, *Trade Information Bulletin*, no. 542, p. 15.

71.   William Victor Strauss, "Foreign Distribution of American Motion Pictures," *Harvard Business Review* 8 (1930): 314.

72.   U.S. Department of Commerce, Bureau of Foreign and Domestic Commerce, "The European Motion-Picture Industry in 1928" (1929), by George R. Canty, *Trade Information Bulletin*, no. 617, pp. 34, 58.

73.   Harold Sugarman, letter to Arthur W. Kelly, 17 July 1933, W. P. Philips file, box 2, folder 3, United Artists Collection.

74.   *Trade Information Bulletin*, no. 617, p. 25.

75.   U.S. Department of Commerce, Bureau of Foreign and Domestic Commerce, "Market for Motion Pictures in Central Europe, Italy, and Spain" (1927), by George R. Canty, *Trade Information Bulletin*, no. 499, p. 17.

76.   *Trade Information Bulletin*, no. 694, p. 3.

77.   See MPPDA, press release, 27 July 1929, Meetings—Exhibition—Production file, reel 7, MPPDA Archive.

78. U.S. Department of Commerce, Bureau of Foreign and Domestic Commerce, "European Motion-Picture Industry in 1930" (1931), *Trade Information Bulletin*, no. 752, p. 62.

79. U.S. Department of Commerce, Bureau of Foreign and Domestic Commerce, "The Motion-Picture Industry in Continental Europe in 1931" (1932), *Trade Information Bulletin*, no. 797, p. 4.

80. Ibid., p. 10.

81. *Trade Information Bulletin*, no. 617, p. 19.

82. See, for example, Douglas Gomery, "Economic Struggle and Hollywood Imperialism: Europe Converts to Sound," in *Film Sound: Theory and Practice*, edited by Elisabeth Weis and John Belton (New York: Columbia University Press, 1985), 25–36.

83. Thompson, *Exporting Entertainment*, 165. As Horak has commented, the economic consequences of the German quota regulations require further research. See Horak, "Rin-Tin-Tin in Berlin," 60.

84. *Trade Information Bulletin*, no. 694, p. 4.

85. Ibid., p. 7.

86. See Harold Smith, cable to MPPDA, 14 February 1930, O'Brien legal file, box 97, folder 5, United Artists Collection. Smith reported that Ludwig Klitsch, director of the German studio Ufa, "believes that contingent is practically ended on account of dialogue films, and that in three months they will be faced with a strong demand for sound pictures, and so few available here that there may be a let up at that time."

87. *Trade Information Bulletin*, no. 694, p. 17. Even so, the French did manage to restrict American imports by limiting the entry of dubbed films and the number of cinemas that could show original-language versions. See Thompson, *Exporting Entertainment*, 165.

88. *Trade Information Bulletin*, no. 752, p. 63.

89. *Trade Information Bulletin*, no. 797, p. 7.

90. See Thompson, *Exporting Entertainment*, 166–67; and Gomery, "Economic Struggle and Hollywood Imperialism," in *Film Sound*, ed. Weis and Belton, 32–33.

91. See Thompson, *Exporting Entertainment*, 111–17.

92. See *Trade Information Bulletin*, no. 617, p. 29.

93. See Thompson, *Exporting Entertainment*, 148–58; and Gomery, "Economic Struggle and Hollywood Imperialism," in *Film Sound*, ed. Weis and Belton, 28–30.

94. In 1930 British studios produced 116 feature sound films, with 8 French, 8 German, and 3 Spanish versions. See *Trade Information Bulletin*, no. 752, p. 16.

95. C. J. North, "Meeting Sound Film Competition Abroad," *Commerce Reports*, 10 November 1930, 374.

96. *Trade Information Bulletin*, no. 694, p. 4.

97. Thompson, *Exporting Entertainment*, 160.

98. See Ginette Vincendeau, "Hollywood Babylon—the Multiple Language Version," *Screen* 20, no. 2 (1988): 24–39; and Nataša Ďurovičová, "The

Hollywood Multilinguals, 1929–1933," in *Sound Theory/Sound Practice*, edited by Rick Altman (New York: Routledge, 1992), 138–53.

99.   "Warners Start Foreign Tongue School to Train Players for Multi-Linguals," *Exhibitors Daily Review and Motion Pictures Today*, 28 April 1930, 1.

100.   *Trade Information Bulletin*, no. 694, p. 5.

101.   Harold B. Franklin, *Sound Motion Pictures* (New York: Doubleday, Doran and Co., 1929), 324.

102.   Henry Blanke, letter to John V. Wilson, 9 June 1930, *The Bad Man* file, PCA Archive.

103.   Joy, letter to Irving Thalberg, 14 August 1930, *Mr. Wu* file, PCA Archive.

104.   Ibid.

105.   Ibid.

106.   See, for example, Fred Eastman, "Ambassadors of Ill Will," *Christian Century* 47 (1930): 144–47.

107.   Hays, letter to Joy, 7 February 1931, *Bachelor Father* file, PCA Archive.

108.   Wilson, memo to Joy, 11 February 1931, *Bachelor Father* file, PCA Archive.

109.   Herron, letter to Wilson, 10 March 1930, *Command to Love* file, PCA Archive.

110.   Quoted in Joy, letter to Thalberg, 29 March 1930, *They Knew What They Wanted* file, PCA Archive.

111.   Herron, letter to Wilson, 5 February 1931, *Bachelor Father* file, PCA Archive. For a discussion of the different application of "moral" standards in the multiple-language versions, see Vincendeau, "Hollywood Babylon," 35–37.

112.   *Trade Information Bulletin*, no. 797, p. 31.

113.   See Ďurovičová, "Hollywood Multilinguals," in *Sound Theory*, ed. Altman, 147–48.

114.   Thompson, *Exporting Entertainment*, 161.

115.   G. F. Morgan, letter to Arthur Kelly, 21 July 1933, W. P. Philips file, box 2, folder 3, United Artists Collection.

116.   This did not always have the desired effect. Harold L. Smith observed in 1935 that none of the people directing the dubbing operations in Paris were in fact French. MGM came the nearest, with a woman of Polish origin whom Smith thought had been naturalized. Smith, letter to Herron, 7 February 1935, W. P. Philips file, box 1, folder 7, United Artists Collection.

117.   In Belgium some versions were simultaneously dubbed in French and subtitled in Flemish, while in Greece and Albania some versions were both dubbed in French and subtitled in Greek. See memo, 1 May 1937, Black Books—Foreign Statistics, box 7, folder 2, United Artists Collection.

118.   G. F. Morgan, letter to Arthur Kelly, 21 July 1933, W. P. Philips file, box 2, folder 3, United Artists Collection.

119.   *Trade Information Bulletin*, no. 797, p. 56.

120.   Ďurovičová, "Hollywood Multilinguals," in *Sound Theory*, ed. Altman, 146.

121.   Australian and Canadian censors continued to use methods of adaptation learned in the silent era: they developed the art of the intertitle and the preface to try to set the tone of the movie and to guide the imaginative experience of the audience. For example, in *The Barbarian* (MGM, 1933) the Australian censors ordered the insertion of the following title: "East is west and west is east, and never the twain shall meet—till earth and sky stand presently at God's great judgment seat—Kipling." Report, Australian censor, *The Barbarian* file, PCA Archive. The most extraordinary preface I have found was inserted by Canadian censors in *Wild Boys of the Road* (Warner Bros., 1933):

"While this presentation is primarily a story of conditions in the United States, yet in our own country the patience of our economically disinherited youth is sadly tried in common with all nations of the earth. . . .

"It may surprise some to reflect that down by the banks of our great tidal rivers boys of teen age as well as older men are living in shacks and ingenious shelters that have been fairly comfortable until now that winter comes. . . . The rainy weather has sodden the low peat country, small mud and sand bars run out from the shallows into the cruel depths of the sullen river and boys stand about in damp clothing around brasiers of disused gasoline cans, cooking the food they have obtained through fishing, panhandling or the rare 'job.' . . . We get a glimpse of them before the fog of a winter's evening closes in. . . . They are fast returning from the higher standard to the level of the coolie and untouchable of the Yangtse-Kiang and other great rivers of the sorrowful of the earth. . . . They are here from all over the Dominion, the drifters who 'ride the freights,' those who cling to that elusive thing they call 'liberty,' which keeps them out of the places provided for unemployed; some have left home where love hemmed them in, breaking hearts of parents who wait in terror and anguish for word that never comes; others have come to the last ditch of the desperate from homes that have been swept away in the tribulation of the workless.

"Shall we escape the menace that grows from such conditions?

"Is it nothing to you that pass by?"

See Report, Canadian censor, *Wild Boys of the Road* file, PCA Archive.

122.   Joy, letter to E. A. Howe, 16 June 1931, *Milly* file, PCA Archive.

Chapter 4. Sophisticated Responses and Displaced Persons

1.   Dorothy B. Jones, "Hollywood's International Relations," *Quarterly of Film, Radio and Television* 11, no. 4 (1951): 367–68.

2.   Clara Beranger, "The Story," in *Introduction to the Photoplay*, ed. Tibbetts, 137.

3.   Robert Gustafson, "The Buying of Ideas: Source Acquisition at Warner Bros., 1930–1949" (Ph.D. diss., University of Michigan, 1983), 141–43.

4.   To some extent this statement reflects Lasky's desire to see the motion picture industry accorded the same status as the popular press. Reporter's transcript, "Proceedings of Conference Held at the Offices of the Association of

Motion Picture Producers, Monday, Feb. 10th, 1930," pp. 96–97, AMPP—
Production Code file, reel 8, MPPDA Archive.

  5. Gustafson, "Buying of Ideas," 79, 113.

  6. *Federal Motion Picture Commission* (1926), 355.

  7. Ibid.

  8. C. L. Roser (Al Ringling Theatre), letter to Hays, 2 December 1927,
Protests file, reel 3, MPPDA Archive.

  9. W. Ward Marsh, "One Moment Please! An Ambassador from the Hays
Office Notes Worries Caused by the Talkies, Podunk and the Revue-Type
Film," *Cleveland Plain Dealer,* 29 September 1929, Books and Plays file, reel 6,
MPPDA Archive.

  10. Frank Wilstach, letter to Joy, 2 April 1929, and Maurice McKenzie,
telegram to Joy, 4 April 1929, both in *The Trial of Mary Dugan* file, PCA
Archive.

  11. See Richard Maltby, " 'To Prevent the Prevalent Type of Book': Censorship and Adaptation in Hollywood, 1924–1934," *American Quarterly* 44, no. 4
(December 1992): 554–83.

  12. "Resolution of Board of Directors of Motion Picture Producers and Distributors of America, Inc., 19 June 1924," Books and Plays Formula file, reel 3,
MPPDA Archive.

  13. *Memorandum between the Authors' League of America, the Dramatists' Guild
of the Authors' League, the Authors' Guild of the Authors' League, and the Motion
Picture Producers and Distributors of America, Inc.* (New York: Motion Picture Producers and Distributors of America, 1927), pamphlet.

  14. Maltby, " 'To Prevent the Prevalent Type of Book,' " 563.

  15. Discussing the sensational appeal of the book, Claud Cockburn observed that Arlen was "the only novelist to have his trouser-bottoms torn off by
mobs of fans on the quay at New York." See Cockburn, *Bestseller: The Books That
Everyone Read, 1900–1939* (London: Sidgwick and Jackson, 1972), 171.
  The contravention of industry agreements did not go unnoticed by other
producers. Harry Warner sent the ads to Hays and told him, "The method now
used, whereby you are allowing people to change stories of condemned plays,
in my opinion, is the biggest joke I have ever heard of. . . . Why beat around
the bush? If you are going to allow plays to be made from any condemned
books, why not do so openly and any way the producer sees fit, because in that
way, he may only hurt his own company and by using a ruse, he is hurting the
business in its entirety." Harry Warner, letter to Hays, 4 January 1929, Books
and Plays file, reel 6, MPPDA Archive.

  16. The origins of adaptations from literature were usually no secret, even
when the titles were changed and the ads refrained from mentioning the book,
since newspapers reported both the studios' acquisitions and the changes of
name. See "Progress of Mr. Hays' Uplift Movement," *Christian Century* 47
(1930): 1438.

  17. Joy, letter to Walter Wanger, 18 September 1929, *Applause* file, PCA
Archive.

18. Lea Jacobs discusses aspects of the MPPDA's policies through which "offensive ideas could survive at the price of an instability of meaning," mainly in relation to the period after Joy departed from the SRC in 1932. See Lea Jacobs, "Industry Self-Regulation and the Problem of Textual Determination," *Velvet Light Trap*, no. 23 (1989): 4–15; and idem, *The Wages of Sin*.

19. Joy, letter to Joe Schenck, 21 March 1930, *Du Barry, Woman of Passion* file, PCA Archive.

20. Maurice McKenzie, letter to Joy, 20 December 1928, *Our Modern Maidens* file, PCA Archive.

21. Gustafson, "Buying of Ideas," 81.

22. See Richard Maltby, "The Genesis of the Production Code," *Quarterly Review of Film and Video* 15, no. 4 (1995): 5–32; and idem, "Documents on the Genesis of the Production Code," 33–64.

23. See, for example, Moley, *Hays Office*, 75–88.

24. After the introduction of the Production Code, Joy's staff consisted of Lamar Trotti (assistant) John V. Wilson (foreign subjects), Florence Sell and Betty Neely (readers), James B. Fisher (reviewer), Douglas Mackinnon (short subjects), and Jack Hutchings (office manager). Alice Winter, nominated to represent the "women of America" by virtue of her former presidency of the General Federation of Women's Clubs, was also accommodated in the office.

25. Joy, letter to Thalberg, 6 March 1931, *Strangers May Kiss* file, PCA Archive.

26. See Joy, letter to Hays, 16 April 1930, AMPP—Code file, reel 8, MPPDA Archive.

27. Robert Pearson, letter to Joy, 9 June 1932, *Ten Nights in a Barroom* file, PCA Archive.

28. See Lamar Trotti, letter to Maurice McKenzie, 19 April 1932, *Woman in Room 13* file, PCA Archive.

29. Zanuck, letter to Joy, 21 September 1932, *Three on a Match* file, PCA Archive.

30. Joy, memo to Hays, 29 April 1931, Production Code file, reel 9, MPPDA Archive.

31. Ibid.

32. Trotti commented to Hays that "most of the MGM pictures have escaped drastic censorship action in this country because of the very fine manner in which the alleged dubious themes are handled." Trotti, memo to Hays, 1 August 1932, *Cock of the Air* file, PCA Archive.

33. Joy, letter to Darryl Zanuck, 17 April 1931, *Bought* file, PCA Archive.

34. See Richard Maltby, " 'A Brief Romantic Interlude': Dick and Jane Go to Three-and-a-Half Seconds of the Classical Hollywood Cinema," in *Post-Theory: Reconstructing Film Studies*, edited by David Bordwell and Noël Carroll (Madison: University of Wisconsin Press, 1995), 434–59.

35. Kuhn, *Cinema, Censorship and Sexuality*, 28.

36. T. B. Fithian, letter to Joy, 20 February 1931, *Where Are My Children?* file, PCA Archive.

37.   Zanuck, letter to Joy, 30 November 1931; Joy, letter to Zanuck, 24 November 1931; and Zanuck, memo, 18 September 1931, all in *Alias the Doctor* file, Warner Bros. Archive.

38.   The well-known economist Roger W. Babson had stimulated the debate on motion pictures and crime in April 1929 with the publication of a report in which he blamed movies for the murder rate in the United States. He claimed that "the greater percentage of pictures are crime-breeding and plant seeds of vice and deceit." See Babson, "Crime Waves," *Babson's Reports*, 8 April 1929, n.p. The subject was revived by a cycle of gangster movies in the production season 1930–31, specifically in relation to the real-life shooting of a twelve-year-old boy, Winslow Elliot, by his sixteen-year-old friend, supposedly in imitation of the MGM film *The Secret Six*. See "A Shot Heard around the Country," *Literary Digest*, 25 July 1931, 20–21. The continuing controversy contributed to the impact of the Payne Fund Studies when they were published in 1933.

39.   Trotti, letter to Harold Fingerlin, 3 November 1930, *Stolen Heaven* file, PCA Archive. Ironically, on a different level of obfuscation, Warner Bros. was advised to *introduce* gambling scenes into *Mandalay* (Warner Bros., 1933), to demonstrate that one of their locations (the Orient Café) was "more of a nightclub" than a brothel. James Wingate, letter to Jack Warner, 20 October 1933, *Mandalay* file, PCA Archive.

40.   Joy had reported on such procedures after visiting censor boards in 1928: "It is the writer's impression that pictures are not judged as a whole but that individual titles and sequences are eliminated often without reference to their relation to the dramatic and moral value of the story. An effort was made to impress the censors with the necessity of judging the picture in its entirety during its first screening and then if necessary to screen it again for the purpose of making eliminations if it contained material which then appeared to be objectionable." Joy, "Résumé of Dinner-Meeting of the Studio Relations Committee," 19 April 1928, Department of Public and Industry Relations file, reel 4, MPPDA Archive.

41.   Joy, résumé, 29 June 1931, *Are These Our Children?* file, PCA Archive.

42.   See Richard Maltby, " 'Grief in the Limelight': Al Capone, Howard Hughes, the Hays Code, and the Politics of the Unstable Text," in *Movies and Politics: The Dynamic Relationship*, edited by James Combs (New York: Garland, 1993), 133–82.

43.   Joy, letter to E. B. Derr (Caddo), 4 June 1932, Caddo—*Scarface* file, reel 9, MPPDA Archive.

44.   See, for example, Robert Sklar, *Movie-made America: A Cultural History of American Movies* (London: Chappell and Co., 1975), 175–94.

45.   Joy, letter to Hays, 21 December 1931, *The Man Who Talked Too Much* file, PCA Archive.

46.   Joy, letter to Darryl Zanuck, 29 May 1930, *The Doorway to Hell* file, PCA Archive.

47.   Trotti, report to Hays, 12 December 1930, and Joy, résumé, 16 December 1930, both in *The Front Page* file, PCA Archive.

48.   Joy, résumé, 16 December 1930, *The Front Page* file, PCA Archive. Eight years later, when the movie was remade as *His Girl Friday* (Columbia, 1939), the Chicago elements were still absent. At the same time, since Hollywood's characterization of reporters and editors had been the subject of considerable criticism in the press, the movie's ironic disclaimer was given a twist. It now read,

"It all happened in the 'Dark Ages' of the newspaper game—when to a reporter 'getting that story' justified anything short of murder.

"Incidentally you will see in this picture no resemblance to the men and women of the press of today.

"Ready?

"Well, once upon a time—"

I am indebted to Kristin Thompson for drawing my attention to this preface.

49.   Trotti, Joy, Wilson, and Fisher, letter to Zanuck, 26 July 1932, *I Am a Fugitive from a Chain Gang* file, PCA Archive.

50.   Hays, letter to Wingate, 14 February 1933, *She Had to Say Yes* file, PCA Archive.

51.   See May, *Screening Out the Past*, 147–66.

52.   Hays, memo, 23 July 1929, *The Boudoir Diplomat* file, PCA Archive.

53.   Joy, memo, 25 November 1929, *The Boudoir Diplomat* file, PCA Archive.

54.   Wilson, letter to Herron, 27 July 1932, *The Painted Woman* file, PCA Archive.

55.   F.S., report, 10 April 1930, *Her Man* file, PCA Archive.

56.   James B. Fisher, report, 26 August 1930, and Herron, letter to Wilson, 17 October 1930, both in *Her Man* file, PCA Archive.

57.   For a discussion of the difficulties inherent in tracing the provenance of prints, see Maltby, " 'Grief in the Limelight,' " in *Movies and Politics*, ed. Combs, 133–82.

58.   T. S. Dellahanty, letter to Herron, 29 October 1930, *Her Man* file, PCA Archive.

59.   Herron, letter to Wilson, 19 April 1932, *The Cuban Love Song* file, PCA Archive.

60.   Joy, letter to Al Rockett, 20 January 1932, *The Gay Caballero* file, PCA Archive.

61.   Al Rockett, letter to Joy, 23 January 1932, *The Gay Caballero* file, PCA Archive.

62.   Luis E. Feliu (Chilean consul), letter to Hays, 28 March 1930, AMPP—Code file, reel 8, MPPDA Archive.

63.   Herron, letter to Joy, 22 December 1931, *The Cuban Love Song* file, PCA Archive.

64.   J. M. Valdez-Rodriguez, "Hollywood: Sales Agent of American Imperialism," *Experimental Cinema* 1, no. 4 (1933): 19.

65.   Hays, letter to Giacomo de Martino, 13 June 1932, Caddo—*Scarface* file, reel 9, MPPDA Archive. Herron commented to John V. Wilson that "we are in the midst of an Italian eruption at the present time, and we never know where they are going to hit next. Our alibi on *Scarface, the Shame of a Nation* was pretty

weak, but at least it has quieted them down for the time being." Herron, letter to Wilson, 27 June 1932, *A Child Is Born* file, PCA Archive.

66. "The Lash," *Variety,* 15 December 1930, n.p.

67. Herron, letter to Joy, 21 March 1931, *The Lash* file, PCA Archive.

68. Joy, letter to Thalberg, 12 May 1932, *As You Desire Me* file, PCA Archive; Joy, letter to Harry Cohn, 12 October 1932, *So This Is Africa* file, PCA Archive.

69. Wingate, letter to Merian C. Cooper, 19 May 1933, *The Headline Shooter* file, PCA Archive; Wingate, letter to David O. Selznick, 22 December 1932, *Our Betters* file, PCA Archive.

70. Fisher, review, 14 January 1931, *Dracula* file, PCA Archive.

71. Hays, letter to Jack Warner, 24 October 1930, *This Is What They're Saying* file, reel 9, MPPDA Archive.

72. After discussions with MGM about *War Nurse* in September 1930, Lamar Trotti reported, "Their attitude has been a little bit queer all the way through. Not the usual Thalberg reaction. Their attitude at the moment is, why should any small group of people decide what the rest of the world should see?" Maurice McKenzie, memo, 30 September 1930, MGM *War Nurse* file, reel 8, MPPDA Archive.

73. Trotti, letter to Hays, 30 March 1931, Production Code file, reel 9, MPPDA Archive.

74. Joy, letter to Joseph Breen, 15 December 1931, *Possessed* file, PCA Archive.

75. See Hays, letter to Robert Cochrane (Universal), 29 April 1931, Production Code file, reel 9, MPPDA Archive. Hays reports a meeting with company heads, held on 20 April, at which it was agreed that the release of gangster pictures should henceforth be staggered. In 1932 Joy suggested limiting the release of movies with sexual themes. See report by Joy included in Hays, memo to company heads, 29 September 1932, reel 10, MPPDA Archive. In 1935 Hays wrote to company heads regarding the "G-man" cycle of pictures, observing, "The quantitative element is a serious factor and it is going to be necessary to stagger the releases." See Hays, letter to Ned Depinet (RKO), 6 September 1935, Production Code file, reel 11, MPPDA Archive.

76. Joy, letter to Julia Kelly (Hays's secretary), 21 June 1930, *The Green Pastures* file, PCA Archive.

77. For example, the publicity for *Glorifying the American Girl* illustrates "how a good picture may get a bad name through its advertising." Joy, letter to Geoffrey Shurlock, 13 December 1929, *Glorifying the American Girl* file, PCA Archive. For a full statement of the Advertising Code and its "uniform interpretation," see Moley, *Hays Office,* 249–50. See also Janet Staiger, "Announcing Wares, Winning Patrons, Voicing Ideals: Thinking about the History and Theory of Film Advertising," *Cinema Journal* 29, no. 3 (1990): 3–31; and Mary Beth Haralovich, "Advertising Heterosexuality," *Screen* 23, no. 2 (1982): 50–60.

78. MPPDA, *This Is What They're Saying* (in-house bulletin), no. 15, 15 May 1930, p. 1.

79. Hays, letter to Aylesworth, 29 September 1932, Production Code file, reel 10, MPPDA Archive.

80. When Joy left he was praised in the press for his ability to mediate diplomatically between public organizations, censors, and producers. See "Joy Quits as Aid of Hays to Join Fox as Adviser," *New York Herald Tribune*, 7 November 1932.

81. See Trotti, letter to Hays, 22 January 1931, *Illicit* file, PCA Archive. Trotti reports Wingate's view that the industry should not be allowed to drift into the position of the stage, writing that "while he recognized the natural temptation to use popular Broadway material, he would nevertheless be utterly opposed to pictures dealing with kept women, etc."

82. For an account of the worsening problems facing the SRC during Wingate's jurisdiction, see Wingate, letter to Zanuck, 3 April 1933, *Mary Stevens, M.D.* file, PCA Archive.

83. See Shearon Lowery and Melvin L. De Fleur, *Milestones in Mass Communication Research: Media Effects* (New York: Longman, 1983), 32–57.

84. Wingate, letter to Hays, 10 March 1933, Production Code file, reel 10, MPPDA Archive.

85. Gustafson, "Buying of Ideas," 72. The decline in the purchase of plays was in line with the general severe reduction in production costs during the 1932–33 and 1933–34 production seasons.

86. Wingate, letter to Hays, 10 March 1933, MPPDA Archive.

Chapter 5. Why Is Mr. Brown Eating Spaghetti?

1. Harry Zehner, memo to Martin Murphy, 26 May 1933, Universal Studios Censorship file, box 778, Department of Special Collections, Doheney Library, University of Southern California, Los Angeles. By 1944 Zehner was overseeing serials for the Production Code Administration. See Jack Vizzard, *See No Evil: Life Inside a Hollywood Censor* (New York: Simon and Schuster, 1970), 78–80.

2. Harry Zehner, memo to Martin Murphy, 26 May 1933, Universal Studios Censorship file, box 778, Special Collections, University of Southern California.

3. Martin Quigley, letter to Hays, 4 August 1932, Hays Collection.

4. For an examination of the Legion of Decency campaign, see Black, *Hollywood Censored*, 149–92. For an alternative account, see Maltby, "Production Code and the Hays Office," in *Grand Design*, by Balio, 37–72.

5. See Paul W. Facey, *The Legion of Decency: A Sociological Analysis of the Emergence and Development of a Pressure Group* (New York: Arno, 1974); and Stephen Vaughn, "Morality and Entertainment: The Origins of the Motion Picture Production Code," *Journal of American History* 77 (June 1990): 39–65.

6. Ruth Inglis, *Freedom of the Movies: A Report on Self-Regulation from the Commission on the Freedom of the Press* (Chicago: University of Chicago Press, 1947), 124. On the other hand, Gregory D. Black cites material from the Hays Collection suggesting that the boycott was only effective in Philadelphia, San Francisco, Cincinnati, and St. Louis and that the Legion's activities actually *stimulated* motion picture attendance overall. According to Black, "The evi-

dence suggests that the Legion was, at least in 1934, a major bluff" (*Hollywood Censored*, 190).

7.   Milliken, letter to Quigley, 23 March 1935, Production Code file, reel 11, MPPDA Archive.

8.   Leff and Simmons, *The Dame in the Kimono*, 42–43.

9.   The PCA continued to consult Catholic authorities about the likely Catholic reaction to story treatments throughout the 1930s. See, for example, *The Garden of Allah* file, PCA Archive.

10.   I have been unable to find a list of the cases brought before this panel and the action taken on them. Moley states that the "Hollywood Jury" was invoked six times under Joy and four times after his departure. Moley claims that "it made its judgments wholly without objectivity" and that "Colonel Joy lost every appeal" (*Hays Office*, 75). However, a report in the press asserts that Joy's position was upheld in relation to *The Common Law* (RKO, 1931) and possibly in relation to *Seed* (Universal, 1931) and *The Maltese Falcon* (Warner Bros., 1931). See "Joy Quits as Aid of Hays to Join Fox as Adviser," *New York Herald Tribune*, 7 November 1932.

11.   For example, according to Olga Martin in *Hollywood's Movie Commandments: A Handbook for Motion Picture Writers and Reviewers* (New York: H. W. Wilson, 1937), under Joy "the Code was more or less ignored by the producers, who generally over-ruled the efforts of the Production Code office to enforce its tenets" (10), while the "moral crusade" of 1934 "forcibly advanced the standards of the modern cinema to embrace moral doctrines" (61). Hays himself claimed, "The industry's buffeted ship reached open water on the Fourth of July, 1934, with the firm establishment of the Production Code Administration. The skies were clearing, and we were free to go full steam ahead" (*Memoirs*, 455). Leonard Leff and Jerold Simmons valorize Breen's role in industry regulation and marginalize the contribution of Joy in *The Dame in the Kimono;* so does Gregory Black in *Hollywood Censored*.

12.   Moley, *Hays Office*, 90.

13.   For a debunking of these myths, see Vizzard, *See No Evil*, 112–20. At the same time, Vizzard cites the case of a PCA "censor," Charles Metzger, who kept meticulous casebook files, but he emphasizes that Metzger's procedure was idiosyncratic (8–12).

14.   Geoffrey Shurlock, memo for the files, 26 July 1934, in *Outcast Lady* file, PCA Archive.

15.   Breen, letter to Thalberg, 13 September 1934, *Outcast Lady* file, PCA Archive.

16.   Breen sometimes brought alarming vehemence to the idea of punishment for sexual transgressors. For example, rather than see Marlene Dietrich's character get off scot-free at the end of *The Devil Is a Woman*, he suggested an alternative whereby she would be choked to death by her lover. See Breen, letter to John Hammell, 19 April 1935, *The Devil Is a Woman* file, PCA Archive.

17.   Breen, letter to H. N. Swanson, 30 December 1933, *The Gay Divorce* file, PCA Archive.

18.   Breen, letter to Jack Warner, 27 February 1934, *Dr. Monica* file, Warner Bros. Archive.

19.   Ibid.

20.   Breen, letter to Jack Warner, 24 April 1934, *Dr. Monica* file, Warner Bros. Archive.

21.   See Jeanine Basinger, *A Woman's View: How Hollywood Spoke to Women, 1930–1960* (New York: Alfred A. Knopf, 1993), esp. 151–59, 392–408.

22.   For another baffling presentation of a pregnancy and abortion, see *Ann Vickers* (RKO, 1933).

23.   Edward S. Schwegler, letter to Breen re *Four Hours to Kill* (Paramount, 1935), 1 September 1935, *The Informer* file, PCA Archive.

24.   Hays, letter to J. Robert Rubin, 4 January 1934, *Men in White* file, PCA Archive.

25.   Breen, letter to Jack Warner, 8 February 1937, *Marked Woman* file, PCA Archive.

26.   Breen, letter to Jack Warner, 13 September 1937, *The Adventures of Robin Hood* file, PCA Archive.

27.   Breen, letter to Jack Warner, 14 February 1935, *G-Men* file, PCA Archive.

28.   This speculation would apply to America's foreign markets as well, although particular historical and constitutional factors tended to make America more susceptible to *armed* criminals than many of its foreign customers. See Richard Hofstadter and Michael Wallace, eds., *American Violence: A Documentary History* (New York: Alfred A. Knopf, 1970).

29.   Martin, *Hollywood's Movie Commandments*, 134.

30.   Examples include *Bullets or Ballots* (Warner Bros., 1936) and *Gangs of New York* (Republic, 1938). Breen was enthusiastic about a proposal that the racketeers in *Bullets or Ballots* should be "of the suave, well-educated, well-dressed, polite type—more like successful bankers or businessmen than like gangsters"; in addition, there should be no showing of guns or gun battles with police. See Breen, letter to Jack Warner, 20 December 1935, *Bullets or Ballots* file, PCA Archive.

31.   For a comprehensive history of black participation in the movie business, see Thomas Cripps, *Slow Fade to Black: The Negro in American Film, 1900–1942* (Oxford: Oxford University Press, 1977); idem, *Making Movies Black: The Hollywood Message Movie from World War II to the Civil Rights Era* (Oxford: Oxford University Press, 1993); and Donald Bogle, *Toms, Coons, Mulattoes, Mammies, and Bucks: An Interpretive History of Blacks in American Films* (New York: Bantam, 1973).

32.   For example, in relation to *Artists and Models*, in which Martha Raye appeared with Louis Armstrong's orchestra in a mock Harlem gangster setting, Paramount received the following complaint from a Louisiana newspaper editor: "For Negroes and whites to be shown in social equality roles is offensive in this part of the country, where the races have nothing socially in common. It never fails to offend the white citizens of this section, and I have

an idea that many Negroes have the same feeling because my lifetime observa-
tion has been that representative Negroes in the Southland wish none of the
social equality ideas." See Dolph Frantz (managing editor, [Shreveport, La.]
Journal), letter to Adolph Zukor, 25 August 1937, Imitation of Life file, PCA
Archive. Frantz circulated his protest to southern exhibitors and to the
MPPDA. Breen wrote to Maurice McKenzie, Hays's executive assistant in the
New York office of the MPPDA: "In this connection, you may be interested in
knowing that we have repeatedly warned the studios about the shooting of
such scenes. Unfortunately, it is not usually set forth in the script that certain
of the dancers are to be Negroes and, consequently, we rarely have an opportunity to discuss this phase of the matter before the picture goes into production." See Breen, letter to Maurice McKenzie, 16 September 1937, Imitation of
Life file, PCA Archive.

33.   Hays, quoted in Islin Auster, memo to Breen, 13 March 1934, Imitation
of Life file, PCA Archive.

34.   Breen, memo for the files, 9 March 1934, Imitation of Life file, PCA
Archive.

35.   Islin Auster, memo to Breen, 13 March 1934, Imitation of Life file, PCA
Archive.

36.   Hays, letter to Robert H. Cochrane, 18 May 1934, Imitation of Life file,
PCA Archive.

37.   In Charleston, Charlotte, Little Rock, Louisville, Memphis, Norfolk,
Richmond, and San Antonio Imitation of Life performed best of the three. In
Baltimore, Dallas, Houston, and New Orleans it came in second. Atlanta was
the only city in the South where it ranked third. See Harry Zehner, memo to
Breen, 24 January 1935, Imitation of Life file, PCA Archive.

38.   H. E. Wilson, vice president of Stuart Silver Fox Ranch (Nebraska),
letter to Breen, 26 August 1936, Bullets or Ballots file, PCA Archive.

39.   Thomas Cripps sees 1942 as a watershed for African Americans in the
movies. In that year the heads of several Hollywood studios agreed to meet
with delegates from the National Association for the Advancement of Colored
People to codify some changes to aspects of black representation. See Cripps,
Slow Fade to Black, 349ff.

40.   Herron, letter to Joy, 26 February 1932, Sunny Side Up file, PCA
Archive.

41.   Hays, memo, 24 October 1934, Meetings—Code file, reel 10, MPPDA
Archive.

42.   Golden, "Brief History and Statistics" (1936), 7.

43.   For example, the Canadian censorship report for Beau Geste (Paramount, 1939) includes the excision of three scenes that had already been removed from the American print: a preface, a bayoneting scene, and the line
"After we kill Markhoff and you I'm going to take off this uniform and spit on
it." See censorship record, Beau Geste file, PCA Archive.

44.   Breen, letter to Vincent Hart, 13 August 1934, Production Code file,
reel 10, MPPDA Archive.

45.   Vincent Hart, letter to W. P. Philips, 13 August 1934, and Hart, letter to Philips, 21 August 1934, both in W. P. Philips file, box 3, folder 13, United Artists Collection.

46.   Hays, memo, 24 October 1934, Meetings—Code file, reel 10, MPPDA Archive.

47.   Martin, *Hollywood's Movie Commandments*, 225.

48.   Censorship record, *East Is West* file, PCA Archive.

49.   Cline M. Koon, *Motion Pictures in Education in the United States: A Report* (Chicago: University of Chicago Press, 1934), 45.

50.   Breen, letter to Herron, 12 February 1937, *The Gay Divorce* file, PCA Archive. In the version of *Star of Midnight* screened on Britain's Channel 4 in 1990, the character does not appear onscreen at all. He may never have done so, although it is possible that he was eliminated in response to the Italian protest. In any case, character names are not supplied with the cast list, so whether he appeared or not the studio presumably would have been able to issue a denial to either an Italian or an Irish protest.

51.   Breen, memo to Hays, 12 February 1937, *The Gay Divorce* file, PCA Archive.

52.   Changes were made in *The Yellow Ticket* (Fox, 1931) and *The Bureau of Missing Persons* (Warner Bros., 1933) at the behest of the Greek association the Order of Ahepa. See *The Bureau of Missing Persons* file, PCA Archive. Breen warned Jack Warner about a Greek characterization in *The Man Who Talked Too Much* (Warner Bros., 1940), on the basis that it might offend Greek exhibitors in the United States. See Breen, letter to Jack Warner, 8 April 1940, *The Man Who Talked Too Much* file, PCA Archive.

53.   See, for example, Beddington Behrens, letter to Murray Silverstone, 13 August 1936, Giannini file, box 1, folder 2, United Artists Collection.

54.   Hays, *Memoirs*, 552.

55.   See, for example, Murray Silverstone, letter to Hubert T. Marsh (British and Dominion Films Corp.), 13 April 1934, W. P. Philips file, box 2, folder 3, United Artists Collection.

56.   D. W. Griffith, "The Rise and Fall of Free Speech in America," *Series of Cinema Classics*, no. 1 (1916; Los Angeles: Larry Edmunds Bookshop, 1967), n.p. Griffith was, however, eventually able to make this project, directing *America* (D. W. Griffith/United Artists) in 1924.

57.   Circuit Court of Appeals, *Goldstein v United States*, Ninth Circuit, 26 May 1920, in Wood, ed., *Film and Propaganda in America* 1:296–303.

58.   Manager of English office, Goldwyn Ltd., letter to Hays, 3 October 1923, Hays Collection.

59.   Wingate, letter to David Selznick, 16 December 1932, *Our Betters* file, PCA Archive.

60.   Herron, letter to Wilson, 21 April 1931, *East of Borneo* file, PCA Archive.

61.   Martin, *Hollywood's Movie Commandments*, 201.

62.   Street, "Hays Office," 37–53. See also Jarvie, *Hollywood's Overseas Campaign*, 151–73.

63.   British censorship provisions forbade the depiction of "men and women in bed together." See Robertson, *British Board of Film Censors*, 182. See also Vizzard, *See No Evil*, 113–15.

64.   "The Censor's Knife," editorial, *Film Weekly*, 5 June 1937.

65.   Max Milder, letter to Sam Morris, 16 February 1937, JLW correspondence, box 59, folder 3, Warner Bros. Archive.

66.   Comments by Max Milder included in Joe Hummel, letter to Jack Warner, 16 March 1937, JLW correspondence, box 59, folder 3, Warner Bros. Archive.

67.   Martin, *Hollywood's Movie Commandments*, 213.

68.   Breen, memo for the files, 29 August 1939, *His Girl Friday* file, PCA Archive.

69.   Breen, memo for the files, 29 August 1939, *His Girl Friday* file, PCA Archive.

70.   Herron, letter to Breen, 13 April 1935, *The Plough and the Stars* file, PCA Archive.

71.   Breen, letter to B. B. Kahane, 18 June 1936, *The Plough and the Stars* file, PCA Archive.

72.   Krisel and Krisel, letter to United Artists, 8 March 1928, Censor—Foreign file, reel 5, MPPDA Archive.

73.   "Trinidad Government Principles of Censorship Applied to Cinematographic Films," internal circular, 31 December 1929, O'Brien legal file, box 97, folder 2, United Artists Collection.

74.   *Report of the Colonial Films Committee, Presented by the Secretary of State for the Colonies to Parliament by Command of His Majesty* (London: HMSO, 1930).

75.   Joy, "Résumé of Dinner-Meeting of the Studio Relations Committee," 17 May 1928, p. 6, Department of Public and Industry Relations file, reel 4, MPPDA Archive.

76.   John V. Wilson, résumé, 18 April 1931, *East of Borneo* file, PCA Archive.

77.   Herron, memo to Wilson, 21 April 1931, *East of Borneo* file, PCA Archive.

78.   See Gina Marchetti, *Romance and the "Yellow Peril": Race, Sex, and Discursive Strategies in Hollywood Fiction* (Berkeley: University of California Press, 1993).

79.   Martin, *Hollywood's Movie Commandments*, 209.

80.   Other European colonial administrations reinforced some central aspects of British influence. For example, Java, which was under Dutch rule, rejected *Affairs of a Gentleman* (Universal, 1934) because "[t]he feature is contrary to the moral standards which must be maintained in favor of the white class in the eyes of the native." Censorship record, *Affairs of a Gentleman* file, PCA Archive. In this connection, *Prestige* (RKO Pathé, 1932) seems to be something of an anomaly, demonstrating the imperfections and inconsistencies that were always a part of industry regulation in the motion picture business. It involves a French colonial administrator in "remote Lao Bao, China," who is too weak to maintain discipline among his native troops until he recovers his

pride and outfaces them at the end of the movie. There is no file for the movie at the PCA (although files were generally kept from October 1931 onward), but there is also no reference to it in any subsequent case files, which suggests that it encountered no particular problems during foreign distribution.

81. DuWayne G. Clark, "South African Motion Picture Industry Distribution Problems," *Motion Pictures Abroad*, 25 March 1931, 4.

82. U.S. Department of Commerce, Bureau of Foreign and Domestic Commerce, "Small Island Markets for Motion Pictures" (1931), *Trade Information Bulletin*, no. 756, p. 16.

83. James H. Smiley (U.S. Department of Commerce), letter to Joy, 17 April 1928, *Beau Geste* file, PCA Archive.

84. Herron, letter to Joy, 14 September 1928, *Plastered in Paris* file, PCA Archive.

85. Joy, letter to Joe Schenck, 21 March 1930, *Du Barry, Woman of Passion* file, PCA Archive.

86. Hal Wallis, memo to William Koenig, 19 September 1933, *Footlight Parade* file, Warner Bros. Archive.

87. Paul K. Whang, "The Boycotting of Harold's Lloyd's *Welcome Danger,*" *China Weekly Review*, 8 March 1930, 51.

88. Report of British Columbian censors, cited in T. B. Fithian, letter to John V. Wilson, 4 December 1930, *East Is West* file, PCA Archive.

89. Herron, letter to Joy, 15 January 1931, *East Is West* file, PCA Archive.

90. Herron, letter to Breen, 16 April 1937, *The General Died at Dawn* file, PCA Archive.

91. American consul general, Tokyo, "The Japanese Motion Picture Market in 1938," *Motion Pictures Abroad*, 1 December 1938, 20.

92. Wolfgang Reinhardt, "Explanatory Note," 15 February 1938, *Juarez* file, Warner Bros. Archive.

93. Jack Warner, letter to Bryan Foy, 8 March 1939, JLW correspondence, box 57, Warner Bros. Archive.

94. *Trade Information Bulletin*, no. 797, p. 63.

95. See "Film Treaty between Spain and San [sic] Salvador," League of Nations *Treaty Series*, vol. 165 (1935), no. 3818, cited in John Harley, *World-wide Influences of the Cinema* (Los Angeles: University of Southern California Press, 1940), appendix 6.

96. Harley, *World-wide Influences of the Cinema*, 264. The Spanish Civil War, which Nathan Golden described as causing American distributors "considerable concern" and resulting in "substantial losses of revenue," may have rendered these treaties irrelevant and/or unenforceable. See Nathan D. Golden, "Effect of Trade Barriers Felt in Foreign Film Markets," *Motion Pictures Abroad*, 15 February 1938, 1.

97. *World Wide Motion Picture Developments*, 15 March 1937, 2; Harley, *World-wide Influences of the Cinema*, 262.

98. Nathan D. Golden, *Review of Foreign Film Markets during 1938* (Washington, D.C.: U.S. Department of Commerce, 1939), 252.

Chapter 6. Diplomatic Representations

1. Interview with Luigi Luraschi by the author, London, 23 February 1988.

2. Sam Morris, letter to Jack Warner, 12 July 1937, JLW correspondence, box 59, folder 8, Warner Bros. Archive.

3. *Trade Information Bulletin*, no. 754, p. 7.

4. Sam Morris, letter to Jack Warner, 12 July 1937, JLW correspondence, box 59, folder 8, Warner Bros. Archive.

5. Memo, 20 December 1923, O'Brien legal file, box 7, folder 25, United Artists Collection.

6. Leo F. Samuels, letter to H. W. Schroeder, 24 May 1937, Giannini file, box 4, folder 6, United Artists Collection.

7. Gomery, *Hollywood Studio System*, 36.

8. Herron, letter to Joy, 26 February 1932, *Sunny Side Up* file, PCA Archive.

9. Censorship record, *Tonight or Never* file, PCA Archive. See also Arthur Garrels (American consul general, Tokyo), "Motion Pictures in Japan and Market for American Films and Sound Motion Picture Equipment," *Motion Pictures Abroad*, 10 October 1930, 2.

10. Arthur Kelly, letter to Joe Schenck, 29 September 1933, W. P. Philips file, box 2, folder 3, United Artists Collection.

11. A. I. Ward, "Motion Pictures in North China," *Motion Pictures Abroad*, 20 May 1931, 3.

12. Walter Gould, memo to H. D. Buckley, 30 December 1936, Giannini file, box 1, folder 3, United Artists Collection.

13. Hall, "Robert M. W. Vogel Oral History," 54. According to Vogel, some of MGM's managers abroad could anticipate the success or failure of the pictures they were to receive on the strength of the number of superimposed titles in the movies: the greater the number of titles, the less the likelihood of success. See Hall, 41, 58.

14. For a discussion of the importance of catering to the foreign market, in this case in relation to the work of Walter Wanger, see Arthur Kelly, letter to A. H. Giannini, 19 November 1937, Giannini file, box 2, folder 6, United Artists Collection.

15. Joy, memo, 17 May 1932, *Cavalcade* file, PCA Archive.

16. Winfield Sheehan, letter to Joy, 9 July 1932, *Cavalcade* file, PCA Archive.

17. Joy, letter to Sheehan, 24 September 1932, *Cavalcade* file, PCA Archive. At the same time, the picture did cause some consternation at the SRC because it violated the "pointed profanity" clause of the Production Code, using "two Hells and one damn." Fox argued that the picture ought to be given some license because it was so thoroughly in tune with the *spirit* of the Code. Although the SRC agreed that it was excellent on balance, they were worried about establishing a precedent. The debate over this issue demonstrates the importance of precedents in guiding the actions of the SRC and the PCA.

18.   When sound was introduced, the reports of the Department of Commerce concentrated on the extent to which "prestige" was being upheld in the face of technical shortcomings. See, for example, *Trade Information Bulletin*, no. 752, pp. 52–53.

19.   Jack Warner, letter to Sam Morris, 9 December 1935, JLW correspondence, box 59, folder 8, Warner Bros. Archive.

20.   Gabriel L. Hess, statement before the House Immigration and Naturalization Committee, 18 February 1937, in opposition to H.R. 30 (the Dickstein Bill), O'Brien legal file, box 101, folder 1, United Artists Collection.

21.   See Gary Carey, "Greta Garbo," in *Cinema: A Critical Dictionary*, vol. 1, edited by Richard Roud (New York: Viking Press, 1980), 415–19; and Hall, "Robert M. W. Vogel Oral History," 40.

22.   She is recorded as being most popular in Algiers, Argentina, Austria, the Baltic States, Belgium, Bulgaria, Chile, Cuba, Czechoslovakia, Denmark, Germany, Greece, Holland, Hungary, Italy, the Netherlands East Indies, Norway, the Philippine Islands, Poland, Portugal, Romania, Spain, Sweden, Switzerland, Turkey, and Yugoslavia. She failed to reach the top of the list in Cristobal (where people preferred Shirley Temple), France, Puerto Rico, and the Straits Settlements.

23.   T. O. Klath, "Sweden," in *Trade Information Bulletin*, no. 694, p. 37.

24.   Hays, *Memoirs*, 509.

25.   Interview with Luigi Luraschi by the author, London, 23 February 1988.

26.   See, for example, John Baxter, *The Hollywood Exiles* (London: Macdonald and Jane's, 1976).

27.   Wallis, memo to G. W. Pabst, 23 November 1933, *A Modern Hero* file, Warner Bros. Archive. See also Jan-Christopher Horak, "G. W. Pabst in Hollywood; or, Every Modern Hero Deserves a Mother," *Film History* 1 (1987): 53–64.

28.   Jack Warner, letter to Sam Morris, 9 December 1935, JLW correspondence, box 59, folder 8, Warner Bros. Archive.

29.   Joseph Breen, letter to Maurice McKenzie, 26 March 1934, *Imitation of Life* file, PCA Archive.

30.   Breen, letter to Herron, 16 April 1935, *The Last Days of Pompeii* file, PCA Archive.

31.   Ibid.

32.   Herron, letter to Breen, 19 April 1935, *The Last Days of Pompeii* file, PCA Archive.

33.   Breen, letter to Herron, 19 April 1935, *The Last Days of Pompeii* file, PCA Archive.

34.   J. B. Wilkinson, letter to Beck, 13 May 1935, *The Last Days of Pompeii* file, PCA Archive.

35.   D. E. Griffiths, letter to Hal Wallis, 8 February 1936, *White Angel* file, Warner Bros. Archive.

36.   Jewell, "RKO Film Grosses," microfiche supplement.

37.   J. G. Mullen (Warner Bros.' Mexico office), letter to Karl G. Mac-

donald (New York Foreign Department), 11 June 1938, *Juarez* file, Warner Bros. Archive.

38. See Delpar, " 'Goodbye to the Greaser' "; and Pettit, *Images of the Mexican American*.

39. M. C. Levee, "Commercial Requirements," in *Introduction to the Photoplay*, ed. Tibbetts, 250.

40. John V. Wilson, memo to Herron, 1 December 1931, *Strangers May Kiss* file, PCA Archive.

41. McKenzie, memo, 2 April 1934, *The Trumpet Blows* file, PCA Archive.

42. Breen, report to Hays, 31 December 1935, *Klondike Annie* file, PCA Archive.

43. Levee, "Commercial Requirements," in *Introduction to the Photoplay*, ed. Tibbetts, 250.

44. Memo from Bill Pine and staff, undated, enclosed in *Woman Trap* script, Performing Arts Research Center, New York Public Library. The same memo makes explicit *Woman Trap*'s project to appeal to several kinds of audience at once, in this case the male and the female: "The ads set forth three separate and distinct types of ads . . . one based on the 'bad man' angle: 'THE BAD MAN COMES BACK' . . . *fighting!* One based on the romance angle: 'FUGITIVE SWEETHEARTS' . . . and the third based on the desperado angle exemplified by such ads as: 'A FORTUNE IN THEIR POCKETS . . . BUT DEATH ON THEIR MINDS' . . . 'DEATH WALKS BELOW THE BORDER' . . . 'THE NET'S CLOSING IN.' "

45. John Hammell, quoted in Jack Cunningham, memo to Harold Hurley, 13 November 1935, *Woman Trap* file, Performing Arts Research Center, New York Public Library.

46. Cunningham, memo to Hurley, 2 January 1936, *Woman Trap* file, Performing Arts Research Center, New York Public Library.

47. Ibid.

48. Bill Pine and staff, memo, undated, *Woman Trap* file, Performing Arts Research Center, New York Public Library.

49. Hays, *Memoirs*, 556.

50. Data on *Woman Trap*'s foreign distribution are currently unavailable.

51. Breen, letter to Herron, 11 May 1937, *Marco Polo* file, PCA Archive.

52. Jack Warner, letter to Sam Morris, 5 August 1937, *West of Shanghai* file, Warner Bros. Archive.

53. Ibid.

54. Sam Morris and Walter MacEwen, telegram to Jack Warner, 7 September 1937, *West of Shanghai* file, Warner Bros. Archive.

55. Morris, letter to Jack Warner, 7 September 1937, *West of Shanghai* file, Warner Bros. Archive.

56. Morris and MacEwen, telegram to Jack Warner, 7 September 1937, *West of Shanghai* file, Warner Bros. Archive.

57. Jack Warner, letter to Morris, 5 August 1937, *West of Shanghai* file, Warner Bros. Archive.

58. Morris, letter to Warner, 7 September 1937, *West of Shanghai* file, Warner Bros. Archive.

59. Breen, letter to Herron, 11 June 1937, *West of Shanghai* file, PCA Archive.

60. Ibid.

61. Foreign Legion movies comprised *Under Two Flags* (Universal, 1922); *Love and Glory* (Universal, 1924); *A Son of the Sahara* (Edwin Carewe/First National, 1924); *Wages of Virtue* (Famous Players–Lasky, 1924); *The New Commandment* (First National, 1925); *The Winding Stair* (Fox, 1925); *Beau Geste* (Paramount, 1926); *The Silent Lover* (First National, 1926); *The Forbidden Woman* (De Mille Pictures/Pathé, 1927); *Beau Sabreur* (Paramount Famous-Lasky, 1928); *The Foreign Legion* (Universal, 1928); *Plastered in Paris* (Fox, 1928), a comedy; *The Desert Song* (Warner Bros., 1929); *Two Men and a Maid* (Tiffany-Stahl, 1929); *Hell's Island* (Columbia, 1930); *Morocco* (Paramount, 1930); *Renegades* (Fox, 1930); *Women Everywhere* (Fox, 1930); *Beau Ideal* (RKO, 1931); *The Devil's in Love* (Fox, 1933); *The Rest Cure* (Condor, Regal/Regal, Grand National, 1936), a comedy; *The Legion of Missing Men* (Monogram, 1937); *Trouble in Morocco* (Columbia, 1937); *Adventure in Sahara* (Columbia, 1938); *Beau Geste* (Paramount, 1939); and *The Flying Deuces* (Boris Morros/RKO, 1939), a comedy.

Devil's Island stories comprised *Love's Wilderness* (Corinne Griffith Productions/First National, 1924); *Devil's Island* (Chadwick Pictures, 1926); *Condemned to Devil's Island* (Samuel Goldwyn/United Artists, 1929); *Hell's Island* (Columbia, 1930); *Escape from Devil's Island* (Columbia, 1935); and *Devil's Island* (Warner Bros., 1939).

This information was derived from Patricia King Hanson and Alan Gevinson, eds., *The American Film Institute Catalog of Motion Pictures Produced in the United States: Feature Films, 1931–1940* (Berkeley: University of California Press, 1993), indexes.

62. George Weltner (assistant manager, Paramount Foreign Department), letter to Garreau Dombasle (French commercial counselor), 1 September 1939, *Beau Geste* file, PCA Archive.

63. Breen's relationship with Hal Wallis, in particular, was strained from the beginning. See Breen, letter to Hays, 19 May 1934, *Merry Wives of Reno* file, PCA Archive. The history of *Dr. Monica* also provides evidence of Wallis' less than cooperative attitude. See Breen, memo to McKenzie, 16 March 1934, *Dr. Monica* file, PCA Archive. For a series of correspondence between Wallis and Breen, see Rudy Behlmer, *Inside Warner Bros. (1935–1951)* (London: Weidenfeld and Nicolson, 1985).

64. Walter MacEwan, memo to Earl Baldwin, 21 January 1937, *Ever since Eve* file, PCA Archive.

65. Press book, *Condemned to Devil's Island* (Samuel Goldwyn/United Artists, 1929).

66. Breen, letter to Jack Warner, 24 June 1938, *Devil's Island* file, PCA Archive.

67. G. Raoul-Duval, letter to Breen, 23 July 1938, *Devil's Island* file, PCA Archive.

68. Herron, letter to Breen, 28 July 1938, *Devil's Island* file, PCA Archive.

69. Breen, letter to Herron, 6 September 1938, *Devil's Island* file, PCA Archive.

70. Hall, "Robert M. W. Vogel Oral History," 47.

71. Herron, letter to Breen, 8 September 1938, *Devil's Island* file, PCA Archive.

72. Breen, letter to Herron, 12 October 1938, *Devil's Island* file, PCA Archive.

73. Breen, memo to Hays, 16 September 1938, *Devil's Island* file, PCA Archive.

74. Herron, letter to Breen, 21 November 1938, *Devil's Island* file, PCA Archive.

75. Herron, letter to Hays, 15 February 1939, *Devil's Island* file, PCA Archive.

76. Review of *Devil's Island*, *Variety*, 17 July 1940, 16.

77. Shurlock, memo for the files, 26 March 1936, *Idiot's Delight* file, PCA Archive.

78. Breen, letter to Herron, 11 April 1936, *Idiot's Delight* file, PCA Archive.

79. Breen, letter to James M. Beck, 20 August 1936, *Idiot's Delight* file, PCA Archive.

80. James M. Beck, telegram to Breen, 15 September 1936, *Idiot's Delight* file, PCA Archive.

81. Breen, letter to "Hunt Schulberg" [Hunt Stromberg], 5 December 1936, *Idiot's Delight* file, PCA Archive.

82. See Douglas Gomery, *Shared Pleasures: A History of Movie Presentation in the United States* (Madison: University of Wisconsin Press, 1992), 57–82.

83. This is reflected in figures from *Variety*, quoted by Joel Finler. In an analysis of North American film rentals in 1939, MGM had a share of 22 percent; Fox, 17 percent; Paramount, 14 percent; and Warner Bros., 14 percent. See Finler, *Hollywood Story*, 35.

84. An example is *The Forty Days of Musa Dagh*. In 1934 MGM acquired the rights for production in 1935, possibly with William Powell in the lead. The story described Armenian resistance to Turkish oppression in 1915, culminating in five thousand Armenians being besieged in a mountain stronghold for forty days, until relieved by the French. Pressure from the Turkish government, conveyed through the U.S. Department of State, persuaded Thalberg not to proceed with the production, even though he was convinced it told a "grand story." The studio was also worried that diplomatic problems would lead to the loss of the French and English markets. Discussions about the project surfaced again at MGM in 1938, but they came to nothing. See *The Forty Days of Musa Dagh* file, PCA Archive; and Martin Quigley, "Viewpoints: The Case of 'Musa Dagh,' " *Motion Picture Herald*, 7 December 1935, 15.

85. See Hanson and Gevinson, eds., *American Film Institute Catalog*, 807–9.

86. Herron, letter to Breen, 7 January 1937, *Idiot's Delight* file, PCA Archive.

87. Moley, *Hays Office*, 175.

88. The rejected pictures were *Beloved Enemy* (Howard Productions/ United Artists, 1936); *The Best Man Wins* (Columbia, 1935); *Ceiling Zero* (Warner Bros., 1936); *Dodsworth* (Samuel Goldwyn/United Artists, 1936); *Fury* (MGM, 1936); *The Garden of Allah* (Selznick International/United Artists, 1936); *The General Died at Dawn* (Paramount, 1936); *Give Us This Night* (Paramount, 1936); *Green Pastures* (Warner Bros., 1936); *Love on the Run* (MGM, 1936); *Mark of the Vampire* (MGM, 1935); *Modern Times* (Charles Chaplin/ United Artists, 1936); *The Plough and the Stars* (RKO, 1937); *Road Gang* (Warner Bros., 1936); *Star of Midnight* (RKO, 1935); *A Tale of Two Cities* (MGM, 1935); *These Three* (Samuel Goldwyn/United Artists, 1936); *A Woman Rebels* (RKO, 1936); a movie identified as *The Rose*, from Paramount, which is not traceable under that title; and an RKO movie of unknown title. See Herron, letter to Arthur Kelly (United Artists), 4 May 1937, *The Plough and the Stars* file, PCA Archive.

89. Herron, letter to Fred Beetson, 7 May 1937, *Idiot's Delight* file, PCA Archive.

90. Robert Caracciolo, letter to Breen, 8 June 1937, *Idiot's Delight* file, PCA Archive.

91. Hunt Stromberg, letter to Breen, 23 June 1937, *Idiot's Delight* file, PCA Archive.

92. Ibid.

93. Hunt Stromberg, cable to Breen, 24 June 1938, *Idiot's Delight* file, PCA Archive.

94. Duke Caracciolo, letter to Breen, 20 June 1938, *Idiot's Delight* file, PCA Archive.

95. Breen, letter to Louis B. Mayer, 26 August 1938, *Idiot's Delight* file, PCA Archive.

96. See statement by Will Hays, *New York Times*, 31 December 1938.

97. F. W. Allport, letter [to Herron?], 23 October 1939, *Idiot's Delight* file, PCA Archive. I wish to thank James Hay for some illuminating correspondence on this subject.

98. Breen, memo for the files, 12 May 1937, *Marco Polo* file, PCA Archive.

99. Herron, letter to Breen, 7 May 1939, *Marco Polo* file, PCA Archive; advertising sheet, *Marco Polo*.

100. Fred Mueller (in Rome), letter to L. W. Kastner (United Artists), 7 September 1938, *Marco Polo* file, PCA Archive.

101. Harold Smith, letter to Herron, 28 April 1939, quoted in Herron, letter to Breen, 5 May 1939, *Marco Polo* file, PCA Archive.

Chapter 7. The Big Picture

1. See, for example, Nick Roddick's discussion of *I Am a Fugitive from a Chain Gang* (Warner Bros., 1932) in Roddick, *A New Deal in Entertainment: Warner Brothers in the 1930s* (London: BFI, 1983), 121–26.

2. "Characterizations of Newspaper Editors, Reporters, and Publishers

in Motion Pictures," reel 12, MPPDA Archive. Although the document is not dated, it contains a survey which extends to 1 April 1938.

3.   McKenzie, letter to Wingate, 24 February 1933, *Constant Woman* file, PCA Archive.

4.   Joy, memo to Hays, 22 April 1931, *Street Scene* file, PCA Archive.

5.   Jane Hoey was the representative nominated. See Arthur DeBra (MPPDA), letter to Jane Hoey, Welfare Council of New York City, 10 July 1929, Pathé—*Godless Girl* file, reel 7, MPPDA Archive.

6.   Joy, memo to Hays, April 1931, *Street Scene* file, PCA Archive.

7.   Janice Pierce (Anthracite Operators Conference), letter to Hays, 8 August 1929, Fox file, reel 7, MPPDA Archive.

8.   McKenzie, letter to Breen, 3 April 1934, *Imitation of Life* file, PCA Archive.

9.   Breen, letter to Jack Warner, 21 January 1935, *Oil for the Lamps of China* file, Warner Bros. Archive.

10.   The film was nevertheless banned in China. See Harley, *World-wide Influences of the Cinema*, 113.

11.   Arthur Houghton, letter to Hays, 2 September 1938, Production Code file, reel 12, MPPDA Archive.

12.   See *Central Airport* file, PCA Archive.

13.   See, for example, "Protect the Movie with National, Uniform Censorship," in both the *Los Angeles Times*, 6 February 1929, and the *Washington, D.C., Herald*, 13 February 1929.

14.   See *The Street of Chance* file, PCA Archive.

15.   Joy, letter to Howard Hughes, 10 December 1930; Lamar Trotti, report to Hays, 12 December 1930; and Joy, résumé, 16 December 1930, all in *The Front Page* file, PCA Archive.

16.   Joy, letter to Hal Wallis, 6 April 1931, *Five Star Final* file, PCA Archive.

17.   "Compendium of Editorials Denouncing Pictures Dealing with Newspaper Life," and Breen, letter to Joy, 5 November 1931, both in *Five Star Final* file, PCA Archive.

18.   Joy, letter to Zanuck, December 1931, *The Strange Love of Molly Louvain* file, PCA Archive.

19.   In 1937 studios were cautioned about their characterizations of newspapermen in *Love is Free* (Fox), *Behind the Headlines* (RKO), *There Goes My Girl* (RKO), *Back in Circulation* (Warner Bros.), *Exclusive* (Paramount), *Atlantic Flight* (Monogram), *Women Men Marry* (MGM), and *Nothing Sacred* (Selznick).

20.   See Charles Wolfe, "*Mr. Smith Goes to Washington*: Democratic Forums and Representational Forms," in *Close Viewings: An Anthology of New Film Criticism*, edited by Peter Lehman (Tallahassee: Florida State University Press, 1990), 300–332.

21.   Breen, letter to Jack Warner, 18 February 1936, *Two against the World* file, PCA Archive. For a discussion of the relationship between the movies and the broadcasting industry, see Michele Hilmes, *Hollywood and Broadcasting: From Radio to Cable* (Urbana: University of Illinois Press, 1990).

22.   Hays, letter to Breen, 27 February 1936, *Two against the World* file, PCA Archive.

23.   Breen, letter to Warner, 26 March 1936, *Two against the World* file, PCA Archive.

24.   Ibid.

25.   Script extract included in *Two against the World* file, PCA Archive.

26.   Martin, *Hollywood's Movie Commandments*, 96.

27.   Breen, letter to Jack Warner, 12 September 1934, *Black Fury* file, Warner Bros. Archive.

28.   Robert Lord, letter to Hal Wallis, 2 May 1934, *Black Fury* file, Warner Bros. Archive.

29.   Clive Hirschhorn, *The Columbia Story* (London: Pyramid, 1989), 53.

30.   Hanson and Gevinson, eds., *American Film Institute Catalog*, 2225. For a discussion of this kind of subject matter in the movies of the 1930s, see Tino Balio, "Production Trends," in *Grand Design*, esp. 280–98.

31.   Walter MacEwen, letter to Henry Blanke, 11 May 1938, *Juarez* file, Warner Bros. Archive.

32.   Blanke, letter to Robert Taplinger, 9 June 1938, *Juarez* file, Warner Bros. Archive.

33.   Breen, letter to Jack Warner, 21 January 1935, *Oil for the Lamps of China* file, Warner Bros. Archive.

34.   Breen, letter to B. B. Kahane, 11 June 1936, *Winterset* file, RKO Corporate Archive, Los Angeles.

35.   Joy, letter to Thalberg, 15 April 1932, Production Code file, reel 10, MPPDA Archive.

36.   Martin, *Hollywood's Movie Commandments*, 223.

37.   Ibid., quoting Quigley, editorial, *Motion Picture Herald*, 22 February 1936.

38.   Thomas Elsaesser, "Tales of Sound and Fury: Observations on the Family Melodrama," in *Home Is Where the Heart Is: Studies in Melodrama and the Woman's Film*, edited by Christine Gledhill (London: BFI, 1987), 47.

39.   Joy, letter to Hal Wallis, February 1931, *The Reckless Hour* file, PCA Archive.

40.   Wingate, letter to Jack Warner, 8 August 1933, *Bureau of Missing Persons* file, PCA Archive.

41.   Lischka, letter to Breen, 12 July 1934, *Evelyn Prentice* file, PCA Archive.

42.   McKenzie, letter to Breen, 17 April 1935, *The Devil Is a Woman* file, PCA Archive.

43.   See, for example, de Mille, "The Future of the Photoplay," in *Introduction to the Photoplay*, ed. Tibbetts, 329–32.

44.   Paul Bern, "The Theory of the Silent Motion Picture," in *Introduction to the Photoplay*, ed. Tibbetts, 76.

45.   Richard Maltby has pointed out that Mae West, the most popular female box office attraction in Hollywood in 1933, was supplanted in 1934 by Shirley Temple. Maltby has speculated on the implications of this shift for the

movies' discourse on female sexuality in the 1930s. See Richard Maltby, "From the Implausible to the Impossible: The Censorship of Sexuality from Mae West to Shirley Temple," November 1986, Day School on Censorship and Sexuality, Plymouth Arts Centre, Plymouth, U.K.

Graham Greene found that this subject had been rendered literally unspeakable when he was successfully sued by Temple and Fox for elaborating on the appeal of her "dubious coquetry" in a review published in *Night and Day,* 28 October 1937. See Greene, "The Films by Graham Greene," in *Night and Day,* edited by Christopher Hawtree (London: Chatto and Windus, 1985), 204.

46. Marilyn Monroe is, of course, the quintessential postwar example of this phenomenon.

47. See Margaret Thorp, *America at the Movies* (London: Faber and Faber, 1945), 49–70.

48. Breen, letter to J. R. McDonough, 3 March 1939, *Bachelor Mother* file, PCA Archive.

49. Review, *New York Times,* 30 June 1939.

50. *Variety,* 28 June 1939, 2.

51. Hays, *Memoirs,* 490.

52. "The Policy and Standards of the National Board of Censorship," in *Federal Motion Picture Commission* (1916), 289.

53. F.S., report, 10 April 1930, *Her Man* file, PCA Archive. Geographic displacement could conceivably occur in the opposite direction as well, when particular problems arose with foreign censorship. When First National was considering an adaptation of *The Bad Man,* Joy pointed out that the subject would probably cause trouble with Mexico, and he suggested relocating the story to the safer environment of the American West. See *The Bad Man* file, PCA Archive. Similarly, Herron commented that *Woman Hungry* (First National, 1931) had "Mexican types in it that are unnecessary entirely. They could have been just ordinary western low-class types of individuals." Herron, letter to Joy, 13 March 1931, *Viva Villa* file, PCA Archive.

54. Joy, letter to Schenck, 27 March 1930, *The Bad One* file, PCA Archive.

55. Martin, *Hollywood's Movie Commandments,* 221.

56. *Variety,* 19 June 1934, 2.

57. Breen, letter to Hays, 22 October 1934, *The Merry Widow,* PCA Archive.

58. Edgar Dale, *The Content of Motion Pictures* (New York: Macmillan, 1935), 30.

59. Robin Wood, *Howard Hawks* (London, BFI, 1983), 17.

60. See Richard Maltby and Ruth Vasey, "The International Language Problem: European Reactions to Hollywood's Conversion to Sound," in *Hollywood in Europe,* ed. Ellwood and Kroes, 68–93. For a contemporary discussion of this issue in a British context, see *The Film in National Life: Being the Report of an Enquiry Conducted by the Commission on Educational and Cultural Films in the Service Which the Cinematograph May Render to Education and Social Progress* (London: Allen and Unwin, 1932).

61. For a discussion of the way in which race has been constructed and

deployed in Hollywood's treatment of sexual themes, see Marchetti, *Romance and the "Yellow Peril."*

62.   Miriam Hansen, *Babel and Babylon: Spectatorship in American Silent Cinema* (Cambridge, Mass.: Harvard University Press, 1991), 256.

63.   *U.S. v Paramount Pictures, Inc.*, 334 U.S. 131 (1948).

64.   See Kindem, ed., *American Movie Industry;* and Mae D. Huettig, "Economic Control of the Motion Picture Industry," in *American Film Industry* (1985), ed. Balio, 285–310.

65.   "Memorandum re the Milliken-Norr-Harmon Committee Report on Jurisdiction of PCA (concurred in by Mr. Breen as revised), Mr. Quigley's reaction thereto, and some comments in reply," 20 September 1938, Production Code file, reel 12, MPPDA Archive.

66.   See Matthew Bernstein, *Walter Wanger: Hollywood Independent* (Berkeley: University of California Press, 1994), 129–37.

67.   *Appeal from Order of Disapproval of Pennsylvania State Board of Censors,* Common Pleas Court no. 6, June Term, 1937, no. 5259. See also Edward de Grazia and Roger K. Newman, *Banned Films: Movies, Censors, and the First Amendment* (New York: Bowker, 1982), 59, 214–15. Although the Pennsylvania hearing identified the film as *Spain in Flames,* it was more widely released under the title *The Spanish Earth.*

68.   *Appeal of Amkino Corporation in the Matter of "Baltic Deputy,"* Common Pleas Court no. 6, December Term, 1937, no. 1694. See also Morris L. Ernst and Alexander Lindey, *The Censor Marches On: Recent Milestones in the Administration of the Obscenity Law in the United States* (New York: Da Capo Press, 1971), 110–12.

69.   Francis S. Harmon, memo, n.d., Production Code file, reel 12, MPPDA Archive.

70.   Ibid.

71.   Breen, memo, 22 June 1938, Production Code file, reel 12, MPPDA Archive.

72.   Hays, memo, 16 March 1938, Production Code file, reel 12, MPPDA Archive.

73.   Breen, letter to Hays, 26 March 1938, Production Code file, reel 12, MPPDA Archive.

74.   This development may have been the more significant since it implied a weakening of the Catholic connection, Harmon being "importantly tied in with the Baptists and the Rockefellers." See Vizzard, *See No Evil,* 51.

75.   Milliken, Norr, and Harmon, "Memo on General Policy," June 1938, Production Code file, reel 12, MPPDA Archive. Martin Quigley, who was convinced that the screen should be free from "propaganda" and that the PCA had a responsibility to make it so, was very much alarmed by these developments. In response to the likely increase in political themes, he proposed a resolution (which the MPPDA seems to have disregarded): "No motion picture," he recommended, "shall be produced which shall advocate or create sympathy for political theories alien to, and subversive of, American institutions, nor any picture which perverts or tends to pervert the theater screen from its avowed

purpose of entertainment to the function of political controversy." Quigley, letter to Hays, 11 July 1938, reel 12, MPPDA Archive.

76. Breen, letter to Goldwyn, 24 August 1938, *Boy Meets Girl* file, PCA Archive.

77. See Adela Rogers St. Johns, "Why Breen Resigned from the Hays Office," *Liberty*, 5 July 1941, 14–15, 43.

78. See, for example, Murray Silverstone, United Artists internal circular, 2 October 1939, O'Brien legal file, box 10, folder 2, United Artists Collection. Silverstone wrote, "Some of our foreign markets have been cut in half and others have been wiped out entirely. Serious money restrictions in many countries throughout the world, together with falling rates of exchange, make it extremely difficult for the producers of important pictures to rely on receiving the kind of revenue it is necessary for them to procure in order to recover their big investments. . . . From now on, the American distributing company has to stand on its own."

79. See Clayton R. Koppes and Gregory D. Black, *Hollywood Goes to War: How Politics, Profits and Propaganda Shaped World War II Movies* (London: I. B. Tauris, 1987); and Thomas Doherty, *Projections of War: Hollywood, American Culture, and World War II* (New York: Columbia University Press, 1993).

80. "Hollywood Wows Wall Street," *Business Week*, 11 May 1946, 60.

Conclusion

1. See Henry Jenkins III, " 'Shall We Make It for New York or for Distribution?': Eddie Cantor, *Whoopee*, and Regional Resistance to the Talkies," *Cinema Journal* 29, no. 3 (1990): 32–52.

2. The demand for westerns was attributed to the tastes of the European market in the 1910s. For example, see editorial, *Moving Picture World*, 7 October 1911, 20: "The stories of Western brigandage and of Indian horrors have of late been horribly overdone. We know that there is today no complaint more frequent among moving picture patrons than the protest against this indefinite multiplication of 'Wild West' reels. It has been said in explanation of this flood of 'Western' and 'Indian' stuff that these reels are made for European consumption and to meet the demand for these pictures in Europe. This may be true, probably it is true, but it contains nothing cheering for either the patrons or the exhibitors of American moving pictures." In 1914 Jacob Schechter of Universal stated that "in the past year the foreign business has increased twice, and perhaps thrice; we are still manufacturing some of those Wild West scenes . . . and the foreign demand is still very great for just that kind of picture. . . . I think the Universal manufactures about 15 or 20 per cent of Wild West scenes, the remainder being those representing the drama and other subjects." Jacob Schechter, cited in *Federal Motion Picture Commission* (1914), 70.

Works Cited

Archives

Will H. Hays Collection. Indiana State Library, Indianapolis.

Motion Picture Producers and Distributors of America, Inc. (MPPDA) Archive. Motion Picture Association of America, New York.

Performing Arts Research Center. New York Public Library.

Production Code Administration (PCA) Archive. Margaret Herrick Library, Academy of Motion Picture Arts and Sciences, Beverly Hills, Calif.

RKO Corporate Archive. Los Angeles.

United Artists Collection. Wisconsin Center for Film and Theater Research, Madison.

Universal Studios Archive. Department of Special Collections, Doheney Library, University of Southern California, Los Angeles.

Warner Bros. Archive. Department of Special Collections, Doheney Library, University of Southern California, Los Angeles.

Unpublished Papers

Gripsrud, Jostein. "Mary and Doug and Modernity: Hollywood Stars in Norway, 1924." Paper presented to the Society for Cinema Studies Conference, New York, 2–5 March 1995.

Hall, Barbara, "Robert M. W. Vogel Oral History." 1991. Margaret Herrick Library, Academy of Motion Picture Arts and Sciences, Beverly Hills, Calif.

Maltby, Richard. "From the Implausible to the Impossible: The Censorship of Sexuality from Mae West to Shirley Temple." November 1986. Day School on Censorship and Sexuality, Plymouth Arts Centre, Plymouth, U.K.

Dissertations

Gomery, Douglas. "The Coming of Sound to the American Cinema: A History of the Transformation of an Industry." Ph.D. diss., University of Wisconsin–Madison, 1975.

Gustafson, Robert. "The Buying of Ideas: Source Acquisition at Warner Bros., 1930–1949." Ph.D. diss., University of Michigan, 1983.

275

Interview

Luraschi, Luigi. London, 23 February 1988.

U.S. Government Proceedings

Federal Motion Picture Commission. Committee on Education, 63d Cong., 2d sess., H.R. 14895 and S. 4941. Washington, D.C.: GPO, 1914.

Federal Motion Picture Commission. Committee on Education, 64th Cong., 1st sess., H.R. 456. Washington, D.C.: GPO, 1916.

Federal Motion Picture Commission. 69th Cong., 1st sess., H.R. 4094 and H.R. 6233. Washington, D.C.: GPO, 1926.

Hearing before Subcommittee of House Committee on Appropriations. 69th Cong., 1st sess. Washington, D.C.: GPO, 1926.

Publications of the Bureau of Foreign and Domestic Commerce, U.S. Department of Commerce

Daily Consular and Trade Reports (Commerce Reports from 1914). Daily, except Sundays and Holidays, 5 July 1910–31 August 1921. Weekly, 5 September 1921–28 September 1940.

Motion Pictures Abroad. Published irregularly, 1927–40 (fortnightly in 1937). Economic and Public Affairs Division, New York Public Library, holds incomplete runs, 1927–32 and 1937–40.

Trade Information Bulletin. No. 467. C. J. North, comp., "The Chinese Motion Picture Market." 1927.

Trade Information Bulletin. No. 499. George R. Canty, "Market for Motion Pictures in Central Europe, Italy, and Spain." 1927.

Trade Information Bulletin. No. 542. George R. Canty, "The European Motion-Picture Industry in 1927." 1928.

Trade Information Bulletin. No. 553. George R. Canty et al., "Market for Motion Pictures in Scandinavia and the Baltic States." 1928.

Trade Information Bulletin. No. 608. "Motion Pictures in Australia and New Zealand." 1929.

Trade Information Bulletin. No. 617. "The European Motion-Picture Industry in 1928." 1929.

Trade Information Bulletin. No. 630. "Motion Pictures in Argentina and Brazil." 1929.

Trade Information Bulletin. No. 694. "European Motion-Picture Industry in 1929." 1930.

Trade Information Bulletin. No. 752. "European Motion-Picture Industry in 1930." 1931.

Trade Information Bulletin. No. 754. "Motion Pictures in Mexico, Central America, and the Greater Antilles." 1931.

Trade Information Bulletin. No. 756. "Small Island Markets for Motion Pictures." 1931.

Trade Information Bulletin. No. 797. "The Motion-Picture Industry in Europe in 1931." 1932.

Trade Information Bulletin. No. 801. James Summervill Jr., "The Motion-Picture Industry in the United Kingdom in 1931." 1932.

Trade Information Bulletin. No. 815. George R. Canty et al., "European Motion-Picture Industry in 1932." 1933.

World Wide Motion Picture Developments. Published weekly, then irregularly, 1937–40. Held in Economic and Public Affairs Division, New York Public Library.

Legal References

Appeal from Order of Disapproval of Pennsylvania State Board of Censors. Common Pleas Court no. 6, June Term, 1937, no. 5259.

Appeal of Amkino Corporation in the Matter of "Baltic Deputy." Common Pleas Court no. 6, December Term, 1937, no. 1694.

Mutual Film Corporation v Ohio Industrial Commission. 236 U.S. 230, 244 (1915).

U.S. v Paramount Pictures, Inc. 334 U.S. 131 (1948).

Trade Papers

Moving Picture World. New York: World Photographic Publishing Co., 1907–12; Chalmers Publishing Co., 1912–27.

Variety. New York: Variety, Inc., 1905——.

Wid's Year Book (*The Film Year Book* from 1922, and *The Film Daily Year Book* from 1928). New York: Wid's Films and Film Folks, 1919–21; J. W. Alicoate, 1922——.

Books, Articles, and Pamphlets

Altman, Rick. *The American Film Musical*. London: BFI, 1989.

Altman, Rick, ed. *Sound Theory/Sound Practice*. New York: Routledge, 1992.

Anderson, Joseph I., and Donald Richie. *The Japanese Film: Art and Industry*. Tokyo: Charles E. Tuttle, 1959.

Arnheim, Rudolph. *Film as Art*. Berkeley: University of California Press, 1957.

Babson, Roger W. "Crime Waves." *Babson's Reports*, 8 April 1929, n.p.

Balio, Tino. *Grand Design: Hollywood as a Modern Business Enterprise, 1930–1939*. New York: Charles Scribner's Sons, 1993.

Balio, Tino, ed. *The American Film Industry*. Madison: University of Wisconsin Press, 1976.

Balio, Tino, ed. *The American Film Industry*. Rev. ed. Madison: University of Wisconsin Press, 1985.

Basinger, Jeanine. *A Woman's View: How Hollywood Spoke to Women, 1930–1960*. New York: Alfred A. Knopf, 1993.

Baxter, John. *The Hollywood Exiles*. London: Macdonald and Jane's, 1976.

Behlmer, Rudy. *Inside Warner Bros. (1935–1951)*. London: Weidenfeld and Nicolson, 1986.

Bernstein, Matthew. *Walter Wanger: Hollywood Independent*. Berkeley: University of California Press, 1994.

Black, Gregory D. *Hollywood Censored: Morality Codes, Catholics and the Movies*. Cambridge: Cambridge University Press, 1994.

Black, Gregory D. "Hollywood Censored: The Production Code Administration and the Hollywood Film Industry, 1930–1940." *Film History* 3 (1989): 167–89.

Bogle, Donald. *Toms, Coons, Mulattoes, Mammies, and Bucks: An Interpretive History of Blacks in American Films*. New York: Bantam, 1973.

Bordwell, David. *Ozu and the Poetics of the Cinema*. London: BFI, 1988.

Bordwell, David, and Noël Carroll, eds. *Post-Theory: Reconstructing Film Studies*. Madison: University of Wisconsin Press, 1995.

Bordwell, David, Janet Staiger, and Kristin Thompson. *The Classical Hollywood Cinema: Film Style and Mode of Production to 1960*. London: Routledge, 1985.

Brownlow, Kevin, and David Gill. "Thames Silents Become Channel Four Silents." Program notes for *The Four Horsemen of the Apocalypse*, London Film Festival, 1993.

"The Camouflagers." *Churchman*, 13 July 1929, 8.

Coben, Stanley. *Rebellion against Victorianism: The Impetus for Cultural Change in 1920s America*. Oxford: Oxford University Press, 1991.

Cockburn, Claud. *Bestseller: The Books That Everyone Read, 1900–1939*. London: Sidgwick and Jackson, 1972.

Collins, Diane. *Hollywood Down Under: Australians at the Movies, 1896 to the Present Day*. Sydney: Angus and Robertson, 1987.

Combs, James, ed. *Movies and Politics: The Dynamic Relationship*. New York: Garland, 1993.

Couvares, Francis G. "Hollywood, Main Street, and the Church: Trying to Censor the Movies before the Production Code." *American Quarterly* 44, no. 4 (December 1992): 584–616.

Cripps, Thomas. *Making Movies Black: The Hollywood Message Movie from World War II to the Civil Rights Era*. Oxford: Oxford University Press, 1993.

Cripps, Thomas. *Slow Fade to Black: The Negro in American Film, 1900–1942*. London: Oxford University Press, 1977.

Dale, Edgar. *The Content of Motion Pictures*. New York: Macmillan, 1935.

Debauche, Leslie Midkiff. "Practical Patriotism: NAMPI Enlists in World War I." *Velvet Light Trap*, no. 23 (1989): 16–38.

deCordova, Richard. *Picture Personalities: The Emergence of the Star System in America*. Urbana: University of Illinois Press, 1990.

de Grazia, Edward, and Roger K. Newman. *Banned Films: Movies, Censors, and the First Amendment*. New York: Bowker, 1982.

Delpar, Helen. " 'Goodbye to the Greaser': Mexico, the MPPDA, and Derogatory Films, 1922–1926." *Journal of Popular Film and Television* 12, no. 1 (1984): 34–41.

Doherty, Thomas. *Projections of War: Hollywood, American Culture, and World War II*. New York: Columbia University Press, 1993.

Dorfman, Ariel. *The Empire's Old Clothes: What the Lone Ranger, Babar, and Other Innocent Heroes Do to Our Minds*. New York: Pantheon, 1983.

Eastman, Fred. "Ambassadors of Ill Will." *Christian Century* 47 (1930): 144–47.

Eckert, Charles. "The Carole Lombard in Macy's Window." *Quarterly Review of Film Studies* 3, no. 1 (1978): 1–21.

Ellwood, David W., and Rob Kroes, eds. *Hollywood in Europe: Experiences of a Cultural Hegemony*. Amsterdam: VU University Press, 1994.

Ernst, Morris L., and Alexander Lindey. *The Censor Marches On: Recent Milestones in the Administration of the Obscenity Law in the United States*. New York: Da Capo Press, 1971.

Facey, Paul W. *The Legion of Decency: A Sociological Analysis of the Emergence and Development of a Pressure Group*. New York: Arno, 1974.

Farber, Stephen. *The Movie Rating Game*. Washington, D.C.: Public Affairs Press, 1972.

Federal Council of the Churches of Christ in America. *The Public Relations of the Motion Picture Industry*. N.p.: Department of Research and Education, Federal Council of the Churches of Christ in America, 1931.

Feldman, Charles M. *The National Board of Censorship (Review) of Motion Pictures, 1909–1922*. New York: Arno, 1977.

The Film in National Life: Being the Report of an Enquiry Conducted by the Commission on Educational and Cultural Films in the Service Which the Cinematograph May Render to Education and Social Progress. London: Allen and Unwin, 1932.

Finch, Christopher, and Linda Rosenkrantz. *Gone Hollywood: The Movie Colony in the Golden Age*. London: Weidenfeld and Nicolson, 1979.

Finler, Joel W. *The Hollywood Story: Everything You Always Wanted to Know about the American Movie Business But Didn't Know Where to Look*. London: Octopus Books, 1988.

Franklin, Harold B. *Sound Motion Pictures*. New York: Doubleday, Doran and Co., 1929.

Galambos, Louis. *Competition and Cooperation: The Emergence of a National Trade Association*. Baltimore: Johns Hopkins Press, 1966.

Galambos, Louis. *The Public Image of Big Business in America, 1880–1940: A Quantitative Study in Social Change*. Baltimore: Johns Hopkins University Press, 1975.

Gardner, Gerald. *The Censorship Papers: Movie Censorship Letters from the Hays Office, 1934 to 1968*. New York: Dodd, Mead and Co., 1987.

Glancy, Mark. "MGM Film Grosses, 1924–1948: The Eddie Mannix Ledger." *Historical Journal of Film, Radio and Television* 12, no. 2 (1992): 127–44.

Gledhill, Christine, ed. *Home Is Where the Heart Is: Studies in Melodrama and the Woman's Film*. London: BFI, 1987.

Golden, Nathan D. *Review of Foreign Film Markets during 1938*. Washington, D.C.: U.S. Department of Commerce, 1939.

Gomery, Douglas. *The Hollywood Studio System*. London: BFI, 1986.

Gomery, Douglas. *Shared Pleasures: A History of Movie Presentation in the United States*. London: BFI, 1992.

Gomery, Douglas, ed. *The Will Hays Papers.* Frederick, Md.: University Publications of America, 1986.

Griffith, D. W. "The Rise and Fall of Free Speech in America." *Series of Cinema Classics,* no. 1. 1916; Los Angeles: Larry Edmunds Bookshop, 1967.

Guback, Thomas. *The International Film Industry: Western Europe and America since 1945*. Bloomington: Indiana University Press, 1969.

Hansen, Miriam. *Babel and Babylon: Spectatorship in American Silent Cinema.* Cambridge, Mass.: Harvard University Press, 1991.

Hanson, Patricia King, and Alan Gevinson, eds. *The American Film Institute Catalog of Motion Pictures Produced in the United States: Feature Films, 1931–1940*. Berkeley: University of California Press, 1993.

Haralovich, Mary Beth. "Advertising Heterosexuality." *Screen* 23, no. 2 (1982): 50–60.

Harley, John. *World-wide Influences of the Cinema*. Los Angeles: University of Southern California Press, 1940.

Hawley, Ellis W., Murray N. Rothbard, Robert F. Himmelberg, and Gerald D. Nash. *Herbert Hoover and the Crisis of American Capitalism*. Cambridge, Mass: Schenkman Publishing Co., 1973.

Hawtree, Christopher, ed. *Night and Day*. London: Chatto and Windus, 1985.

Hays, Will H. *The Memoirs of Will H. Hays*. New York: Doubleday and Co., 1955.

Hilmes, Michele. *Hollywood and Broadcasting: From Radio to Cable*. Urbana: University of Illinois Press, 1990.

Hirschhorn, Clive. *The Columbia Story*. London: Pyramid, 1989.

Hofstadter, Richard, and Michael Wallace, eds. *American Violence: A Documentary History*. New York: Alfred A. Knopf, 1970.

"Hollywood Wows Wall Street." *Business Week*, 11 May 1946, 60.

Horak, Jan-Christopher. "G. W. Pabst in Hollywood; or, Every Modern Hero Deserves a Mother." *Film History* 1 (1987): 53–63.

Horak, Jan-Christopher. "Rin-Tin-Tin in Berlin; or, American Cinema in Weimar." *Film History* 5, no. 1 (1993): 49–62.

Hullinger, Edwin W. *Free Speech for the Talkies?* Rpt. from *North American Review.* N.p., June 1929. Pamphlet.

Inglis, Ruth. *Freedom of the Movies: A Report on Self-Regulation from the Commission on the Freedom of the Press*. Chicago: University of Chicago Press, 1947.

"Is the Stage Like the Augean Stables?" *Literary Digest,* 25 October 1930, 20–21.

Izod, John. *Hollywood and the Box Office, 1895–1986*. London: Macmillan, 1988.

Jacobs, Lea. "Industry Self-Regulation and the Problem of Textual Determination." *Velvet Light Trap,* no. 23 (1989): 4–15.

Jacobs, Lea. *The Wages of Sin: Censorship and the Fallen Woman Film, 1928–1942*. Madison: University of Wisconsin Press, 1991.

Jarvie, Ian. *Hollywood's Overseas Campaign: The North Atlantic Movie Trade, 1920–1950*. Cambridge: Cambridge University Press, 1992.

Jenkins, Henry, III. " 'Shall We Make It for New York or for Distribution?':

Eddie Cantor, *Whoopee,* and Regional Resistance to the Talkies." *Cinema Journal* 29, no. 3 (1990): 32–52.

Jewell, Richard B. "RKO Film Grosses, 1929–1951: The C. J. Tevlin Ledger." *Historical Journal of Film, Radio and Television* 14, no. 1 (1994): 37–49.

Jones, Dorothy B. "Hollywood's International Relations." *Quarterly of Film, Radio and Television* 11, no. 4 (1951): 362–74.

Kaminsky, Stuart M. *American Film Genres: Approaches to a Critical Theory of Popular Film.* Chicago: Pflaum, 1974.

Kennedy, Joseph P., ed. *The Story of the Films.* Chicago: A. W. Shaw Co., 1927.

Kepley, Vance, Jr., and Betty Kepley. "Foreign Films on Soviet Screens, 1922–1931." *Quarterly Review of Film Studies* 4 (1979): 429–42.

Kerr, Paul, ed. *The Hollywood Film Industry.* London: BFI, 1986.

Kindem, Gorham, ed. *The American Movie Industry: The Business of the Motion Pictures.* Carbondale: Southern Illinois University Press, 1982.

Koon, Cline M. *Motion Pictures in Education in the United States: A Report.* Chicago: University of Chicago Press, 1934.

Koppes, Clayton R., and Gregory D. Black. *Hollywood Goes to War: How Politics, Profits and Propaganda Shaped World War II Movies.* London: I. B. Tauris, 1987.

Kuhn, Annette. *Cinema, Censorship and Sexuality, 1909–1925.* London: Routledge, 1988.

Leff, Leonard J., and Jerold L. Simmons. *The Dame in the Kimono: Hollywood, Censorship, and the Production Code from the 1920s to the 1960s.* New York: Grove Weidenfeld, 1990.

Lehman, Peter, ed. *Close Viewings: An Anthology of New Film Criticism.* Tallahassee: Florida State University Press, 1990.

Low, Rachael. *The History of the British Film, 1918–1929.* London: Allen and Unwin, 1971.

Lowery, Shearon, and Melvin L. De Fleur. *Milestones in Mass Communication Research: Media Effects.* New York: Longman, 1983.

Maltby, Richard. " 'Baby Face'; or, How Joe Breen Made Barbara Stanwyck Atone for Causing the Wall Street Crash." *Screen* 27, no. 2 (1986): 22–45.

Maltby, Richard. "Documents on the Genesis of the Production Code." *Quarterly Review of Film and Video* 15, no. 4 (1995): 33–64.

Maltby, Richard. *Dreams for Sale: Popular Culture in the 20th Century.* London: Harrap, 1989.

Maltby, Richard. "The Genesis of the Production Code." *Quarterly Review of Film and Video* 15, no. 4 (1995): 5–32.

Maltby, Richard. *Harmless Entertainment: Hollywood and the Ideology of Consensus.* Metuchen, N.J.: Scarecrow, 1983.

Maltby, Richard. *Hollywood Cinema: An Introduction.* Oxford: Blackwell, 1995.

Maltby, Richard. "*The King of Kings* and the Czar of All the Rushes: The Propriety of the Christ Story." *Screen* 31, no. 2 (1990): 188–213.

Maltby, Richard. " 'To Prevent the Prevalent Type of Book': Censorship and Adaptation in Hollywood, 1924–1934." *American Quarterly* 44, no. 4 (December 1992): 554–83.

Marchetti, Gina. *Romance and the "Yellow Peril": Race, Sex, and Discursive Strategies in Hollywood Fiction.* Berkeley: University of California Press, 1993.

Marill, Alvin H. *Samuel Goldwyn Presents.* New York: A. S. Barnes, 1976.

Martin, Olga. *Hollywood's Movie Commandments: A Handbook for Motion Picture Writers and Reviewers.* New York: H. W. Wilson, 1937.

Mast, Gerald, ed. *The Movies in Our Midst: Documents in the Cultural History of Film in America.* Chicago: University of Chicago Press, 1982.

May, Lary. *Screening Out the Past: The Birth of Mass Culture and the Motion Picture Industry.* New York: Oxford University Press, 1980.

Mayne, Judith. "Immigrants and Spectators." *Wide Angle* 5, no. 2 (1982): 33–40.

McEvoy, J. P. "The Back of Me Hand to You." *Saturday Evening Post,* 24 December 1938, 8–9, 46–48.

Memorandum between the Authors' League of America, the Dramatists' Guild of the Authors' League, the Authors' Guild of the Authors' League, and the Motion Picture Producers and Distributors of America, Inc. New York: Motion Picture Producers and Distributors of America, 1927.

"Michael Takes the Mickey." *TV Times,* 13–19 October 1990, 26–27.

Moley, Raymond. *The Hays Office.* Indianapolis: Bobbs-Merrill, 1945.

Motion Picture Producers and Distributors of America, Inc. *The "Open Door."* New York: Motion Picture Producers and Distributors of America, Inc., 1924.

North, C. J., and Nathan D. Golden. "The European Film Market—Then and Now." *Society of Motion Picture Engineers Journal* 18 (1932): 442–44.

Pettit, Arthur G. *Images of the Mexican American in Fiction and Film.* College Station: Texas A&M University Press, 1980.

"Progress of Mr. Hays' Uplift Movement." *Christian Century* 47 (1930): 1438.

Quigley, Martin. "Viewpoints: The Case of 'Musa Dagh.' " *Motion Picture Herald,* 7 December 1935, 15.

Report of the Colonial Films Committee, Presented by the Secretary of State for the Colonies to Parliament by Command of His Majesty. London: HMSO, 1930.

Richards, Jeffrey. "The British Board of Film Censors and Content Control in the 1930s: Foreign Affairs." *Historical Journal of Film, Radio and Television* 2, no. 1 (1982): 39–48.

Robertson, James C. *The British Board of Film Censors: Film Censorship in Britain, 1896–1950.* London: Croom Helm, 1985.

Roddick, Nick. *A New Deal in Entertainment: Warner Brothers in the 1930s.* London: BFI, 1983.

Rogin, Michael Paul. *Ronald Reagan, the Movie: And Other Episodes in Political Demonology.* Berkeley: University of California Press, 1987.

Roud, Richard, ed. *Cinema: A Critical Dictionary.* Vol. 1. New York: Viking Press, 1980.

Rubin, Joan Shelley. *The Making of Middlebrow Culture.* Chapel Hill: University of North Carolina Press, 1992.

Salt, Barry. *Film Style and Technology: History and Analysis.* London: Starword, 1983.

Saunders, Thomas J. *Hollywood in Berlin: American Cinema and Weimar Germany.* Berkeley: University of California Press, 1994.

Schatz, Thomas. *The Genius of the System: Hollywood Filmmaking in the Studio Era.* New York: Pantheon, 1988.

Seabury, William Marston. *Motion Picture Problems: The Cinema and the League of Nations.* New York: Avondale Press, 1929.

Sellin, Thorsten, ed. *The Annals of the American Academy of Political and Social Science.* Philadelphia: American Academy of Political and Social Science, 1947.

Short, William Harrison. *A Generation of Motion Pictures: A Review of Social Values in Recreational Films.* New York: National Committee for the Study of Social Values in Motion Pictures, 1928.

"A Shot Heard around the Country." *Literary Digest,* 25 July 1931, 20–21.

Sklar, Robert. *Movie-made America: A Cultural History of American Movies.* London: Chappell and Co., 1975.

Sklar, Robert, and Vita Zagarrio, eds. *Frank Capra and Columbia Pictures: Authorship and the Studio System.* Philadelphia: Temple University Press, forthcoming.

Staiger, Janet. "Announcing Wares, Winning Patrons, Voicing Ideals: Thinking about the History and Theory of Film Advertising." *Cinema Journal* 29, no. 3 (1990): 3–31.

Stallings, Penny. *Flesh and Fantasy.* New York: Harper and Row, 1978.

Stanfield, Peter. "The Western, 1909–14: A Cast of Villains." *Film History* 1 (1987): 97–112.

Steele, Rufus. *7 News Stories about the Movies.* Rpt. from the *Christian Science Monitor,* 30 July 1926. New York: Motion Picture Producers and Distributors of America, n.d. Pamphlet.

St. John, Adela Rogers. "Why Breen Resigned from the Hays Office." *Liberty,* 5 July 1941, 14–15, 43.

Strauss, David. "The Rise of Anti-Americanism in France: French Intellectuals and the American Film Industry, 1927–1932." *Journal of Popular Culture* 10, no. 4 (1977): 752–59.

Strauss, William Victor. "Foreign Distribution of American Motion Pictures." *Harvard Business Review* 8 (1930): 307–15.

Street, Sarah. "The Hays Office and the Defence of the British Market in the 1930s." *Historical Journal of Film, Radio and Television* 5, no. 1 (1985): 37–55.

That Marvel—the Movie: A Glance at Its Reckless Past, Its Promising Present, and Its Significant Future. New York: G. P. Putnam's Sons, 1923.

Thompson, Kristin. *Exporting Entertainment: America in the World Film Market, 1907–1934.* London: BFI, 1985.

Thorp, Margaret. *America at the Movies.* London: Faber and Faber, 1945.

Tibbetts, John C., ed. *Introduction to the Photoplay.* 1929; Shawnee Mission, Kans.: National Film Society, 1977.

Valdez-Rodriguez, J. M. "Hollywood: Sales Agent of American Imperialism." *Experimental Cinema* 1, no. 4 (1933): 18–20.

Vaughn, Stephen. "Morality and Entertainment: The Origins of the Motion Picture Production Code." *Journal of American History* 77 (June 1990): 39–65.

Vincendeau, Ginette. "Hollywood Babylon—the Multiple Language Version." *Screen* 20, no. 2 (1988): 24–39.

Vizzard, Jack. *See No Evil: Life Inside a Hollywood Censor.* New York: Simon and Schuster, 1970.

Walker, Alexander. *The Shattered Silents: How the Movies Came to Stay.* London: Harrap, 1978.

Walsh, Francis R. " 'The Callahans and the Murphys' (MGM, 1927): A Case Study of Irish Catholic and Catholic Church Censorship." *Historical Journal of Film, Radio and Television* 10, no. 1 (1990): 33–45.

"Warners Start Foreign Tongue School to Train Players for Multi-Linguals." *Exhibitors Daily Review and Motion Pictures Today,* 28 April 1930, 1.

Weis, Elisabeth, and John Belton, eds. *Film Sound: Theory and Practice.* New York: Columbia University Press, 1985.

Whang, Paul K. "The Boycotting of Harold Lloyd's *Welcome Danger.*" *China Weekly Review,* 8 March 1930, 51.

"What Hays Can Do for the Movies." *Literary Digest,* 28 January 1922, 12–13.

Woll, Allen. *The Latin Image in American Film.* Rev. ed. Los Angeles: UCLA Latin American Center Publications, University of California, 1980.

Wood, Richard, ed. *Film and Propaganda in America: A Documentary History.* Vol. 1. New York: Greenwood, 1990.

Wood, Robin. *Howard Hawks.* London: BFI, 1983.

Yallop, David A. *The Day the Laughter Stopped: The True Story of Fatty Arbuckle.* London: Hodder and Stoughton, 1976.

Young, Donald Ramsey. *Motion Pictures: A Study in Social Legislation.* Philadelphia: Westbrook, 1922.

Index

285